More Advance Praise for
Leadership Secrets of Elizabeth I

"This is a 'must read' for all managers of contemporary organizations."
—Hedy Ratner, Co-Director,
Women's Business Development Center

"While female leaders will find this book of special interest, it's not for women only. Elizabeth reigned in an all-male world and her androgynous leadership style provides countless good lessons in managing today's mixed gender workplace."

—Rick Cronk,
President, Dreyer's Grand Ice Cream

"Offers fascinating insights into Elizabethan England's rise to greatness, and makes them relevant in today's world with excellent examples provided by top 21st Century executives."

—Cheryl D. Broussard,
Author of *Sister CEO*

"Higgins and Gilberd have provided a terrific mix of history, contemporary management theory, and 21st Century business practice to produce one of the most interesting and informative books of its kind."
—Kay Fredericks,
President and CEO, Trend Enterprises

"At last, a book that uses a great, historic female leader to provide insights for today's business world!"
—Julie Chaiken,
Owner and President, Chaiken Clothing

Leadership Secrets of
Elizabeth I

Leadership Secrets
of
Elizabeth I

Shaun O'L. Higgins
Pamela Gilberd

PERSEUS PUBLISHING
Cambridge, Massachusetts

Many of the designations used by manufacturers and sellers to distinguish their products are claimed as trademarks. Where those designations appear in this book and Perseus Publishing was aware of a trademark claim, the designations have been printed in initial capital letters.

Copyright © 2000 by Perseus Publishing

Cataloging-in-Publication Data is available from the Library of Congress
ISBN 0-7382-0390-4

Perseus Publishing is a member of the Perseus Books Group.

Find us on the World Wide Web at http://www.perseuspublishing.com

Perseus Publishing books are available at special discounts for bulk purchases in the U.S. by corporations, institutions, and other organizations. For more information, please contact the Special Markets Department at HarperCollins Publishers, 10 East 53rd Street, New York, NY 10022, or call 1–212–207–7528.

Text design by Heather Hutchison
Set in 11.5 point Electra by Perseus Publishing Services

First printing, September 2000
1 2 3 4 5 6 7 8 9 10—03 02 01 00

Contents

Acknowledgments

THE AUTHORS WISH TO acknowledge with gratitude the assistance of all the executives whose comments are quoted in Leadership Secrets of Elizabeth I. In addition to the executives we have quoted, we are grateful for the comments, suggestions, and assistance of Maureen Bausch, Lois Bolin, Jennifer Bowman, Anna Davis, David Hochberg, Kathy Kolbe, Ray Lawton, Laura Lawton, Patt Morrison, Nancy S. Mueller, Jose Natori, Carrie Ponder, Richard N. Sobanski, Dr. Sol Weingarten, Shanette Westphal, Dori Wilde, and Marie Wood.

In addition, we are grateful to Colleen Striegel, Lynn Dahmen, and Ann Glendening, each of whom read, chapter by chapter, advance copies of the manuscript and offered their astute comments for adding relevance and clarity. We are particularly grateful to Glendening who, in addition to being a formidable researcher, is also Shaun Higgins's wife. She assisted the authors with countless hours of library research at the Spokane Public Library and the Foley Center Library at Gonzaga University, whose staffs were extremely helpful in locating historical and management texts.

Jacqueline Murphy, our editor at Perseus, was tremendously supportive throughout the process of drafting and shaping the manuscript, keeping us on point and on time throughout its development. Our appreciation for her keen commentary and extraordinary dedication to seeing the book into print cannot be overstated. We would also like to thank our agent, Michael Snell, for bringing us together and helping us see the power of combining Elizabeth's secrets with those of the countless modern Elizabeths running twentieth-century organizations.

Shaun O'L. Higgins
Pamela Gilberd

Foreword

A LEADER IS SOMEONE WHO inspires and brings out the best in people with her spirit, energy, and vision. Leaders are role models who set high ethical standards for others to follow. Leaders are intellectual pragmatists, willing to take risks for causes they believe are important. They are good listeners who show compassion for people.

Queen Elizabeth I was a leader who exemplified these traits. She used her leadership and influence to reinvigorate her country. In the process, she created the legendary Elizabethan Age that bears her name and was best noted for achievements in the arts and exploration of new lands.

Shaun O'L. Higgins and Pamela Gilberd have written a fascinating book based on the life of Queen Elizabeth I, who was one of history's great leaders and one of my favorite role models. Interestingly, I found many parallels between the establishment of Elizabeth's reign centuries ago and the beginning of my mail-order business in 1951. Elizabeth and I were almost the same age when she took the throne and I became an entrepreneur. We were young visionaries, ready to make some much needed changes in the male-oriented societies we both lived in. As I noted in my autobiography, *An Eye For Winners*, the mail-order business forty-nine years ago was a man's domain, much like Elizabeth's England. Capable and ambitious women were regarded warily, but I never gave much credence to these prejudices and neither did Elizabeth. I believe this is the reason for our success.

Realistically, women in business still face many hurdles today, but on the whole, we are treated with the respect we have earned. I am proud that my company's success has contributed to this change of attitude and has opened some minds and more than a few doors. Elizabeth's example has certainly inspired twenty-first-century women to seek leadership roles.

When Elizabeth became queen of England, her nation was on the verge of bankruptcy. Her country's coinage was debased, and England was caught in a power struggle between two strong neighboring countries, Spain and France. Leaders in both countries believed the new queen would marry a member of their own royal families. Instead, Elizabeth chose to be her own woman, assuming full responsibility for the throne and relying on no one for help. She overlooked prejudice about a woman's ability to lead a nation. I also overlooked prejudice in favor of self-reliance. Simply put, I began working because I wanted to help supplement my husband's income. But I began my business at home so I could still perform my role as a wife and mother.

The Tudor monarchy needed money, but, more important, it needed to regain lost credibility at home and among foreign rivals. Elizabeth had serious goals to achieve, and she carried them out effectively. In both cases, the tasks were too important to succumb to prejudice and conventional wisdom. As this book notes, all the leaders represented, including myself, share common traits similar to

Elizabeth's style of management. We have learned how to switch managerial approaches when the situation warrants and we know that perseverance pays off.

So, whether you are starting a small business as I did on my kitchen table with $2,000 of wedding gift money or serving as CEO of an established corporation, Elizabeth's reign is a timeless example of leadership at its best.

In retrospect, today's leaders can learn much from Elizabeth's legacy. One of the greatest lessons Elizabeth teaches us is that managing a business, and in her case a country, is only one aspect of a life well lived. Although she denied herself the pleasures of marriage and children, Elizabeth was an outgoing leader, known for her wit and her commitment to the arts, especially William Shakespeare's plays. She delighted taking part in conversations on a broad range of subjects and perfected her language, music, and horsemanship skills throughout her nearly forty-five-year reign and long life. She inspires business leaders like myself to give back to their communities by being charitable. Whether we are rulers of nations or CEOs of corporations, humankind is our business and we must do our best to help make the world a better place.

Lillian Vernon
Founder and Chief Executive Officer of
Lillian Vernon Corporation

INTRODUCTION

Gloriana:
Elizabeth I as a Role Model for
Twenty-First-Century Leaders

"So great a lady that there could be no hold taken
of her."

SHORTLY AFTER 7 O'CLOCK on the cold, dreary
morning of November 16, 1558, a lone horseman named
Nicholas Throckmorton rode from Greenwich Castle in
London to the nearby royal estate of Hatfield. Throckmorton had been dispatched from the deathbed of Queen Mary
I with orders to carry an engagement ring taken from the
dead queen's hand to Mary's chosen successor, Elizabeth
Tudor. The courier found the new queen on Hatfield's
grounds where, bundled against the severe weather, she sat
beneath an oak tree reading a Greek version of the Bible.
Throckmorton presented his new sovereign with the ring as

proof of Mary's death. Elizabeth then knelt upon the frigid ground and quoted a verse from Psalm 118: "This is the Lord's doing; it is marvelous in our eyes."

———————

So began the remarkable reign of one of history's most illustrious leaders, Elizabeth the First, Queen of England, Ireland, and Wales, Defender of the Anglican Faith, Protector of the People, genius, "spin doctor," diplomat, linguist, poet, vivacious beauty, and nurturer of the English Renaissance.

In her nearly forty-five-year reign Elizabeth created and directed one of the most dynamic political and cultural transitions in the history of the world. Her achievements stemmed from her extraordinary intelligence, unsurpassed communication skills, clear vision, and passionate belief in her nation and its people. The queen's natural gifts were enhanced by her application of learned leadership behaviors and management skills that were uncommon in her time and rare in our own.

Elizabeth's strengths are timeless and universal: commitment, excellence, focus, teamwork, communication, and fairness (though many of those around her often considered her unfair.) This is the stuff of modern leadership as expounded in countless books on the subject. With the exception of Machiavelli's *The Prince*, however, Elizabeth had no such books to guide her and she lived long before concepts like "paradigm shift" and "360-degree feedback" became part of the leadership lexicon. This meant the queen had to create and evolve her management style from her own intelligence and the advice of those around her.

To better understand Elizabeth's management principles, we have tried to discover them as she did—by looking at historical examples and asking our own advisers and peers for their input and interpretation. Just as Elizabeth studied her forebears on the throne and the lives of noble Greeks and Romans, we have studied Elizabeth. And just as the queen consulted her Privy Council and noted scholars, we have called upon modern management gurus and practicing CEOs to help us interpret the queen's strengths.

Elizabeth transcended her century's prejudice against women leaders as well as the ardent desire of her closest advisers that she marry a *man* who would serve as England's behind-the-throne king. Queen Bess could simply have presided over England, but she chose, instead, to actively reform, direct, manage, and rule it. And she was able to rule because she often went directly to the English people who, unlike her advisers, viewed her first as their Great Ruler and only second as a woman. Because Elizabeth drew her strength from the people she led, she is a powerful role model for all who would lead through empowerment, rather than on the basis of title alone. This has made her a source of personal inspiration for both male and female leaders throughout the four centuries since her passing.

The authors interviewed more than 100 modern executives to find out if Elizabeth's lessons were valid today and if the queen had served them as a role model. Although many said they had not studied Elizabeth's life formally, a number said the queen's life and practices had been helpful to their careers. The variety of their responses illustrate the broad range of appeal Elizabeth has for contemporary leaders. For example, Helen Whelan, president of the Internet company MyPrimeTime, said she has often considered Elizabeth a role model because "she bucked convention, stayed single [and] was very solid and strong in being a leader." Every aspect of the queen's life was unconventional, Whelan told us, "yet she focused on moving forward when she could have settled into what was easy — conforming."

Carol Stephenson, president and CEO of Toronto-based Lucent Technologies Canada, praised Elizabeth's strengths as an inclusive leader. "Whether you are the leader of an empire, a corporation, or a family, diversity is key," Stephenson said. "As Queen Elizabeth I so evidently knew, surrounding yourself with the best and the brightest, embracing diverse points of view, and fostering free expression leads the way to unleashed creativity, unmatched innovation, and unlimited success."

Dr. Judith Rosener, the best-selling author who has made a specialty of studying differences in the management styles of men and women, found in Elizabeth an outstanding example of "female leadership style." Among the strengths Rosener finds in Bess's style are the queen's "comfort with ambiguity," her vivaciousness, her inclusiveness, her pragmatism, her flexibility, and the fact that Elizabeth "harnessed the talents of the creative and courageous people of her time."

"She surrounded herself with strong people," Rosener said. "She didn't seek power in a hierarchical fashion. She was charismatic and drew people to her in an inclusive manner. She's not sitting there telling people what to do because 'I'm the Queen.'"

Harriet Mosson, former president of Liz Claiborne Dresses and Suits in New York, cited the importance of Elizabeth's having had "a definite point of view." Mosson noted that the queen had "no experience when she started, but she had a point of view and a vision for what she wanted England to be. How else could she have had the courage of her convictions to push people in those directions?"

Marilee Winiarski, senior director for West Online Content Development in Eagan, Minnesota, was the most enthusiastic Bess fan among our interviewees and has studied the queen for years. "Elizabeth I has been a role model for me ever since I read *A Crown for Elizabeth* [by Mary M. Luke] when I was a teenager," Winiarski told us. "At the time, the early and mid–1970s, I was impressed with her ability not only to survive but also to be a powerful political force in a world dominated by powerful men . . . As I grew older, I became even more impressed not only with her considerable intelligence, but also with her ability to turn into assets what many men of her age labeled her feminine weaknesses: 'vanity' (in actuality, brilliant image management—'Gloriana, the Virgin Queen'); 'vacillation' (usually the playing off of political enemies against each other); and 'fear of war' (her absolute conviction that war was a ridiculous waste of human life and financial resources). She was not above using her femininity to get what she wanted, but as she said, 'My sex cannot diminish my prestige.'"

Elizabeth is unquestionably interesting, but is she relevant in the twenty-first century? Winiarski makes the case: "Translating Elizabeth's precepts into modern business leadership is actually pretty easy: know your ultimate goal and stay the course, surround yourself with highly competent and intelligent people, and nourish the source(s) of your ultimate influence/power/authority."

To better understand the relevance of Elizabeth's management techniques to modern business organizations, let's "translate" her situation into a contemporary setting.

Imagine yourself as a stockholding member of a family that has long held the controlling interest in a large but struggling public corporation. Imagine that for years you have received your meager annual dividends, but have been locked out of an operational position that might help you improve company performance. Since its founding more than twenty years ago, the company has been managed first by your larger-than-life father, then by your sickly brother (with help from an old, nonfamily employee), and more recently by your estranged sister (with help from a husband who headed a rival firm). Each successive manager has led the company according to a different management philosophy and employees are tired of all the changes. Suddenly, health problems force that sister to step aside. Estranged from you as she is, your sister has decided that it's better to keep the business in family hands — even *your* hands — than to let "outsiders" take control. (You'd made a similar decision years ago when you helped your sister gain control of the company when outsiders tried to supplant *her*). Now, with your sister's reluctant blessing, you find yourself in the CEO's job. Having previously been excluded from all matters dealing with the governance of the firm, you now have access to its books. You quickly learn to your chagrin that your company is in dire fiscal straits, having expended far more than it takes in. Your youth and inexperience will make it difficult to quickly reestablish confidence in your firm's financial viability. In addition, you are beset with internal administrative problems. Your management team is filled with people loyal to rivals for your job. There is no clear company philosophy except that of survival. That survival is threatened externally by two strong competitors, each of whom is trying to take over your company by whatever means possible. Lacking vision, wracked by internal dissension, hounded by creditors, and preyed on by powerful external foes, your company is paralyzed and crumbling. The company has made no significant capital investments in decades; your sales force is understaffed, ill equipped and demoralized; most of your strategic planners are ready to sell out before potential buyers learn just how weak your position is. The most unfortunate aspect of these problems is that they have surfaced at a time when major new opportunities abound. A new global market is being developed and exploited by your competitors, but you have failed to stake a claim in that market because you've been focused on competition close to your home office. Getting your company back on track will require you first to establish your authority, consolidate your power, and build a management team you can trust. To do this you decide that your best strategy is to win the affections of the company's stockholders, appealing to them directly and using their support as a wedge against your entrenched and often unsupportive management team. You must become a master "spin doctor" and win the support of the shareholders by articulating a clear vision that inspires commitment.

In the end, you not only survive but thrive, sending your competitors into disarray, seizing market share from them at every turn, and creating a dynamic, financially strong, and independent firm that becomes the rising star in its field.

The story above closely parallels the challenges Elizabeth faced when she ascended the throne of England in 1558. Born in the Greenwich section of Greater London in 1533, Elizabeth was the daughter of King Henry VIII by his second wife, Anne Boleyn. Throughout her youth Elizabeth was viewed as a threat to the succession interests of her rivals, who were divided not only by personal jealousies but also by vicious religious partisanship. When Henry VIII died in 1547, his ten-year-old son by Jane Seymour succeeded to the throne as Edward VI. But Edward was a sickly child and died six years later of tuberculosis, setting off a battle for succession between Elizabeth's pro-Catholic half-sister, Mary, and Edward's choice, Lady Jane Grey, who was supported by militant Protestant leaders. Lady Jane reigned for only nine days, however, as the Protestant sympathizer Elizabeth sided with Mary to force Jane's abdication. Shortly after Mary ascended the throne, she became suspicious of Elizabeth's ambitions and of her religious leanings. In 1554, Mary had the future queen briefly imprisoned in the Tower of London and later placed under house arrest. Upon "Bloody Mary's" death, Elizabeth succeeded to the throne and, despite many plots to overthrow her, held it until her own death in 1603.

When Elizabeth ascended the throne, England was impoverished, weak, and demoralized. When she died, it was confident and had a sense of direction and destiny. Among her accomplishments:

- She permanently established the Church of England in 1559.
- She reestablished the authority of the British Crown at a time when other monarchies were weakening and wracked by civil war. After early years of turbulence, her long reign was largely one of stability and unity.
- She raised England's standing in the international community, defying Spain and frustrating King Philip II's attempts to take over England and France.
- She reestablished England's coinage, which had become "bad money"—thoroughly adulterated by mintings that replaced gold and silver content with base metal.
- She laid the foundations of the British Empire, competing with Spain, France, and Portugal for New World territories by encouraging the voyages of English explorers like Sir Francis Drake, who circumnavigated the globe, and Sir Walter Raleigh, who led three expeditions to North America.
- She encouraged the flowering of culture that produced England's Golden Age of literature, theater, and music. The names Shakespeare, Marlowe, Tallis, Byrd, and Spenser are only the greatest among many talents that flourished during her reign.

- She survived frequent internal and external conspiracies to oust her from the throne. Her forces
  defeated Spain's invasion forces in 1588; her intelligence service uncovered and destroyed assassination plots; and, while fighting Catholic conspirators who wanted her dead, she worked diligently to
  check the threats to her power posed by the Puritan faction of the Church of England.

Although the lessons of Elizabeth's life and reign are
valuable for *any* executive, the sixteenth-century queen is
a particularly compelling role model for twenty-first-century *women* executives. Elizabeth was frequently torn by
conflicts between her public responsibilities, her private
life, and continual demands that she marry and produce
children, specifically a male heir. Such conflicts parallel
those many modern women face in balancing work, social
life, and family life. Elizabeth had a number of romantic
relationships, but chose not to marry, claiming that her
love of England and its people precluded matrimony.
Only her relationship with Robert Dudley, the Earl of
Leicester, touched her deeply. (She dismissed him when
she discovered he was already married.) She used her marriageable status as a diplomatic tool, often hinting to foreign monarchs and princes that she might consider a
union, but always dropping the matter when pressed to say
"yes."

A strong-willed, astute, yet often capricious woman, the
queen not only presided over the English Renaissance but
also was a Renaissance woman herself. She kept elaborate
diaries, wrote exemplary letters, was fluent in Latin, Greek,

Italian, and French, and understood Spanish and Welsh. She was an accomplished lutenist and keyboard player. She delighted in dancing, studied divinity, wrote poetry, and was noted for her wit.

Elizabeth is often cited as not only the most important woman leader in Western history, but also as one of the greatest world leaders of all time. She has been the subject of countless books and figured in dozens of films, including 1998's *Elizabeth* and the Oscar-winning *Shakespeare in Love*. On television, Bess was the subject of a six-part *Masterpiece Theatre* docudrama, *Elizabeth R*, starring Glenda Jackson, as well as the target of Roland Atkinson's wicked humor (and Miranda Richardson's zany performance) in the PBS comedy series, *Black Adder II*. The A&E program *Biography* recently ranked Elizabeth among the Top 100 leaders of the Millennium and described her as "the spin doctor of a 45-year reign." The queen's skills at "spin" were critical in helping her transform her tiny island nation from a bankrupt pawn of France and Spain into a global powerhouse that dominated the market for political clout, religious influence, and trade for centuries.

Elizabeth's life is as exciting as it is instructive. It is the stuff of great drama—as playwrights and filmmakers have long known. Conflict abounds in her story and the cast of characters surrounding the queen is as interesting as Elizabeth herself. She was aided by a remarkably talented group of advisers including Sir Francis Walsingham, her dark and mysterious spymaster; Sir Francis Drake, the dashing and patriotic privateer who sailed around the world and preyed on Spain's gold-laden ships; William Cecil (later Lord Burghley), the loyal and subtle analyst who served as her chief counselor for nearly forty years; and Sir Thomas Gresham, who revalued her coinage, restructured England's debt, and restored the queen's credit. Her inner circle also included Lord Essex, the unruly and arrogant military leader who fought for her in Ireland, but with whom she quarreled incessantly and eventually had beheaded for leading an uprising against her. And, of course, there was Robert Dudley, Earl of Leicester, her childhood friend, Master of Horse, and love of her life. Dudley intrigued and entertained her, but later betrayed both her love and his country and was cast out of court and favor because of those betrayals.

Elizabeth's rivals add further drama to her story. They included the Three Marys: Her half-sister and predecessor, Queen "Bloody" Mary I, who burned religious dissidents at the stake; the wily Mary of Guise, French wife of King James V of Scotland; and, most famous of all, Mary, Queen of Scots, daughter of Mary of Guise, foremost challenger to Elizabeth's throne and mother to its eventual heir, James I. Elizabeth's greatest rival, however, was a rejected suitor, her former brother-in-law, and the most powerful man on earth—King Philip II of Spain. England and Spain fought for decades to gain global dominance in battles over New World gold, European cultural hegemony, religious philosophy, and the allegiance of foreign nations. In the end, Elizabeth won and her greatest victory—defeat of Spain's Armada—became Philip's worst defeat.

Elizabeth, like all great leaders, was controversial in her time and has remained so since. Her detractors, including revisionist historians, have often cast her in a less flattering light than do we. Throughout *Leadership Secrets of Eliza-*

beth I we have expounded the best interpretations of her actions, thoughts, and methods. Like all great leaders, of course, Elizabeth had her flaws. Although we have praised her for avoiding decisions until they could no longer be postponed, her contemporaries often described her as vacillating and indecisive. She was often damned, too, for being petulant and mercurial, vain and obsessed with her image. We have viewed these aspects of the queen as minor, human failings rather than as significant detractions from her leadership ability.

It would be easy, from a modern viewpoint, to dismiss Elizabeth as a role model because she was born to power, rather than having had to earn it. Biographer Jane Resh Thomas has noted, however, that the advantages of Elizabeth's royal birth carried with it many emotional, political, and psychological burdens. "If she was charmed," wrote Thomas, "then her enchanter must have been an evil fairy whose charm was at least in part a curse. For many of Elizabeth's subjects despised her from infancy. Her father put her mother to death and neglected Elizabeth for much of her childhood. Wealthy though she was, money constantly worried her, for her personal fortune, derived from her lands and investments, was not always enough to support the government, the army and navy, and her several enormous households." Elizabeth's obliging and supportive friends were sometimes as dangerous as her most vicious enemies. The former mounted plots on her behalf, causing her to be implicated by association in their treason; the latter launched rebellions and attempted her assassination. On a personal level, Bess had to deal with family dysfunction (Henry fathered two illegitimate children, divorced two of his six wives, and had two others beheaded). Elizabeth also faced threats to her health, avoiding the Black Plague that struck rich and poor alike, and surviving a near-death battle with smallpox. Through all adversity, however, Bess triumphed, re-creating herself as one of history's most respected leaders and building her nation into a powerful, modern state.

Elizabeth is a particularly challenging study in leadership because of the uniqueness of her mental powers, the complexity of her personality, and the particular political climate of her day. Books based on the attributes of famous historical leaders often reduce the leaders to stereotypes and their wisdom to platitudes. Such oversimplification would be a particular disservice to Elizabeth, who was perhaps the most intellectually and emotionally complex monarch in history. Indeed, her leadership skills show at their best when they defy conventional wisdom. For example, many of her advisers accused her of lacking decisiveness. A more charitable, less conventional view—and ours—is that Elizabeth made conscious decisions *not* to decide and that her approach both advanced her goals and served her country well. The queen's use of pragmatic delays contrasts sharply with the nostrums to "act decisively" found in so many of the "different leader, same advice" books that have proliferated in contemporary business publishing. Elizabeth's advice often cannot be reduced to conventional platitudes. Although she was a master of delegation and teamwork and fostered excellence, her secrets lie in the nuances of such mastery. The queen was multifaceted, multitalented, and subtle in her dealings—and that subtlety alone separates her from the "bold action" school of the historic-figure-as-manager genre. The queen's abstemious attitude toward food and drink, her emphasis on virginity, and the very fact that she was a woman leading in a man's world stand in sharp contrast to the personal and leadership attributes of figures such as Generals Ulysses S. Grant, Dwight David Eisenhower, and George S. Patton.

The value of Elizabeth's often unconventional leadership is proven by her achievement. Her reign was marked by extensive global exploration, growth of England's political prestige, and unparalleled artistic achievement. She was highly contemporary in her approach to the revolutionary changes taking place around her as well as in her use of public relations techniques. She was adept in dealing with the ambiguities that faced her and that, in different form, now confront twenty-first-century executives. Like many historic *male* leaders, Elizabeth exemplified commitment, tenacity, and charisma. Like many of them she combined skill and judgment with grace and charm. But her scope of achievement transcends the relatively brief moments of glory achieved by military heroes such as Robert E. Lee. Elizabeth was more than a hero—she was mistress of an Age. The variety of her achievements deservedly places her in the pantheon of leaders that includes Moses, Julius Caesar, Napoleon Bonaparte, and Winston Churchill who, in addition to their political and military accomplishments, are remembered for lasting achievements in other fields. Caesar, for example, was not only an outstanding military leader, but also an exemplary historian and literary stylist, as was Churchill. Arguably, too, Napoleon's greatest monument is not his brief military career (which, despite his tactical brilliance, ended in defeat and exile), but rather the Napoleonic Code which stands, like that of Moses, as one of the principle legal achievements in human history. Like theirs, Elizabeth's credentials as a leader are based not only on the length of her reign and her diplomatic prowess, but also on her powerful rhetoric, her nurturing of one of the major artistic flowerings in history, and on her status as incarnate proof that women are capable not only of ruling, but of ruling well. The lessons of such breakthrough leadership overshadow those of transitory leaders. Their achievements are bound to a specific time and place, whereas Elizabeth's legacy has extended into our own.

Because Elizabeth was a woman, we have made a particular effort to seek out women CEOs to help us assess the queen's techniques and their relevance to the twenty-first century. But we have not written a book "for women only." That, too, would be a disservice to Elizabeth who, though she was a woman leader, was not a leader of women. She headed an all-male government and she led it with an androgynous style designed to transcend gender issues. On the one hand, she consistently referred to herself as a prince or king. On the other hand, she often played on her status as a "weak and feeble woman" to inspire her soldiers to fight and on her fickleness as a marriage prospect to play rival suitors against one another to achieve her political goals. It was said of her that she was as "proficient in the reading of men as of books," and she was highly proficient at reading both. Although Elizabeth is a powerful role model for modern women leaders, she was a leader, period—a view underscored by the comments of the male CEOs we interviewed. One said, upon learning how the queen had handled a disciplinary problem, not only that he would hire her, but that he would like to work for her.

Interviews with modern executives revealed some pronounced differences among male and female attitudes toward history and the relevance of history in the modern workplace. For example, when we asked respondents to name other historic women leaders they admired we were struck that most of the men named no one and that most of the women named female leaders from the twentieth century, many of whom are still living. Only two respondents named women from prior periods: Joan of Arc and Catherine the Great of Russia. The most popular choice among all respondents was former First Lady Eleanor Roosevelt, followed closely by Margaret Thatcher, the former British prime minister, and Elizabeth Dole, the former U.S. Secretary of Labor, head of the American Red Cross, and presidential candidate. But most of our respondents named nonofficeholders and social activists, including Mother Teresa, Rosa Parks, and Oprah Winfrey. Three of our female respondents selected women whose influence had been intimate and personal: a mother, an aunt, and a grandmother, each of whom had broken new ground in social or business circles. When we explored these responses we received additional anecdotal evidence that many female interviewees, in particular, had little interest or affection for history as it is taught in school, viewing it as a matter of "kings and wars" or "dates and battles." For them, history is *now* and should emphasize leaders who achieved social progress, fostered individual empowerment, and exemplified inclusion in decision making. In the final analysis, that type of history was what Elizabeth was about. Although she had to deal with "kings and wars" (and dealt with them well), she was more interested in uniting her people in peace and hope.

The authors are neither professional historians nor management theorists, but practical people of business. As a result, our focus in this book is to approach history as a tool for contemporary business practice and contemporary organizational leadership. Elizabeth's relevance to modern leaders lies not in the battles won by her soldiers and sailors, not in the negotiations of her diplomats, nor in the battles with Parliament over budgets and succession; rather, it lies in Elizabeth as a complete, extraordinary, and complex human being who was able to unite people in a common cause, foster the growth of the arts, provide protection for the poor, and allow for dissent both in her councils and in the private lives of her subjects.

Since we are not historians, our book is not intended as a history of Elizabeth's reign. Major episodes and issues are omitted entirely or mentioned only in passing, including the Irish campaigns, the Rebellion of the Northern Earls, most of the Queen's relationships with her various suitors, and the repercussions of the 1572 Saint Bartholomew's Day Massacre in Paris. Likewise, several relatively minor aspects of Elizabeth's reign—such as the appointment of her agent in Turkey—receive far more attention here than in most biographies of Elizabeth because they are particularly germane to modern management issues. Finally, we have avoided dwelling on the nuances of the religious conflict so critical to understanding the history of sixteenth-century

Europe. Rather, in dealing with religious strife, we have adopted the approach of biographer Jasper Ridley who, in his aptly titled work *Elizabeth I: The Shrewdness of Virtue*, held:

> Today, the religious hatreds have passed away in England and America, and the conflict between Catholics and Protestants in sixteenth-century Europe can be seen, not as a struggle between true and false religion, but as another phase in the never-ending contest in which the conservative upholders of the established order, the revolutionary youth, the martyrs, the careerists and the Foreign Offices of the great powers all played their parts.

That type of "never-ending contest" between "conservative upholders of the established order" and revolutionary forces exists in the twenty-first-century economy and its workplaces, where the "old" natural resource, product-based economy competes with the "new" electronic, service-based economy for talent and capital; where the forces of globalization and free trade battle those of import-replacement and protectionism; and where traditional organizational hierarchies and their legions of middle managers are being replaced by cross-departmental, self-directed work teams.

By the time Elizabeth died in 1603, England had established the most extensive empire the world had known. The queen had vanquished her foes, laid the groundwork for peaceful succession that brought Scotland into the kingdom, and fostered the age that bears her name. Elizabeth's balanced pragmatism made her an effective leader; her personal charisma, speaking skills, and emphasis on excellence in herself and those around her have made her a legend. Beloved by the English people, to whom she had dedicated her life, she was their "Great Queen," "The Virgin Queen," "Good Queen Bess"—and, as the glory of her age and nation, she was and remains "Gloriana."

In the chapters that follow you will witness Elizabeth's rise to power and learn how she consolidated her position, inspired her people, built her management team, and sent her competitors into disarray. Along the way you'll find comments from dozens of modern leaders whose organizations have benefited from their application of Elizabethan practices—"Bess" practices that can help you establish the "best practices" for your own organization.

1

Leadership

My state requires me to command that [which] I know my people will willingly do from their own love to me.

ON NOVEMBER 30, 1601, the Speaker and 140 members of the House of Commons traveled to Whitehall to hear Elizabeth defend her reign, her policies on taxation, and her controversial grants of lucrative monopolies to court favorites. Although she often responded to Parliamentary concerns with argumentative scorn, Elizabeth was in a mood of reconciliation and appealed to the House in terms of her integrity, her love of the people, her service to the realm, and, significantly, her appreciation for Parliament's service to the cause they shared—a strong England. Though she delivered what appeared to be an impromptu address, the queen's remarks were later called the Golden Speech because, as one listener said, they should have been "written in gold."

"There is no jewel," she said, "be it of never so rich price, which I set before this jewel: I mean your love. For I do esteem it more than any treasure or riches; for that we know how to prize, but love and thanks I count invaluable. And, though God hath raised me high, yet this I count the glory of my Crown, that I have reigned with your loves . . . I do not so much rejoice that God hath made me to be a Queen, as to be a Queen over so thankful a people. Therefore I have cause to wish nothing more than to content the subject and that is a duty which I owe . . . Of myself I must say this: I never was any greedy, scraping grasper, nor a strait fast-holding Prince, nor yet a waster. My heart was never set on any worldly goods. What you bestow on me, I will not hoard it up, but receive it to bestow on you again . . . . I have ever used to set the Last Judgment Day before mine eyes and so to rule as I shall be judged to answer before a higher judge, and now if my kingly bounties have been abused and my grants turned to the hurt of my people contrary to my will and meaning, and if any in authority under me have neglected or perverted what I have committed to them, I hope God will not lay their culps and offences in my charge . . .

". . . I know the title of a King is a glorious title, but assure yourself that the shining glory of princely authority hath not so dazzled the eyes of our understanding, but that we well know and remember that we also are to yield an account of our actions before the great judge. To be a king and wear a crown is a thing more glorious to them that see it than it is pleasant to them that bear it . . . And though you have had, and may have, many princes more mighty and wise sitting in this seat, yet you never had nor shall have, any that will be more careful and loving."

The Golden Speech is a composite statement of Elizabeth's leadership secrets in practice. In it, the queen *establishes her authority*, noting that it derives not only from God, but also from the people at whose pleasure and for whose benefit she serves. She then *defends her actions, takes responsibility* for them, and notes that she, like her subjects, is not above the law, but *accountable to higher authority*. She affirms her *commitment and energetic support of public interest*. She notes that *leadership is often a burden*, arguing that "to be a king and wear a crown is a thing more glorious to them that see it than it is pleasant to them that bear it." In the section that separates her intentions in making grants from the actions of those who receive them, Elizabeth *deflects criticism from herself* and onto those who have failed in their stewardship of the public trust. If she has erred, it has not been through intent and *never from desire for personal gain or glory*.

It was a perfect speech, perfectly delivered to the ideal audience at the precise moment it needed most to be heard—and it worked! Many of the Commons left with tears in their eyes! They knew the truth of what they had heard, recalling the benefits of Elizabeth's reign. Reading the speech today, we are tempted to find in it the insincerity and false self-deprecation that has marked the resignation speeches, apologies, and defenses of dozens of late-twentieth-century world leaders. But Elizabeth's words did not ring hollow. The queen's actions during more than forty years on the throne tacitly underscored every sentence she uttered and reaffirmed her mastery of leadership.

Modern business libraries are filled with books on the theory and practice of leadership, but in Elizabeth's day there was only one such book: Niccolo Machiavelli's *The Prince*. Machiavelli wrote his classic in 1513 but it was not published until 1532, the year he died and a year before Bess's birth. *The Prince*, written to endear Machiavelli to the ruling Medici family in Florence, codified rules for retaining monarchical power. As a work of realpolitik, the book stood in sharp contrast to other political works of the period, which focused on philosophical issues such as the source of political authority. *The Prince*, however, gives short shrift to the sources of power, focusing instead on the exercise and maintenance of power, regardless of its origin or legitimacy.

Elizabeth must certainly have read *The Prince*. She was fascinated with things Italian, had mastered the Italian language, and was a longtime observer of Catherine de Medici, whose sons, the French dukes of Anjou and Alençon, were among her suitors. Not least, Elizabeth would have been drawn to *The Prince* because Pope Clement VII, her father's bitter foe, had condemned the book. Certainly, the queen (perhaps as a princess) would have been intrigued by Machiavelli's argument that Italy's city-states could be liberated from the influence of foreign governments only through the establishment of strong, indigenous governments. That argument, applied to England, became the goal of her life.

Elizabeth's statements and actions also bear the marks of Machiavelli, although she had little in common with Cesare Borgia, the ruler after whom Machiavelli modeled his ideal of princely power. In phrases that echo those of *The*

Prince, she said on one occasion, "The word 'must' is not to be used to Princes." At another time, she told Parliament: "The head [meaning her] is not ruled by the foot [meaning them]." And, in perhaps her most Machiavellian statement, she said, "Princes . . . transact business in a certain way, with princely intelligence, such as private persons cannot imitate." These statements were balanced (as the villainous Borgia's were not) by values deeply instilled in Elizabeth in her childhood, and by the queen's strong identification with the welfare of her people. Elizabeth's imperious comments were frequently tempered not only by the type of self-deprecating and humble phrasings that graced the Golden Speech of 1601, but also by Bess's actions. As a young princess, Bess frequently consulted a book of advice prepared for her by one of her caretakers. The book was filled with what we would today call "affirmations" and with instructions on selfless stewardship of the needs of the less fortunate. Among its dictums: "Think of the needy once a day" and "Further the just suit of the poor." As queen, Elizabeth didn't just give lip service to these ideals; she acted to see them realized. In one remarkable instance, for example, Elizabeth furthered a "just suit" with a vengeance. Historian Christopher Hibbert tells the story of the queen's visit to a town during one of her "progresses" to the countryside:

> There were those who grumbled about the expense of it all, and those who had cause to complain that the royal purveyors were unconscionably slow in paying for the goods they ordered, that they not infrequently requisitioned them without payment at all. The story was told of a Kentish man who was

evidently bold and angry enough to approach a group of royal attendants to demand, "which is the Queen?"

"I am your Queen," said Elizabeth who was standing nearby. "What would thou have with me?"

"You are one of the rarest women I ever saw, and can eat no more than my daughter Madge, who is thought the properest lass in our parish, though short of you. But the Queen Elizabeth took for devours so many of my hens, ducks and capons as I am not able to live."

The man's case was examined and the [queen's] grasping purveyor, so it was widely reported, was hanged.

Although hanging is no longer an approved punishment for theft or embezzlement, there has been no change in the need for leaders to take prompt and effective action in situations like that of the crooked purveyor.

Leadership is a complex topic and Elizabeth is one of the most complex leaders in history. The hallmark of Elizabeth's leadership style might best be described as "balanced pragmatism." Her leadership was *balanced* because she expertly juggled rival interests that could have destroyed her reign. These included rival suitors for her hand, rival political and religious factions, rival foreign powers, and rival views within her Privy Council. The queen's leadership was *pragmatic* in that she invariably acted with rational self-interest, adopting expedient short-term actions, and never losing sight of her long-term goals.

Elizabeth also believed in the philosophy of "divide and rule," and was one of the most dedicated centrists in history, striving always to preserve as much of the status quo as she could and driving as much change as was required to achieve her ends. She was by nature conservative—supportive of the order of things, especially the ordained right of kings and queens. This made Elizabeth anxious to avoid establishing dangerous precedents and may have contributed to her reluctance to behead Mary, Queen of Scots. After all, if Mary's head rolled, a change of political tide could well put Elizabeth's head on the block!

Leadership is a popular topic, in part, because of the philosophical questions it begs—questions that make for interesting, but unresolvable, debate. Are leaders made or born? Do leaders define their times, or are they merely reflections of them? Is leadership only a matter of effectiveness, or does it require that its goals be ethical and progressive? These questions have been argued for centuries and have attracted thinkers as diverse as Aristotle, Machiavelli, Tolstoy, Thomas Carlyle, and St. Thomas Aquinas. At a more practical level, leadership becomes a psychological study, as we attempt to unravel the mystery of how leadership works—regardless of its origin or the purpose to which it is put. What are the actions of a leader? Just what do leaders do that nonleaders don't? Are some styles of leadership more effective than others and, if so, why? Here the answers are somewhat clearer than with the philosophical questions—and they help us decipher the secrets and understand the strength of Elizabeth's leadership.

Leadership guru Daniel Goleman analyzed generic styles of leadership and their application in an article published in the March-April 2000 edition of the *Harvard Business Review*. Goleman analyzed findings from research conducted in 1999 by the Hay, McBer consulting firm, which surveyed a randomly selected sample of nearly 4,000 executives from a list of 20,000 executives worldwide. The survey focused exclusively on leadership attitudes. Analysis of the findings identified six generic leadership styles. First, said Goleman, there is the Coercive style, briefly encapsulated in the phrase "demand compliance." Then there is the Authoritative style, best used to "mobilize people toward achieving a vision." There are also Affiliative, Democratic, Pacesetting, and Coaching styles, characterized, respectively, by their goals of "creating emotional bonds and harmony"; "building consensus through participation"; "expecting excellence and self-direction"; and "developing people for the future."

Goleman found that different styles work best in different situations. Some were less productive (even counterproductive) when used exclusively. Significantly, Goleman found that the best leaders had high levels of emotional intelligence that told them which style worked best in a given situation.

The Hay, McBer survey found (as we did in our own interviews with more than 100 executives), that leadership is most often defined as the ability to "get results."

Although Elizabeth faced constant challenge and crisis (the best situations in which to use Coercive techniques), she used each of Goleman's six styles of leadership during her rise to power and throughout her reign.

In her "Coercive" mode the queen could take quick action to order compliance in matters that required it. A fine example of Elizabeth at her most coercive is found in a letter of 1573, sent to Richard Cox, Bishop of Ely. Cox had refused to vacate property Bess had granted him and for which she had another use. In a stingingly short letter, she cut to the point and wielded her "divine" right with the up-start divine. "Proud Prelate," she wrote, " You know what you were before I made you what you are now. If you do not immediately comply with my request, I will unfrock you, by God."

Charles Decker, a former executive with Proctor & Gamble, compared Elizabeth's note with a terse personnel evaluation. "If you are unhappy with someone's performance . . . you have to clearly lay out in writing . . . where the shortcomings are and say, 'here is an action plan of what you need to do to improve this.' Only then can you really go to the next step and say, well it didn't work, you're out of here." (Or, as in the case of Bishop Cox, "you didn't move, so we're moving you—not only out of the house but out of your bishopric!")

Elizabeth most often used the "Authoritative" style of leadership, invoking her status as a servant of God and the people as a means of mobilizing her advisers and Parliament toward her vision of England as an independent and respected nation. Faced in the early years of her reign with a petition from Parliament that she marry and produce or name a successor, the queen responded by first establishing her credentials to hold the throne, then demanding respect for her position, her viewpoint, and her word; and then citing reasons of state for her noncompliance with the petition's demands:

"Was I not born in the realm?" she asked, rhetorically,

> Were my parents born in any foreign country? Is not my kingdom here? Whom have I oppressed? Whom have I enriched to other's harm? What turmoil have I made in this commonwealth

that I should be suspected to have no regard to the same? How have I governed since my reign? I will be tried by envy itself. I need not to use many words, for my deeds do try me . . . I did send them answer by my council, I would marry (although of mine own disposition I was not inclined thereunto) but that was not accepted or credited, although spoken by their Prince . . . I will never break the word of a prince spoken in a public place, for my honour's sake. And therefore I say again, I will marry as soon as I can conveniently . . . Your petition is to deal in the limitation of the succession. At this present it is not convenient, nor never shall be without peril unto you, and certain danger to me. But as soon as there may be a convenient time and that it may be done with least peril to you, although never without great danger to me, I will deal therein for your safety and offer it unto you as your prince and head without request.

As an "Affiliative" leader, Elizabeth was at her best. Her frequent linking of her goals and derived powers to the interests of the people provided the ultimate "affiliation" of Elizabeth's self-interest with the interests of her constituents. Biographer Mary Luke has noted this characteristic in her astute observation of Elizabeth's personal motivation involving the throne:

"Acknowledging the deprivation—the physical, emotional and spiritual loneliness of her first twenty-five years," writes Luke,

it must be remembered that this was no ordinary individual who ascended the throne of England in 1558. Given any other position in life, Elizabeth Tudor would have made her mark, perhaps in the arts and sciences of the day. Given the power of royalty, there was nothing she could and would not attempt. She had had scant security, less love and small hope for most of her life. To Elizabeth, the throne represented freedom — freedom to do as she chose as long as she remembered wherein lay her real popularity and strength: in the hearts and affections of her people. She spent forty-five years preserving her subjects' love and her appeal to them. This preservation of her Queenship was the prime reason for which Elizabeth Tudor lived. Never, under any circumstances or for any one individual would she endanger her popularity or risk her royal freedom. Once this is accepted, many of the perplexing questions involving Elizabeth — from her reluctance to marry to her reluctance to make war — become clear and understandable.

Elizabeth was, perhaps, least skilled in the Democratic style of leadership (but, it must be remembered, democracy was little practiced in her age). She was, however, inclusive in her councils, which consisted of nominal Catholics, mainstream Anglicans, and radical Puritans, among others, representing a wide range of styles, temperaments, and talents.

In our own age, with its strong emphasis on empowerment and group decision making, the Democratic style has become a sine qua non for leaders. Andrew Schorr, editor of HealthTalk.com, a Seattle-based online medical service, discussed democratic leadership skills not only in the workplace, but in dealing with customers. Schorr says leaders show others "how they can win by working together in a positive way." At HealthTalk.com, he does that by encouraging interactivity and acting on suggestions of people who use the website, as well as those on the site-development team. "Leadership is having people see how they can have a common win, [how they] can do remarkable things," Schorr says. "You simply have to ask and give them an opportunity to do it in a way that they are comfortable. When you call on people to help or follow, as long as they respond in a positive way it still can have value even if it doesn't fit your exact image of how you think it should be." Schorr says there's a "gloriousness" in leadership that enables people to express their individuality within a context of a higher purpose.

Bess's skill as a "Pacesetter"—a leader who expects excellence and self-direction—is illustrated by her mastery of delegation. The ability to delegate was cited as a primary attribute of outstanding leaders in many of the interviews we conducted with prominent modern leaders, including Brigadier General (USAF-retired) Karen S. Rankin. Rankin, now a senior executive with Johnson Controls, described outstanding leadership as "the ability to express a vision for an organization, define the appropriate strategies to achieve that vision, and then delegate to subordinates the responsibility and authority to execute the strategies as well as insuring subordinates have sufficient resources."

Elizabeth's use of delegation and the "Pacesetter" style exemplify Rankin's view of how delegation should be handled. When the queen handed off a responsibility, she passed along the authority needed to meet that responsibility. The powers she conferred, in some instances, were equal to her own. For example, in establishing the Turkish Company to trade with the Ottoman Empire, she also appointed the company's head, William Harborne, to serve as her ambassador to Turkey. In Elizabeth's day, travel and communications were slow and unreliable—especially across the Mediterranean, where English ships were subject to capture by Spanish ships, as well as pirates. If a crisis required instant action in Turkey to protect English interests, there would be no time for Harborne to send to London for instructions. Consequently, when Elizabeth named him her agent in 1582, she assigned him three broad commissions:

1. The power and authority to confirm the league of friendship and to ratify the grant of privileges and to command and enjoin by the authority of the Queen all English merchants to obey the prescription and orders of these privileges and in default thereof, to administer justice and punishment accordingly.

2. The power to designate the ports and cities where Englishmen might trade and to prohibit their trading elsewhere within the limits of the Ottoman Empire; and to make and create consuls or governors in whatever places he might choose to establish trading centers; and,

3. The power to enact laws and statutes for the governing of all English subjects having business with Turkey and to punish all offenders against these laws.

Having told Harborne what he was to do, the queen then gave him the power to it, authorizing him to "doe and fulfill all and singular things whatsoever, which shall seeme requisite and convenient for the honest and orderly government of our said subjects and of the manner of their traffic in those parts."

And, if he erred in his judgments? Having given Harborne the authority to act on his judgment, she also vowed to back his actions (malfeasance excepted): "Whatsoever shall be done of our sayd Orator and Agent, in all, or in any of the premisses, not repugnant and contrary to the lawes, shall be accepted, ratified and confirmed by us."

Elizabeth's grant of such authority and support to Harborne (and countless other appointees), demonstrates a key distinction modern leaders find between good managers and bad managers. Liz Dolan, former vice president of Global Marketing for Nike, put it this way: "A bad leader is a back seat driver who says 'take a right here, a left here.' A good leader says, 'Okay, we're meeting in Dodge. Here's a map. There are 10 different ways to get there. Good luck!'" Elizabeth was most often that second kind of leader.

In "Coaching" mode, Elizabeth could be formidable. She set clear standards for behavior and dress and surrounded herself continually with young advisers and courtiers with whom she could model behavior and discuss ideas and practices. She could also coach some of the "old pros" in her cabinet. Elizabeth's "coaching" sometimes involved shoring up the confidence and helping demoralized councilors. This is seen in several of her letters to her advisers. At one point, Lord Burghley was discouraged because of criticism he received from other councilors, notably Dudley, whose influence over the queen he bemoaned. Elizabeth wrote him a letter in which she referred to him as "Sir Spirit," joking that she called him that because "spirits" were known for having no sense and that he must be one because "I have seen lately that if an ass kick you, you feel it too soon." She then went on, in a light but clearly supportive tone to tell Burghley how much she needed him. Burghley stayed on as a result of this written "pep talk."

Because Elizabeth was a skilled leader, the queen set a standard, not only for future political leaders, but also for leaders of any organization, in any age.

In our interviews with executives we found common elements in their practical definitions of leadership and its qualities: vision, persuasiveness, openness to differing points of view, passion, integrity, ability to link strategies to goals, strong team-building skills, mastery of delegation, and the ability to inspire commitment in others. Our interviewees also noted that although Elizabeth's techniques were ahead of her time, we have learned much about leadership since 1603—much that Elizabeth would no doubt have incorporated into her style were she dealing with today's organizations.

But the techniques of leadership must be separated from the ends to which they are put, which is one reason Machiavelli's *The Prince* has been found to be a useful guide by leaders who advance worthy causes, as well as those who use effective means to achieve questionable—if not evil—ends.

The pragmatic Elizabeth recognized that occasionally the niceties of "right" had to be sacrificed in order to obtain a higher good, a justification she noted in a letter to Sir Henry Sydney, her governor of Ireland. "If the right must be violated," she told him, "it must be for the sake of rule." But the queen kept an eye out at all times to avoid such ethical dilemmas and urged her contemporaries to do likewise. In a letter to France's King Henry IV in 1593, she reminded him that "It is a dangerous thing to do evil, even for a good end."

Dr. Judith Rosener, who frequently cites Machiavelli's ideas in her management courses at the University of California–Irvine, spoke to us about the age-old controversy involving confusion of the means with the ends of leadership. "This is not original, I don't know where I've heard it, but I think the definition of leadership is a lot like the concept of pornography," Rosener says. "You can't describe it but you know it when you see it. You can't measure it or define it. Leadership takes so many forms. Gandhi was a leader and Hitler was a leader. The question is, 'Is leadership necessarily implicit [if what you are doing is taking] you where you want to go?' Hitler was a great leader. We don't approve of what he did, but that doesn't detract from the fact that he was able to mobilize people. If you took leaders in all their forms, what is the one underlying consistent pattern? I think it's the ability to motivate others to behave in a desired way for some desired goal."

No less an authority than Arthur Schlesinger, the Pulitzer Prize–winning historian and biographer of President John F. Kennedy, has written that, whether they are considered good or bad human beings, "great leaders are those men and women who leave their personal stamp on history."

According to Schlesinger, "the very concept of leadership implies the proposition that individuals can make a difference. This proposition has never been universally accepted. From classic times to the present day, eminent thinkers have regarded individuals as no more than the agents and pawns of larger forces, whether the gods and goddesses of the ancient world, the will of the people, the spirit of the times, or history itself. Against such forces, the individual dwindles into insignificance."

It is difficult to imagine a leader less eclipsed by her age and the forces of history than Elizabeth. Her age was named after her and she remains a cultural icon throughout the English-speaking world nearly 400 years after her death. This might be true in part because, though she reigned in an era of divine right in which the duty of followers was to obey, her style made her a forerunner of the more democratic world to come.

According to Schlesinger,

> . . . the single benefit the great leaders confer is to embolden the rest of us to live according to our own best selves, to be active, insistent and resolute in affirming our own sense of things. For great leaders attest to the reality of human freedom against the supposed inevitabilities of history. . . . Great leaders, in short, justify themselves by emancipating and empowering their followers.

In the view of executives we interviewed, what is true for political leaders is valid for business leaders: empowerment of others is the single most important key to a modern executive's success. Amal Johnson, principal of Weiss, Peck & Greer Venture Partners in San Francisco, put it this way: "I believe as a leader you have to create opportunities within your environment so that there are moments of leadership that everyone can display. Leadership defines creating an environment where everyone in the organization can feel that they can take the moment of leadership and exercise it. There is a tremendous expectation that the leader has to be the leader every time, all the time, on every topic at every occasion. That's unrealistic. No one can know everything about every topic and be there all the time."

Elizabeth chose her team of advisers well, striving for diverse viewpoints in her cabinet. Carol Stephenson, president and CEO of Lucent Technologies Canada Corp. in Toronto, noted the criticality of this "Bess" practice. "Whether you are the leader of an empire, a corporation or a family," Stephenson told us, "diversity is key. As Queen Elizabeth I so evidently knew, surrounding yourself with the best and the brightest, embracing diverse points of view and fostering free expression leads the way to unleashed creativity, unmatched innovation and unlimited success."

In stating her personal definition of a leader, direct-mail merchandising legend Lillian Vernon described not only what many have said of Vernon herself, but succinctly summed up the key points that made Elizabeth the great leader she became. Said Vernon: "A leader is someone who inspires and brings out the best in people with their spirit, energy and enthusiasm. Leaders are role models who set high ethical standards both in their personal and professional lives. A leader is an intellectual thinker yet pragmatic, and is willing to take risks for a cause they believe is important. A leader must also be a sensitive person who is a good listener and shows compassion for others."

We have focused on the key traits that characterized Elizabeth's pragmatism, foremost of which was her flexibility in matching leadership style to the circumstances at hand. Throughout this book, you'll find examples of how, as a "radical centrist," she balanced opposing interests to maintain her independence and that of her realm.

It is common to think of leaders in terms of massive changes, great leaps forward, revolutionary practices, but Elizabeth was not that kind of leader. Conservative by nature, she favored, in most instances, an evolutionary approach. But she forced things to evolve. Her goal, on many issues, was to drive progress at a pace acceptable to all parties (with the possible exception of those who would marry her!). She was well positioned to understand that changes occurring in her reign were more likely to last if allowed to "sink in" rather than being forced with a heavy hand. She had, after all, seen revolutionary attempts at change lead to disorder and bankruptcy for her country.

Contrasting Elizabeth's style to that of her father, Henry VIII, and her sister, Mary, shows the wisdom of her "make haste slowly" style. Henry had, of course, established the Church of England in a precipitous move designed to affirm his divorce from Catherine of Aragon. Henry's Church continued, but weakened, under the reign of the tubercular adolescent Edward VI. Upon his death, Mary I rescinded the Church's mandate and precipitously reestablished Catholicism as England's religion. Upon her coronation, Elizabeth quickly reestablished the Anglican Church, but she made a point of keeping both Catholics and Protestants in her government and adopted aspects of the Catholic mass in her personal worship. She also declined to take retaliatory steps against Catholics that would further the interests of the Puritans, the most radical wing of the Protestant movement. By allowing a period of adjust-ment and justifying any perceived persecution of Catholic rebels on grounds of "treason to the state" rather than dif-ferences of religious viewpoint, her reestablishment of An-glicanism survived her and the Church of England re-mained an established institution from her day to our own.

Although she could be inordinately impatient in her per-sonal affairs, Elizabeth exercised extraordinary patience in matters that would lead to lasting change in affairs of state. Her reluctance to authorize the executions of Mary, Queen of Scots and, earlier, the Duke of Norfolk, often frustrated her less-patient advisers. But her deliberateness served the queen well. It was not, as some of her advisers thought, a matter of "a woman's weak will," but of the pre-scient mind of a genius: delay enabled the queen and her partisans not only to develop compelling cases for her ac-tions but also—and, more important—to ensure that the people, upon whose good will the queen's future rested— understood why the queen acted as she did.

Elizabeth's attempts at balance enabled her to consoli-date her base of support. In a time when news traveled slowly, she made a point of making sure the reasons for her actions and the nature of her deliberations were dissemi-nated well in advance of any significant action. As a leader who did not like to be unfavorably surprised by the actions of others, she was diligent in not surprising others with her own. The value of leading with information, then follow-ing with action, was illustrated in one of our executive in-terviews. The interviewee told her story this way:

I have been with this company two months and we haven't made any dramatic process changes yet, but there's something happening already with the culture, and recognized by people who have been in the company for a long time, that is changing the outcomes in just two months. . . . Before I got here, I sent out a letter to all the management staff. I told them about my basic beliefs about running a "people first" company, taking care of our customers both internal and external, the need to create value for our associates, our customers, our community at large, and our investors. I try to be very clear about my expectations. When I go in we look at how we are going to do this [and develop the path together].

That manager's approach emulates Elizabeth's during the first months of her reign. Weeks before her coronation she established the criteria she would use in choosing her cabinet; she outlined the rules for who would stay and who would go and let people know that those asked to step aside would incur no retribution for their services to Elizabeth's predecessor. Prior to her coronation and during the first two months of her reign, the queen spoke of her values and laid the philosophical groundwork that would rule her decisions concerning religious tolerance, her own marriage, and the succession. In her choice of ministers, her outreach to the people, her avoidance of punitive measures against old foes, and her outreach to dissidents, Elizabeth established a climate of stability and reason to erase fears that could have brought her reign down before it had had a chance to succeed.

Had times been different, Elizabeth might well have chosen a different leadership path, but at a time when her kingdom was beset by civil dissent, fear of war, and concern over her lack of experience, the queen chose "balanced pragmatism" as the leadership style best suited to the times, her position, and her character. The length and success of her reign proved the wisdom of her choice.

2

Managing Finances

I never was any greedy, scraping grasper . . . nor
yet a waster. My heart was never set on any
worldly goods. What you bestow on me, I will not
hoard it up, but receive it to bestow on you again.

HENRY VIII LIKED TO SPEND MONEY. In fact, his
fun-loving, oft-married highness was a spendthrift and left
his heir, the boy-king Edward VI, with huge debts that he
and his regent Lord Somerset passed on to Mary I, who
passed them on to Elizabeth. The personal fortunes of the
English monarchs in the sixteenth century were, in effect,
the national treasury. Although Parliament could enact special taxes for the purpose of carrying out wars, taxation was
neither common, nor were the proceeds large—certainly
not by twenty-first-century standards. In effect, the
monarch's coffers and lines of credit with European bankers
maintained their administrations, financed their wars, and
paid for all expenses of both their households and the na-

tion. Since the concept of "national debt" was nonexistent, monarchs relied on a number of clever techniques to keep things going when their outflows exceeded their incomes. Faced with serious cash flow problems, Henry and his immediate predecessors, for example, had tried to balance their books by adulterating the coinage (a practice that wags might say fitted perfectly with Henry's sexual behavior!). Their scheme was this: Take an English coin, which at the beginning of Henry's reign was minted of solid gold or silver, and as new coins were minted start mixing in a little base metal, while maintaining the face value of the coin. Ideally, the coin would trade within England at face value and maintain its purchasing power. The gold no longer used in the coins could be used to pay off the foreign bankers. By Elizabeth's time, most English coins contained only about 25 percent gold or silver. Of course, as the English people figured this out, prices began rising and inflation was the rule of the day. The people also began hoarding older coins containing more precious metal while spending as quickly as possible the debased coinage, whose composition was in question. This meant that gold was harder for the mints to come by and consequently, they used even less precious metal in the coins as time passed.

The English also practiced the art of melting down the coins to extract the gold, which was hoarded, and of "clipping" the gold from the edges of the coins and then trying to pass the coins off at face value. When Elizabeth came to power, no one had faith in the coins issued by the monarchs—and lack of faith in the money created lack of faith in the monarchy itself. If Elizabeth was to restore faith in the monarchy, she had to restore faith in the money it issued; she had to spend less than she took in; and, if she was to pay off debt, she would have to find new sources of revenue. With the help of Lord Burghley, Sir Thomas Gresham, and Sir Francis Drake, she did just that, while maintaining a splendid court and beating the Spanish Armada to boot!

———————

Although Elizabeth's skills at leadership, communication, and spin doctoring have been highly praised, she is less well known for her extraordinary acumen as a businessperson and financial manager. Bess was notoriously tight with her money, especially when it was sought for the purpose of financing foreign entanglements that might throw England into bankruptcy or cause the queen to risk her popularity through the imposition of burdensome taxes.

The queen's "balanced pragmatism" became a hallmark of her decisions to loosen or tighten the purse strings while maintaining her popularity, her image, and her ability to keep aggressors at bay. One of her first financial achievements was that of restoring the credibility of her coinage, which demonstrated not only her understanding of monetary issues, but also her ability to heed advice from experts whose genius matched her own. In money matters, that "genius" was none other than Thomas Gresham, who earned himself a place in history by articulating "Gresham's Law," which holds that "bad" money drives "good" money from circulation. On a personal level, we intuitively recognize the truth of Gresham's Law. If we have a torn, worn, or defaced dollar bill in our wallets, we invariably tend to get rid of it as soon as possible, sometimes even trading it in at the teller's window. Gresham, of course, was dealing with a much more onerous type of "bad" money. Sir Thomas was the first person in history to observe that if two coins bearing the same face value and supposedly possessing the same purchasing power were circulated at the same time, people tended to hoard coins containing the most gold or silver, while quickly passing on debased coins that contained mostly base metal. Thus, the bad money drove the good money out of circulation. A corollary phenomenon was that "bad" money also drove prices up and undermined the purchasing value of all money.

In 1560, England had mostly "bad" money—so bad, in fact, that many historians have called it the most debased coinage in history. Although precious-metal content had been reduced to an average of only 25 percent over a period of twenty-five years, many coins contained far less. One coin, for example, was made primarily of copper and then lightly coated in silver. The coating was so thin that it tended to quickly wear off as the coin was passed, revealing a reddish image of King Henry's face—and well his face should have been red, given the scam he was pulling on his subjects! Debased coinage fueled inflation, pulled good money from the market, and undermined faith in Elizabeth's administration. Inflation meant, of course, that Elizabeth's gold would buy less and that there would be less gold in circulation (unless, of course, Sir Francis Drake came home with more of the stuff in his hold). The queen could, with Parliament's permission, perhaps raise taxes (as on occasion she did), but heavy taxation could well kill the profit incentive that might drive the creation of new monopolies and the revenues to be derived directly from her investments in them. In addition, if the people were over-burdened with taxes they might find their affections alien-ated from their monarch in ways that might lead to addi-tional costs for security. Elizabeth required a strong economy; restored coinage and an avoidance of taxes on her people would fuel the trade and investment growth needed to attain it.

Guided by Gresham, Elizabeth acted quickly to fix things. In 1560, she instructed Gresham to call in the bad money, melt it down and issue new coins of pure precious-metal content. Within a year, he completed the task and England had real money again.

Gresham's Law has applications beyond finance. Any time standards are lowered, one runs a risk of losing value. If, for example, a college lowers its admission standards to maintain entry-class sizes, then over time better students will begin choosing to attend institutions with higher stan-dards. The same exodus will eventually occur if the institu-tion lowers its standards for faculty. Although a college may be able to maintain its reputation for excellence in the short term, when the best and brightest students and teach-ers realize the quality of graduates has suffered, the school will lose its reputation as a place of academic excellence and will be tempted to further lower admission and faculty standards in order to maintain entry-class size, faculty size, and solvency. Or, in an example from business, think of what happens when a firm tries to capitalize on its estab-lished reputation for quality, but reduces that quality in an attempt to control costs. Several former Commonwealth governments have learned the lessons of Gresham's Law in terms of their issuance of postage stamps—a major source of revenue for many small countries. Having built a reputation among collectors for issuing infrequent new designs in limited editions valued by collectors for their rarity, during the late 1970s many began issuing new designs more frequently and in larger quantities. Ignoring Gresham's Law, these nations believed that collectors would continue collecting the new stamps in order to maintain the integrity of their collections. At first, revenues soared, but as the new issuing policies became apparent, collectors switched their interests to countries with more value-oriented issuance policies, or began focusing on collecting a country's older stamp issues in the secondary market, from which the governments derived no income. What was true for Commonwealth stamps is true anytime quality is reduced: consumers reject lower quality and flock to higher quality when "face value" remains the same.

J. E. Neale, arguably Elizabeth's finest biographer, held that "finance is the essence of Elizabeth's story." When she came to power she inherited about £350,000 in debt (close to $280 million in today's money) from Mary's government and soon had another £650,000 (about $520 million today) to cover the costs of driving the French out of Scotland and trying to reclaim Calais by force. These sums may seem small in the twenty-first-century world of trillion-dollar national debts and billion-dollar-a-year CEO compensation, but were formidable amounts in Elizabeth's time, in which an unskilled laborer might earn the modern equivalent of only $4,000 a year. They were especially burdensome on a country with less than 4 million inhabitants. (Costs are relative, however, and it should be noted that a loaf of bread cost only about seven cents and a chicken less than four cents in modern terms.)

In approaching her financial woes, Elizabeth did what any smart executive should do. In addition to getting rid of bad money, she took five other actions that eventually gave her government a surplus. Her program consisted of:

1. Reducing ongoing expenses.
2. Avoiding costly new ventures with high risk of loss.
3. Restructuring debt.
4. Selling off (or renting) nonproductive Crown properties.
5. Investing the proceeds from interest savings and the sale of less profitable properties in growth opportunities.

Let's look at each strategy with an eye to its relevance today:

Point 1: Reducing ongoing expenses. Bess had learned to be tight with a dollar as a young woman. Her father had granted her a small bequest of £3,000 a year until she married, at which time a payment of £10,000, mostly in goods, would be turned over to her. The stipend was designed as short-term maintenance in the belief that Elizabeth would, in fact, marry, and be provided for by others. She had learned to count her pennies as a result, keeping household expenses low and learning to live within a budget. Although Elizabeth was frugal, it would be wrong to imply that she was impoverished. Biographer Jane Resh Thomas cites figures indicating that Princess Elizabeth's average annual income was about £4,800 pounds a year. As Thomas notes, using a calculation that one Tudor pound (actually, they were called "sovereigns" back then) was equal to about 500 modern pounds, the princess had to survive on a mere £2.4 million in today's currency, or about $3.8 million! But Elizabeth, even as a princess, had to maintain a large household and several estates—and, if she became queen, she would have to absorb the debts run up by her predecessors and virtually all costs of maintaining the government. So she learned to live within her means.

William Cecil, later Lord Burghley, in defending the queen to Parliament, once remarked that "the parsimony of her Majesty hath been a great cause of her majesty's riches, [enabling her] to perform these actions whereof heads are inquisitive." Although never allowing her cutbacks to diminish the level of splendor necessary to retain her image of power both at home and abroad, Elizabeth studiously avoided the profligacy that had characterized her father's reign. "As for her private expenses," it was said. "they have been little in building. She hath consumed little or nothing in her pleasures. As for her apparel, it is royal and princely, beseeming her calling, but not sumptuous nor excessive."

Elizabeth also used modern compensation approaches to controlling payroll costs, keeping fixed wages low, but bestowing gifts and "bonuses" based on performance or enabling her subordinates to profit from their offices. Burghley, for example, had an official wage of only about £100 a year ($80,000 today), but it is estimated his annual income was as often as much £4,000 (or $3.2 million—pocket change in comparison to top CEO compensation in our time!). As with many contemporary efforts to control payrolls, the queen's moves were not always greeted with enthusiasm by those who labored on her behalf and, in truth, the queen was not always fair in whom she chose to reward. Sir Francis Walsingham, in particular, was more impoverished by his office than enriched by it and complained in 1578 that "none hath more cause to complain than myself, being rather decayed than advanced by my long and painful service." Upon Burghley's urgings, the queen eventually granted Walsingham the right to farm a number of royal manors, but unlike Burghley (who died an extraordinarily rich man), Walsingham was pursued to his grave by creditors.

Finally, the queen took advantage of vacancy savings, particularly as they related to Anglican bishoprics, where a vacancy meant not only that she could reduce "middle management salaries," but also keep the money expended on them for other purposes. Historian Christopher Hibbert describes her methods this way:

> When opportunities to make more money presented themselves, the Queen was never overscrupulous in seizing them, whether it be in clandestine investments in piratical expeditions or in fleecing the Church. Not only were bishoprics kept vacant for long periods so that she could lay her hands on the revenues . . . but she also took advantage of a clause in the Act of 1559 to insist upon bishops granting long leases to the Crown either for her own benefit or for that of some councilor or courtier whom it was in her interest to reward. As her godson, John Harington, punned, her courtiers were more often to be found preying on the Church than [praying] in the church.

Point 2: Avoiding costly new expenditures.   For Elizabeth, avoiding costly new ventures meant avoiding foreign entanglements that might lead to expensive wars that would drain her coffers. This often frustrated her advisers, particularly militants like Walsingham, who argued that her concern for fiscal responsibility and obsession with bean-counting were holding her own security and England's future hostage to her parsimony. In reading over contemporary documents detailing the arguments advanced both in support of and against the queen's reluctance to fund Walsingham's foreign programs, we were struck by their similarity to those that often exist in modern corporations between financial and marketing divisions, as well as those that exist between political partisans who argue for reducing the national debt and trimming the budget, while their opponents call for social and economic programs that would increase government spending in the short term but might reduce expenditures and increase revenues over time. In modern terms, Elizabeth, as CEO, basically backed and encouraged Lord Burghley's view that England would have no future unless it was on a sound financial footing in the present. She firmly believed short-term dollars should be used for short-term purposes and only after those had been met, should surpluses be spent on foreign interventions with, at best, long-term benefits, if any at all. Walsingham, Nicholas Throckmorton, and Dudley argued, on the other hand, that forgoing long-term investment in their foreign-policy initiatives would, if postponed, do more to undermine England's future than would the queen's tightfistedness assure its present.

We asked the CEOs we interviewed how they balanced long- and short-term considerations in their own budget decisions and found general agreement with Elizabeth's approach.

Like Elizabeth, Brenna Bolger, president of PRx, a large public relations firm in San Jose, California, said financial decision-making should be a matter of return on expenditure. "Trying to postulate and project what return might come from a projected expenditure is the best way to determine whether or not to take risk." Bolger cited three expenditures she'd recently decided to make: the cost of a bigger office, the purchase of new equipment for a conference room, and investments in her company's website, www.prxinc.com. In each case, she says, the decision was based on a determination that the outlays in cash would be covered by lowered costs of operations, time savings, customer satisfaction, and employee productivity. "My bottom line on how I spend money is what kind of return I'll get on it."

Although Elizabeth was focused on solvency rather than margin, the issue for modern organizations—particularly not-for-profit organizations—often involves arguments over margin goals.

"Look, it's as simple as this," one executive told us. "If my shareholders don't get an adequate return, they pull their funds. That means I have to scramble to find new ones—and no one is going to be attracted to a company that has a margin of, say 5 percent, when other companies can give them 30 percent. In addition, when margins fall, I have to spend more time focusing on shareholder relations, which distracts me from finding new revenue sources and restructuring for cost control. Less money for the shareholders makes me less likely to have money for big raises and rewards for my people, which means more turnover, more training costs, more time spent finding new people — another distraction. The more profit at high margin I have, the more money I have to invest in R&D, pay out to shareholders, and reward my employees. I think this is a slam-dunk, QED thing. Elizabeth didn't just do the best thing, she did the only thing a good steward can do. And she modeled it by not overrewarding herself and showing restraint in her personal expenditures."

Another executive said it even more succinctly: "A demand for strong financials in the present doesn't rob the future; it enables the future."

Point 3: Restructuring her debt and obtaining lower interest rates.   Elizabeth cut nonproductive expenditures to free up money to invest in more productive ones. But restructuring alone was not enough. If, for example, she had done what too many people do when they consolidate credit-card payments, pay them off with a contemporary "home equity" loan, and then use the savings for a long European vacation, she would not have improved her financial situation. She refused to accept interest rates of more than 10 percent and the strength of her government and attention to prompt payment helped her get the rate she demanded.

Point 4: Selling off unproductive properties.   Elizabeth had never heard of portfolio matrix analysis, but she practiced it nonetheless. Matrix analysis (sometimes called four-box analysis) was created years ago by Boston Consulting Group to assess investment portfolios for its clients. In its original application, a shareholder's stocks were segmented on the basis of their current returns, on the one hand, and their potential for future returns on the other. If a stock was found to have low current earnings and virtually no hope for future growth it was assigned to the lower-left section of a box that had been divided into four quadrants. This quadrant became known as the "doghouse." If a stock had great current returns but was unlikely to show growth in the future, it was assigned to the lower right quadrant, the "milk barn," and labeled a "cash cow." Stocks that produced little current income, but had high growth potential were assigned to the upper-left-hand quadrant, the "nursery," and labeled "problem children"; with a little nurturing they might grow up to be productive citizens. Finally, stocks that had both strong current earnings and strong prospects for growth were assigned to the upper right-hand quadrant and labeled "Stars." Once investments had been assigned to the quadrants, analysts could proceed with recommendations. In most cases, this meant selling off the dogs and milking the cash cows, then reinvesting in efforts to nurture the problem children and buy more stock in the "Stars." By selling off unproductive Crown lands and other fallow assets, Elizabeth's freed up cash to fix the problem kids and invest more in lucrative monopolies and high-growth foreign-trading companies.

Many of the executives we interviewed use matrix analysis routinely to assess not only investment and product-development decisions, but also to analyze their staffs.

"It's simple—sometimes I think too simple, but it's one of the most effective thinking tools in a manager's bag of tricks," said one CEO. "Whenever a manager wants me to magically find money we don't have to fuel a new initiative, I suggest that she look for some dogs we can unload for reinvestment purposes. It's surprising how often we uncover resources that can be used more productively."

Harriet Mosson, former president of Liz Claiborne Dresses and Suits, told us that the fast-changing world of fashion requires quick changes in product lines. "The sooner you make the decision to drop [a losing product], the better off you are. Because if something is bad, whether the product is bad or the dress isn't selling or the inventory isn't moving or the whole concept isn't working, you have to get past it. You have to get rid of it and start over again, or revamp it. You have to address it. Ignoring it won't make it go away. The worse it gets the more money you lose." Of course, the more money one loses, the less money one has to develop and market products that *will* sell.

Point 5: Investing in growth opportunities to drive revenues.   To become financially stronger, Elizabeth needed not only to spend less, she also needed to bring in more. She had to plow the benefits of improved cash flow into income-producing ventures. She did this by investing in Drake's voyages (we don't recommend backing pirates, though in her case and her times, it was justifiable in the national interest). The executives we interviewed applauded Bess's financial astuteness in putting the money she saved from restructuring her debt and selling off her "dogs" to productive use rather than, say, gold-plating her palace. Elizabeth realized that she could not simply save her way to prosperity; she had to put her savings to work.

Backing the likes of Drake was only one of her strategies. She backed other voyages to the New World—notably Raleigh's—and she sought trade relations around the world. Her support went beyond policy; she actually became an investor in new joint public-private trading ventures like the Turkish Company and the East India Company, as well as in domestic monopolies on internal trade. Elizabeth's support for these companies was essential in securing their recognition by foreign rulers, who had to approve access to their markets. Domestically, the queen's imprimatur assured the profits in trade and manufacture of goods such as linen, tobacco, and whiskey.

Once Elizabeth had expanded her income potential, she found she had created new ways of saving money through business alliances and additional "vacancy savings." As a major shareholder in the joint-stock companies, Elizabeth was astute in using her clout to reduce the costs of government by passing them along to the private interests that benefited from her support. For example, when she was negotiating with the Turkish Company, she insisted that its agent also serve as her ambassador to the Ottoman Empire—and that the private shareholders cover the expense of his state role! The deal was a hard one for the Turkish Company's investors to swallow, but they agreed to it in recognition of the profits they were likely to enjoy from having a monopoly on trade with Turkey. Modern corollaries to Elizabeth's actions to reduce the fixed costs of business abound in the form of outsourcing and joint-venturing. Elizabeth outsourced a diplomatic job to a TC employee, while sharing in overall development costs and proceeds of the company's success as an investor and partner. That model was followed in other joint ventures, both foreign and domestic throughout her reign.

As a historical note, Elizabeth did not invent the public-private joint venture. Prior to her reign, the Russia Company had been formed in 1553, primarily as an outgrowth of efforts to find a Northeast Passage to Asia. The queen did, however, enable formation of the first domestic joint-stock companies in 1568, when the Mines Royal and others were established. Her reign also saw the founding of the Turkey Company (1580) and the London East India Company (1600).

Elizabeth was a strong believer in both collecting and paying her debts on time—and nothing infuriated her more than a fellow prince who engaged in slow pay, or no pay practices. Her "collection" letters, written to Henry IV after she'd helped him defend his throne against Spanish intrigue and internal rebellion, seem tame by modern collection standards, but are classics in the early history of debt-collection techniques. Having extended him credit during his time of trouble and waited patiently until she knew he was in a position to pay, she hounded him incessantly for repayment, threatening to cut off relations and shame him in the eyes of his fellow rulers if he didn't come through with payment—which, reluctantly and with little grace—he eventually did.

Elizabeth's emphases on avoiding long-term debt, keeping her financial promises, maintaining the credibility of her coinage, avoiding unjustified taxation, spending wisely, and investing aggressively in growth ventures were not only a hallmark not only of her shrewdness in financial matters—but set a standard for future governments and organizations seeking success through sound fiscal policy.

The Queen's Money Men

Sir Francis Drake (c. 1543–1596)

The Spanish called him El Draque ("The Dragon") and believed him to be in league with the devil and endowed with supernatural powers of perception and movement. An accomplished sailor who had made his first voyages, starting in 1563, with his cousin John Hawkins, a trader in slaves and commodities, Drake had seen both Africa and the New World before his twenty-fifth birthday. His first command resulted in disaster when Drake's ship, the *Judith*, was ambushed at San Juan D'Ulloa, leaving him with a lifelong hatred of the Spanish. His swashbuckling ways and ability to torment the Spanish at sea made him a folk hero among the English and a favorite of the queen. In 1577, she secretly authorized him to raid Spanish ships during what was ostensibly a voyage of discovery in search of the Northwest Passage to the Orient—a voyage that she helped finance. His circuitous route around Cape Horn and through the Straits of Magellan gave him ample opportunity to stumble upon gold-laden Spanish ships, which he confronted and pillaged before proceeding up the California coast, which he claimed for England. He returned in 1580, and though he had failed to find the Northwest Passage, his ships were filled to capacity with expensive spices from the Orient and with the booty from the Spanish ships that had crossed his path. Elizabeth enjoyed a large and much-needed profit from the voyage. Drake had also made England's first (and history's second) circumnavigation of the world and was knighted the following year. In 1587, he "singed the beard" of Philip II-when he led a raid on Cadiz, leaving thirty destroyed

(continues)

Spanish ships in his wake. Drake was instrumental as both a commander and strategist in the English defense against the Armada, but lost some of his luster when, in 1589, he led an unsuccessful attack on Spanish ports. Shortly thereafter he retired from the navy and served a short term in Parliament before heading to sea with Hawkins in a failed effort to raid Spanish holdings in the New World in 1595. He died on the return voyage in January 1596. A dashing military man and explorer, Drake's greatest contribution to Elizabeth was as "a rainmaker"—a privateer who was able to find the revenues that fueled the second half of her reign and in large part guaranteed her solvency.

Sir Thomas Gresham (c. 1518–1579)

Gresham, the son of a wealthy London merchant, was Henry VIII's chief financial agent from 1551, a post he continued to hold under Edward VI, Mary I, and Elizabeth. His first task upon his appointment was that of convincing bankers in Antwerp to accept lower interest rates on Henry's debt while obtaining a better rate of exchange for payments on the principle. From 1560 to 1563, he was Elizabeth's ambassador to the Netherlands, where in addition to his financial tasks he served as a source of political and military intelligence. When the Netherlands banned the export of its solid-gold coinage, Gresham abrogated the ban by smuggling it to England in cargoes of munitions, gunpowder, and spices. He not only convinced the queen to stop the practice of debasing English coinage, but also devised the program for recalling the debased coins and distributing the newly minted and fully valued ones. The program began in 1560, as the bad coinage was collected and melted down so that the precious metal could be extracted and minted into the new coins. The whole program took a year to accomplish. An astute businessman, Gresham enjoyed large commissions on his government transactions, later using his riches to establish the precursor of the London Stock Exchange. He is best known today for having propounded "Gresham's Law," which holds that bad money drives good money from the market.

3
The Art of "Spin"

WHEN SUMMMER CAME to Britain, the queen usually went "on progress," traveling her realm with a large retinue of courtiers and servants. These annual excursions served both as royal vacations and as opportunities for the queen to escape the incessant political buzz of her Privy Council and establish direct contact with the public she served.

The processions were carefully orchestrated to enable direct contact with the queen so that the common folk could not only see her, but also chat her up, be touched by her, sing her praises, and sometimes kiss her hand. Whether riding on horseback at the head of the procession or being carried in an open litter, the queen frequently halted so she could speak to or receive presents from those who lined her path. When out among her people, Elizabeth was magnanimous, charming, approachable—working the crowd for days at a time and winning their affection wherever she went.

The queen's progress was an entertainment for the towns through which she passed, a spectacle of unmatched splendor. After witnessing her on progress in 1579, the French ambassador Michel de Castelnau described his awe of the queen who "more beautiful than ever, bedizened like the sun, and mounted on a fine Spanish horse; and with so many people before her that it was a marvelous thing. They did not merely honour her, but they worshipped her, kneeling on the ground, with a thousand blessings."

Elizabeth was as at home among the throng as she was in her council chambers, prompting Edmund Grindal, a contemporary observer, to capture the essence of her appeal when he wrote, "I believe no prince living that was so tender of honour, and so exactly stood for the preservation of sovereignty, was so great a courtier of the people, yea of the commons, and that stooped and declined lower in presenting her person to the public view, as she passed in her progresses and perambulations."

The queen was simultaneously perceived both as Gloriana, the near-God, and as Good Bess, servant of the common people. Her public relations skills enabled her to merge the two into one without contradiction—and the image served her well.

When *Biography*, the A&E channel's prize-winning history program, described Elizabeth as "the spin doctor of a forty-five-year reign," it recognized both the extent and the modernity of the queen's skills in public relations. These skills manifested themselves in three areas:

Image Development,
Promotion, and Protection

The queen developed, promoted, and vigorously protected her image as Gloriana, the divinely ordained Virgin Queen married to her people. Because near-gods must be nearly perfect, they cannot afford to make egregious errors, so Elizabeth became not only a Virgin Queen, but a Teflon Queen as well. Failure would simply not stick to her reputation. Although some of her advisers criticized her for being too apt to take credit for success and avoid taking blame for failures, the queen and her wisest councilors recognized that protecting Elizabeth's image as the perfect ruler required bruising the egos of those whose glory could be enhanced only at their monarch's expense.

Communication of Her Mission

Elizabeth regularly carried her message directly to the people, using both visual and spoken language to embody their hopes. Although the queen was noted for her speaking abilities, she could also be a patient listener, particularly when visiting with local officials, whose views she heard less often than those of her Privy Councilors.

Damage Control

The queen was quick to respond to criticisms of her policy, attacks on her honor, and formal attempts to portray her as too weak to rule. In such instances, she responded immediately and in full to questions raised by her opponents.

Bess's techniques in all three arenas remain in widespread use by twenty-first-century corporate practitioners and political "spinmeisters," which testifies to their timeless utility. Even more remarkably, Elizabeth carried out her public relations program without benefit of modern media and communications technology—no television, no radio, no Internet, no computerized databases, no newspapers, and, most important, no public opinion polls. The success of her efforts depended entirely on her emotional intelligence and intuitive understanding of human nature, and her efforts were so successful that it is difficult to imagine that even with the benefit of modern techniques and technology, she would have been able to manage her public relations any better. Indeed, the queen's skills at "spin" were critical in transforming her tiny island nation from a bankrupt pawn of France and Spain into a global powerhouse.

Brenna Bolger, president of PRx, a public relations firm in San Jose, California, described Elizabeth as "a born PR woman [who] would accomplish even more extraordinary things than she did if she could be here now." Bolger noted that, important as public relations was to Elizabeth, it plays an even more critical role in today's world of high-speed and specialized communication. "This is a period of the greatest innovation in human history and those of us in the communications and promotion business now get to be an integral part of it."

Elizabeth was, first and foremost, a great communicator. Although her subjects had to *listen* to her because she was queen, they *heard* her because she was able to articulate and personify their hopes.

To help us understand Elizabeth's strengths as a spin doctor, we called not only upon our own experiences in the public relations and speaking fields, but also upon the expertise of outstanding lobbyists, public relations specialists, and brand managers. One of them, Maureen Kindel, president of Rose & Kindel, an integrated public affairs company with offices in Los Angeles, Sacramento, and Washington, D.C., spoke specifically to Elizabeth's strengths. "She had two very important points [in her favor]," Kindel told us. "She understood that people want to worship something better than themselves [and] she understood how to communicate directly to the people and jump across the medium. In her days the media were her advisers and the opinion makers, probably the major landowners and church leaders. Today the medium is television."

"In U.S. political history, the first person to understand modern communications and use it wisely was Franklin Delano Roosevelt," Kindel said. "He used the radio. More close to our time is Ronald Reagan, who was absolutely a perfectionist at using the television and his speechmaking to jump right over his handlers, right over reporters, and right to the people. He spoke to the hearts of most men and women."

Kindel said modern communicators face more complex challenges than Elizabeth because "there is much more diversity in the population." Consequently, "a leader has to speak with many tongues and nuances to diverse audiences."

Elizabeth, of course, could literally speak many foreign languages, but her audience, the English people, was relatively homogeneous. There were fewer than 5 million people in Elizabeth's nation and, except for their religious differences, most shared a common language, common cultural and racial heritage, and a common history. Clearly, however, the high-sounding speeches sprinkled with Latin and Italian that characterized Elizabeth's formal speeches to elite audiences were unlikely to be understood by or appeal to the masses. When speaking to them, she had to express herself in a different language altogether, so she adapted her style, using the "language of the people" and creating public relations opportunities that became the basis for stories that could be told about her and widely disseminated by her advocates. The queen's summer progresses provided ample opportunities to create such stories and Elizabeth's history is filled with them. A frequently cited example involves an incident in Huntingdonshire in which a brash country fellow waylaid the queen. The queen was a stickler for protocol and fine dress at court, but she was informal on the road and found the behavior of the common folk refreshing, spontaneous, naturally gracious, and often amusing. At Huntingdonshire, one Sergeant Bendlowes stepped in the path of the queen's open carriage and impertinently demanded the coachman stop. "Stay thy cart, good fellow! Stay thy cart, that I may speak to the Queen." The coach halted, its passenger laughing as if she had "been tickled." With a show of graciousness that matched the sassiness of her petitioner, the queen listened to Bendlowes (no one knows what he said), then thanked him and stretched forth her hand to receive his kiss. Such informality was a hallmark of Elizabeth's processions and progresses.

The queen's passages often, though not always, accrued to a city's benefit. But the queen did not come cheap. Towns had to make costly preparations to welcome her. They were expected to stage elaborate and expensive entertainments; and they had to cover the costs of increased security and cleanup activities both before and after the entourage arrived—just as communities graced by presidential visits do in our own time. The towns were also expected to make a gift to the queen and the gifts had to be appropriately grand. The queen's gracious comments upon receiving these gifts were duly recorded and are masterpieces in the expression of politically savvy gratitude. For example, on a visit to Coventry Elizabeth was presented with a silver-plated cup holding £100 in gold (equal to nearly $80,000 in 2000). She praised the generosity of the town leaders, saying that "it was a good gift . . . I have few such gifts." Coventry's mayor replied, "If it please your Grace, there is a great deal more in it." The queen then asked what else there might be and received the reply: "It is the hearts of all your loving subjects." To which she replied, "We thank you, Mr. Mayor, it is a great deal more indeed." She so prized the good efforts and gifts of the people of Norwich that she left the town with tears in her eyes. And though quick to accept the gifts, she told the mayor of one town that "Princes have no need of money . . . we come for the hearts and allegiance of our subjects." Apparently, as in Coventry, the hearts and minds were intermixed with the gold for she kept both the cup and its contents!

Biographer Anne Somerset noted in her 1991 biography of Elizabeth that the queen's visits "were not necessarily just passing excitements, for if properly exploited, direct contact with the sovereign could yield solid advantage."

Somerset wrote: "When Elizabeth went to Stafford in 1575, for instance, she was told by one of the city magistrates that the city was in decline partly because the county assizes were no longer held there, and she promptly promised that in future they would be. Similarly, during a visit to Coventry ten years earlier the recorder of the city mentioned in his speech to the queen that the town had been unjustly deprived of lands that Henry VIII had set aside for the purpose of founding a free school there, and Elizabeth asked to be given more details about this."

In 1573, on a progress through Sandwich, Elizabeth showed she could well match the most vote-hungry modern politician in working the crowd at a political picnic. Abandoning her usual practice of dining lightly, Bess played the trencherman, sampling more than 140 dishes, praising the women who had prepared them, and then, noting that some of the food was so good she could not bear to part from it, asked that it be "doggy-bagged" so she could take it home! (Imagine the positive PR that existed in Sandwich for generations as recipes bearing names like "The Queen's Biscuits" were handed down from mother to daughter, perhaps noting that "grandmother prepared these for Good Queen Bess who called them the best she ever ate!")

Kindel said that, regardless of the audience one is trying to reach, "likeability" is the most important thing to convey and it is best conveyed by "the ability to speak in plain terms, terms with which average people can identify." Elizabeth was always in "the zone" when she was on progress. And although her trips were technically vacations, she always chose to go where her presence was most likely to shore up popular support and indicate her awareness and concern for the issues affecting the people who lived there. In 1575, for example, she visited the city of Worcester, where 5,000 textile workers were unemployed. Here she listened patiently while one of the town's leading men presented a long speech on the town's troubles and called for higher tariffs and lower quotas on imports to improve things. Although the queen made no promise of action, her presence and her willingness to endure the speaker's haranguing and tedious argument were enough in themselves to buoy the spirit of the townspeople. Her visit showed she was both sympathetic and willing to listen — and that alone is often enough to win the hearts of those in despair. The visit had a remarkable parallel in American politics more than 400 years later when President Ronald Reagan visited the economically devastated city of Flint, Michigan, where thousands of workers had been thrown out of work by cutbacks at General Motors. The president toured the city, met with city leaders, and even visited a pizza parlor, where he listened, one-on-one, to the concerns of auto workers for their future.

Elizabeth's progresses were filled with acts of compassion, including the distribution of alms to the poor; the ritual washing of her subjects' feet; and the examination of subjects' sores and injuries. Her propagandists capitalized on her image as a healer of supernatural power. William Tooker, one of the queen's chaplains, even wrote a tract about Dr. Bess, claiming that there was in her the "power inherent in the rightful English sovereign of curing the King's Evil" (also known as scrofula or tuberculosis of the lymph nodes, particularly in the neck), a disease that was rampant during a portion of Bess's reign. People believed Gloriana's touch alone could rid them of the disease and Tooker credited her with having cured, on a single day, thirty-eight people!

Tooker's account was only one of many tracts, stories, paintings, odes, and songs designed to foster Elizabeth's popular image as a messenger and representative of God, ordained by Him to care for her subjects and deliver England from its enemies. Gloriana, the Virgin Queen married to her people, was more than just a persona, it was a brand. It stood not just for Elizabeth, a tangible being, but for all of the things her subjects might wish her, and themselves, to be: pure, prosperous, devout, beloved of God, strong in war, and magnanimous in peace. In the 1998 motion picture *Elizabeth*, the queen remakes herself and establishes herself as the embodiment of that brand. She cuts her hair and adopts a mask of white makeup, symbolizing her purity and giving her a rather severe look that enhances the seriousness of her commitment. Her clothing becomes not only more ornate but also enlarging, almost armorlike. Billowing sleeves and multiple layers of oversized, outspreading collars and rabatos make her seem taller and more massive, enhancing her nearly six-foot frame, making her look even taller and more warlike. In one portrait she wears a headdress, its base mounted low on her forehead with two large feathers rising upward like long antennae. The effects combine to create an almost mythical creature not unlike a heavily carapaced insect whose major defense mechanism is its ability to evoke fear in its enemies through its appearance alone. This, of course, is only one portrait of Elizabeth, who sat for only one painting and demanded that she personally see all paintings of her before they were released—literally controlling her image!

The continual emphasis on the queen's virginity was central to elevating her stature from that of a mere ruler to that of a near god—a secular, if ordained, counterpart to the Virgin Mary herself. As a "woman" ruler, she was open to attack; as a secular saint or demigod, she could transcend the arguments of those who regretted her gender. Virginity also symbolized, as with nuns, the sacrifice of personal interest and human joys to a higher purpose. Whether she was a demigod, political nun, or very clever politician, when Elizabeth opted to demonstrate her allegiance to the God she believed had ordained her she became the fulfillment of her subjects' need for that "thing greater than themselves." She knew and skillfully modeled behaviors that enhanced her popular image as a queen who, like Jesus of Nazareth and Mary his mother, combined elements of the human and the divine. Elizabeth is arguably the only European monarch to have pulled off such an association with the majority of her constituents for a reign of such length.

Although a near-God benefits from an image of power, the power advantage is soon lost if she seems unapproachable and remote—so Elizabeth carefully cultivated a counterbalancing image of herself, that of Good Queen Bess. If Gloriana was strong, Good Queen Bess was gentle; if Gloriana was fierce, Good Queen Bess had to be gracious and charming; if Gloriana was majestic and remote, Good Queen Bess would be approachable, outgoing, and, most of all, likeable.

In the twenty-first century, marked by diversity and audience fragmentation, a leader's chosen image and methods for reinforcing it must be different, but the basics remain much the same. Lynda C. McDermott is the president of EquiPro International, Ltd., a consulting firm based in New York that specializes in leadership development and management training. McDermott cites "symbolism" — Elizabeth's forte — as a necessary tool for modern leaders. "I have advocated increasingly to the leaders I work with that they use stories and symbolism as a way of getting peoples' attention and making their mark," McDermott told us. And, she said, symbolism is not just for world leaders, but works at all levels of any organization. After taking her leadership-training courses, one of McDermott's clients came up with a symbol for his department. "He chose an octopus," she said, explaining that the client managed a corporate legal affairs department. Why an octopus? "Because he felt his staff needed to have their feelers out in all different places." Having selected a symbol, the manager made sure he established it. Octopus imagery quickly became more common than even a Gloriana could have hoped for. The manager even "bought some octopus Beanie Babies and gives them out as awards."

McDermott recently launched a leadership storytelling program. "We invite executives to a leadership storytelling circle [that runs] two hours. They tell stories about being a leader, about being led. I teach them storytelling principles. What's the story about? [What's] the meaning of the story. I actually start them with 'Once upon a time.' I think that storytelling has always been a way of passing history and values on to subsequent generations. In this age of information overload and technology, you have to think of a way to stand out and be memorable. The marketers call it branding. It's about branding your leadership." And it's what Elizabeth did.

The value of "progresses" as a public relations tool is not limited to presidential visits and royal processions. Maureen Kindel cited an example of a particularly effective "progress" in which an affable and credible spokesperson represented Native American efforts to obtain gambling rights for their reservations in California. "[They] put ads on TV and went around the state visiting targeted audiences and opinion makers and they were just really nice. We had something to do with that campaign and people who were inherently against gambling looked at the fairness of the issue and said, 'Oh, you represent the nice Indians.' That's where likeability comes in. [Spokesperson] Mark Macaro was featured in the ads [and] and Mark Macaro is very nice. The ads really reached people . . . my role in the campaign was to have him meet elite opinion makers. He was as excellent one-on-one as he was with groups or on television. Very likeable. Someone the average person could identify with. The message was universal [and] based on fairness. Basically, it said, 'We're not coming for a handout after hundreds of years of suffering tremendous poverty on the reservation, [but] this is a way we can make our living and we will set money aside to lift up our people.' Even though the cause was controversial, the message resonated with voters and the measure passed."

Among modern leaders, Kindel praised Ronald Reagan as a "superb" communicator. "Even when he had real problems in his administration [as with the Iran-Contra affair], he was able to separate himself from that in a very brilliant manner by just saying 'I really didn't know.' And people believed him. He was a very believable person. He had spent years building up his likeability." Like Reagan and other successful leaders, Elizabeth was known for her ability to distance herself from unpopular decisions—including, in her case, the executions of the Duke of Norfolk and Mary, Queen of Scots. Although she had signed death warrants in both cases, she claimed, in Mary's case, that she was not notified of the actual time and date of the event and therefore not given the chance to change her mind! Some people believed her, others felt she was lying, but no one knew for sure. Ironically, Elizabeth's perceived "indecisiveness," was an asset in the matter, providing her critics a reason for granting her "benefit of the doubt" in the matter.

President Clinton, too, has been advantaged by benefit of the doubt—particularly during his 1999 impeachment trial. Both Reagan and Clinton are considered great communicators, but their styles, issues, and audiences are different. "Clinton speaks to a much more diverse group of people," Kindel told us, noting that whereas Reagan's message often addressed the interests of mostly white, moderate conservative men, Clinton has spoken to the interests of women, blacks, Latinos, and other nonmale, nonwhite, and less conservative audiences. "I think [Clinton's] personal brilliance has carried him maybe farther than he would have otherwise been carried," Kindel said. "I would not denigrate in any way his ability to use the media. But I don't know about his general likeability since his impeachment. Again, it goes back to people wanting to worship something better than themselves. I think Clinton suffered mightily on that in his impeachment trial and will not be able to overcome that." So what must Clinton do to recover from such image damage? Kindel says, "He will always have to be stressing his good programs, his incredible intelligence, and his ability to marshal the facts and master the situation." Which is, in fact, what Bill Clinton has been doing since the impeachment proceedings in an effort to assure his presidency a positive legacy.

Kindel emphasized that likeability, credibility, and sincerity can't be faked—particularly today. "You have to be the person you aspire to be," she told us. "The veneer cracks very quickly under the scrutiny of the year 2000, which is a different kind of scrutiny than Elizabeth had. If I put myself back in time, there were many fewer people that Elizabeth had to deal with in terms of population. Nevertheless, she still was observed by many and interpreted by many of her observers to the rest of the population. In a way, she had to deal with the very same thing modern leaders face, but on a smaller scale." Kindel noted that Elizabeth had to be what she set up herself to be. Whether, in fact, the queen was a virgin may always remain an open question for historians, but it and questions like it are often irrelevant in terms of image. What is important, says Kindel, is that once Elizabeth adopted the role of Gloriana, Virgin Queen, she had to play it well and always: there could be no "fooling around."

The queen and her advisers encouraged the use of Elizabeth's virgin image in poems, plays, and songs. This cer-

tainly helped maintain the advantages of the queen's desired associations with purity, self-denial, dedication, and
the Virgin Mary, but there were other reasons at work as
well. For an aging queen, the nuances of the word "virgin"—with its connotations of youth, purity, and nonsubju-
gation to the desires of men—was critical. Certainly, Elizabeth could not allow herself, as an unmarried woman in
the sixteenth century, to be described as a "spinster" or "old
maid." Those terms were frequently associated with a lack
of desirability, sometimes with poverty, isolation, debility,
and, not uncommonly, with witchcraft! Because Elizabeth's opponents often characterized her as a witch, there
was all the more reason for her to portray herself as God's
uncorrupted creature.

The queen not only promoted her image, but literally
protected it—and vigorously. Only two painters—Isaac
Oliver and Nicholas Hilliard—were authorized to do her
portraits. If she didn't like what they did, she had it destroyed. Although this may, as many commentators suggest, have been motivated by vanity, it's just as likely that
she simply didn't want pictures circulating that failed to
project her favorably. Since most of her subjects would
never see her in person, she wanted them to see her at her
best. By controlling the paintings, the queen was merely
ahead of her time in practicing the basics of branding.

Sheila Murray Bethel, a noted lecturer, consultant, and
author of the book *Making a Difference, 12 Qualities that
Make You a Leader*, serves on the advisory board of America's Promise and has worked closely with the organization's leader, General Colin Powell, for the past two years.
Powell's name tops most surveys when Americans are asked

to name men they admire. One poll named him "the world's most admired man," and ranked Powell ahead of South African bishop Desmond Tutu, former president Jimmy Carter, and former South African president Nelson Mandela, among many others. What's Powell's secret? "He's an incredible communicator," Bethel said. "He wins you over—bam!—because he knows where *you're* coming from. He knows how to determine how someone listens. I've watched him. I've seen him do it to me! . . . It's a delight to see someone who is that powerful, that personable, and watch him use his skills. I've seen him do that with 10,000 people."

Bethel says, "The wisest leader is someone who finds the common ground right off the bat and starts from there. A leader, by definition, is someone who influences human beings by their communication skills to look at their way of thinking. You don't just influence people to follow you, you influence them to think, to act. . . . That comes from being able to put your own ego aside and say "Where is that other person, how can I get through to them?

"The most powerful leaders," Bethel told us, "are humble enough to know that they don't know it all, and when they talk to someone they will try to delve into how that person operates in order to communicate in a fashion that [gets] everyone listening."

Powell's secret was Elizabeth's as well—a point Bethel underscored. "Elizabeth had excellent communication skills . . . [she] lived in an era of total power and control, but she didn't do it that way," Bethel said. "[Elizabeth] understood that power and control really comes when you don't put them first and are willing to listen first. Then peo-

ple will walk through fire with you. That's why she is remembered today and that's why she is considered a leader
400 years later."

A final note on Elizabeth and public relations: her
celebrity helped her keep her PR costs down. As we have
noted, the queen was notoriously tight with a pound and
her progresses were expensive affairs involving hundreds of
accompanying members of the court and their servants.
These costs were borne in very large part by the people she
stayed with and the towns she passed through. In some
cases, her hosts all but paid her to come, but in other cases,
hosts were virtually impoverished by the cost of entertain-
ing her. The status that derived from having the queen stay
at one's estate was formidable and, in most cases, she
stayed at the homes of political supporters who had been
enriched, not directly from the Exchequer, but through the
profits they had enjoyed from the queen's preferment in
granting trade monopolies, tillage rights, and other
benefices. In a sense, the queen's visiting rights were a form
of high-bracket income taxation on her well-heeled hosts.
Certainly, shifting the costs of her progresses onto her hosts
allowed her to stage an extensive public relations program
that was as cost-efficient as it was effective.

4
Building and Managing Teams

To Cecil, on his appointment: This judgment I
have of you, that you will not be corrupted with
any manner of gift, that you will be faithful to the
State, and that without respect of my private will
you will give me that counsel that you think best.

ONE OF THE FIRST CHALLENGES Elizabeth faced
following her coronation was that of forming her Privy
Council, the team of key advisers who would help her govern. The council in place was that of Mary, comprised of
powerful Catholic nobles, suspicious of Elizabeth, her suspected Protestantism, her youth and inexperience, her gender, and her apparent unwillingness to quickly wed and produce an heir. Her first formal address, following the
three-day official mourning period for her predecessor, attempted to reach out to those councillors, and the nobility

that supported them. She did this first by stating that having been found fit by God to govern, she would demand of the nobility and her advisers the same service she would render to the deity. She also assured them that she would honor their experience and past service and be guided by well-intentioned advice from them.

"I mean to direct all mine actions by good advice and counsel, and therefore at this present, considering that divers of you be the ancient nobility having your beginnings and estates of my progenitors, Kings of this realm, and thereby ought in honor to have the more natural care for the maintaining of my estate and this commonwealth. Some others have been of long experience in governance and ennobled by my father of noble memory [Henry VIII], my brother [Edward VI] and my late Sister [Mary I] to bear office. The rest of you being upon special trust lately called to her service only, and for your service considered and rewarded.

"My meaning is to require of you all nothing more but faithful hearts, in such service as from time to time shall be in your powers towards the preservation of me and this commonwealth. And for counsel and advice I shall accept you of my nobility and such others of you the rest as in consultation, I shall think meet, and shortly appoint; to the which also with their advice I will join to their aid and for ease of their burden, others meet for my service. And they which I shall not appoint, them not think the same for any disability in them, but for that I consider a multitude doth make rather disorder and confusion than good counsel, and of my good will you shall not doubt, using yourselves as appertainth to good and loving subjects."

As one commentator has noted "it was a reassuring speech: it made no promises, it told no lies, but it gave Elizabeth and Cecil the time they needed to get the machinery of government under control, and to assess the dependability of the Marian councilors they wished to retain in office."

Elizabeth began forming her council almost immediately upon Mary's death. Her first appointee was the thirty-eight-year-old William Cecil (later Lord Burghley), a man who had served both Edward VI and, in minor ways, Mary I. Though Protestant, Cecil was tolerant in matters of religion and known as an excellent analyst who weighed the pros and cons of alternative courses of action in any situation. Upon appointing Cecil, Elizabeth stated clearly her expectation of him: "This judgment I have of you, that you will not be corrupted with any manner of gift, that you will be faithful to the State, and that without respect of my private will you will give me that counsel that you think best." It was what she expected from all her councilors and it was an expectation that Cecil, in particular, fulfilled completely.

Cecil's first task was that of helping the new queen choose her other councilors. Like Elizabeth, Cecil was a balanced pragmatist with a bias for transitional, rather than revolutionary change. As Elizabeth's subsequent appointments were announced it became clear that the queen would, as she had vowed in her speech, keep those advisers who had served the state well, without regard to internal religious issues, replacing those who had been appointed to further the religious interests of Mary. Elizabeth's team would thus evolve as she sought to maintain stability within the country—again an example of her faith (and Cecil's) in progressive change and her desire to balance competing interests as a means of maintaining control.

The Privy Council was the chief instrument of administration in the Elizabethan era. It was flexible in composition, wide-ranging in its duties, and unique in both regards. The councilors exercised three primary functions: they advised the queen on policy; they acted, at times, as judicial review boards; and they handled the day-to-day administrative functions of the government. The choice of who sat on the council was entirely the queen's. Many privy councilors also held other state positions, such as Lord Treasurer, Lord Admiral, or, as did Cecil and later Walsingham, secretary of state, but no one served on the council in an ex officio capacity.

Full council meetings were usually attended by only six to twelve councillors. Except during the early months of her reign, Elizabeth seldom joined full meetings of the group. The council's business was transacted on a day-to-day basis by only a handful of the queen's most trusted councilors, who invariably also held major state offices. In both function and methods, the council was therefore similar to the boards of many modern corporations in which the full board of directors meets infrequently, whereas executive directors and officers of the corporation run the company on a day-to-day basis, advising and seeking advice from the company chairman, who may or may not meet with them routinely.

With Cecil in place, the other appointments came in short order. Elizabeth needed to establish a government that appeared inclusive of the major religious factions and thus ease fears that the new regime would, in any way, create precipitous change that might spur insurgence. She also made a decision that clearly signaled that her administration, while taking into account religious interests, would focus on this world, not issues relating to the next: she reduced the council's size and she reduced the influence of churchmen. Under Mary I, the Privy Council had grown to some fifty members and was loaded with clerics. Elizabeth's council never numbered more than nineteen and had only one churchman on it: the archbishop of Canterbury. Symbolically the clerical reduction was important because it indicated that religion would be viewed as an instrument of state, rather than dominating state interests. The reduction in the council's overall size was practical: it created a group of manageable size that could be filled with only the most trustworthy councilors.

Elizabeth's appointments reflected great wisdom. She kept longtime, personal loyalists on her household and private staff, maintaining a factional balance in the public offices of state and on the council. She tended to choose personal attendants who were younger than she was. In filling key public offices, however, she balanced her own youth and inexperience by reappointing some of Mary's oldest and most experienced councilors. The seventy-year-old marquess of Winchester was reconfirmed, for example, as Lord Treasurer. She also reappointed the sixty-year-old earl of Shrewsbury Lord Lieutenant of seven province, and the earl of Pembroke (William Herbert), one of four peers chosen to give Mary away on her wedding day. Other Marian counselors who kept their jobs included the earl of Derby, a powerful northern lord and firm opponent of religious change. Catholics also remained in the offices of High Admiral, Lord Steward of the Household, the Lord Deputy of Ireland and, in a new Catholic appointment, the Lord President of the Marches of Wales. Except for Cecil, her youngest major appointee at age thirty-eight, and the elderly Winchester and Shrewsbury, most of the appointees were in their fifties.

With the Marian holdovers reappointed and the remaining vacancies identified, the queen began appointing aides and councilors from Protestant factions. She cleaned house when it came to her ladies in waiting and maids of honor. Almost all of them were dismissed and replaced with the daughters of prominent Protestant families. She also rewarded those loyal retainers from her preaccession days. Her longtime nurse Katherine "Kat" Ashley was named First Lady of the Bedchamber, and Kat's husband, John, was named Keeper of the Queen's Jewels. To her Privy Council she named, among others, Nicholas Throckmorton, the man who had carried Mary's ring to Bess at Hatfield and a fiery Protestant. He was appointed Chamberlain of the Exchequer and Chief Butle,r and despite his fervid religious factionalism, urged the queen to approach reform slowly. She must, he said, "strive to succeed happily through a discreet beginning . . . with a good eye that there be no innovations, no tumults or breach of orders." Robert Dudley, another staunch Protestant and the queen's childhood friend and longtime favorite, was named Master of Horse. Dudley, who had been chief councillor during the reign of Edward VI and had plotted on behalf of Jane Grey's failed succession effort, was soon granted an earldom and placed on the Privy Council (where he often stood in sharp opposition to Cecil's centrist advice).

Elizabeth was neither the first nor last public leader to opt for a philosophy of stability in her appointments. If, as she said, Time had brought her to the throne, Time, God, and her own good judgment would sustain her long enough to build, step by step, the team she would need to achieve her goals. In her early years, that meant the formation of a coalition council representative of all major points of view in the kingdom.

In naming her council, biographer J. E. Neale argues that "Elizabeth desired to be neither weak nor rash; not to have an unwieldy Council, nor one whose complexion was old-fashioned, not yet to alienate those who must find themselves in retirement."

Perhaps no political figure in recent history has been more Elizabethan in her approach to reorganizing her cabinet than former Canadian prime minister Kim Campbell. The major achievement of her short term in office during 1993 was to reduce the Canadian cabinet from thirty-five to twenty-five. Like Elizabeth, Campbell also strove for inclusion in her government—an especially important act for any prime minister in a nation that is a constitutional confederation, has two official languages, and is continually wracked by East-West, French-English, provincial-national, and other splits, as well as an economy that, like that of Elizabethan England, was deeply troubled!

Campbell, a Progressive Conservative and the only woman who has served as Canada's prime minister, tells what she did and how she did it in her insightful autobiography, *Time and Chance*. During her election campaign, Campbell committed herself to reducing the size of the cabinet from thirty-five (it had reached a high of thirty-nine under predecessor Brian Mulroney) to about twenty-five ministers. Such a reduction could not be achieved by consolidation alone, but would require a complete restructuring of the cabinet functions, including the possible creation of new departments. Campbell realized, too, that her new cabinet would have to be geographically, culturally and, ideally, gender balanced to adequately reflect Canadian diversity. She knew, too, that her appointments had to reflect the electorate's desire for an energetic government that would carry out a new Progressive Conservative agenda. Attempting to simultaneously reduce and replace cabinet ministers, Campbell had fewer positions to fill, which meant more potential and existing appointees—like Elizabeth's clerics—would have to face disappointment. Campbell approached her task much the way Elizabeth and Cecil approached theirs. In Campbell's case the process looked like this:

1. She assessed the government's needs, preserving departments with clear and necessary focus; combining departments with overlapping jurisdictions into new, larger departments under a single cabinet member; and eliminating or absorbing unnecessary, freestanding departments.

2. She analyzed appointment considerations: regional balance, gender balance, linguistic balance, experience.

3. She determined and personally confirmed the intentions of cabinet ministers who might be planning to retire from office, identifying openings
that would be created by retirement and attrition.

4. She discussed the list of potential appointees and
her approaches to reform with key analysts, party
leaders, opinion leaders and predecessors.

5. She met with potential appointees and tendered
offers of appointment.

"Unfortunately, with the decision to reduce the size of
the cabinet, the hopes of some very worthy candidates had
been dashed," Campbell wrote. "Beyond regional and gender balance, my decisions were based on a need to combine stability in the short period available before an election with new energy and ideas. With the smaller cabinet, I
could only maintain the same proportion of woman as before. I hoped that after an election we could have a larger
percentage of women MPs. (We did—50 percent in fact!)

"The final makeup of cabinet reflected the many factors
I had worked to balance as well as my goals for the new
government," Campbell says.

In our interviews with contemporary executives and
business experts, we found broad consensus concerning
the qualities one should look for in choosing one's advisers.
Their comments, ranked in order of most frequent mention, appear below as a checklist of qualities to assess. Few
candidates for a key position will rank high on a list of all
factors, but candidates who fail on three or more items
should, in our view, be dropped from consideration for ap-

pointment. The first three listed factors—integrity, intellectual honesty, and a sense of humor—far outranked the other traits—and the reasons given by some of the interviewees underscore their importance.

Liz Dolan, former vice president of Global Marketing for Nike, argued the need for intellectual integrity this way: "Experimenting can only work if it comes hand and hand with honestly assess the results of that experimentation. One thing about the Nike culture that I really loved; there was this great sense of honesty. It was almost ridiculous. It was your job to confess your own mistakes before anyone said to you, 'that didn't work.' There was almost a competitiveness coming into a meeting to say, 'Boy, did we blow it!' There was a real value in that culture for being self-critical, which is part of being honest. When you're honest you set really clear goals that people understand. People who are honest tend to engage less in behind-the-scenes machinations that can undermine a team of people working toward a goal."

Dolan, now a partner in Dolan St. Clair Marketing Consultants of Portland, Oregon, is involved in the production of programming for the National Public Radio show *Satellite Sisters*. She is also a great believer in advisers with a sense of humor. Although a sense of humor may, at first, seem less critical than many of the other factors on the list, it appeared with remarkable regularity in our interviews. Dolan told us why: "We are creating a business and a creative product and imagining who our audience will be. NPR audiences are educated, active, public affairs–

Traits for Advisers

- Integrity
- Intellectual honesty
- A sense of humor
- Intelligence
- Willingness to question the boss
- Creativity (ability to think "outside the box")
- Drive
- Resilience
- Healthy sense of competition
- Insight
- Debate skills (as opposed to arguing)
- Flexibility
- Teamwork skills
- Self-awareness
- Broad range of life experience

oriented, somewhat affluent. We come on after the No. 1–rated show of the week, *Car Talk.* [It's] done by two brothers who talk about cars. They are hilarious. So the programming will go from a show about two brothers to a show about five sisters. We want both men and women listeners. I bring this up because creating a business with your sisters really makes you think a lot about the qualities you look for in your partners and advisers. Honesty, competitiveness for success not against each other, and a sense of humor. Not only is the show supposed to be funny, but we better have a good time doing this together or it's not worth doing."

Whatever criteria are used to select advisers, all of our interviewees agree that they have to be selected with care — advice Elizabeth may have gotten from Machiavelli, as well as Cecil.

Dr. Judith Rosener, the noted author, lecturer, and professor at the graduate school of management of the University of California–Irvine, whose students read Machiavelli, underscores the point. "You want people who will tell you the truth, and give you what you want, but not want your job," she says, adding, "that's hard to do. You don't want to pick people who will undermine you because they want your job, and you don't want people who will 'yes' you because then you're not getting good information. A lot of people choose people who agree with them which means frequently they don't hear the bad news.

"When it comes to qualities of key advisers," says Rosener, "I would look for somebody who questions and is constantly questioning what I'm saying and testing me. Making sure that I really know what I'm talking about because it's too easy when you're in a position of power to think whatever you think is good. I want someone to bring me the bad news, but with a solution. I would want someone with really good analytic skills, someone who can identify problems or issues ahead of time and how they would impact us negatively or positively, how we can leverage what we've got. I call these 'Issues Management' people."

Rosener is also a strong advocate of the need for initiative so "you don't have to be telling people what to do [because] they know what to do."

Marilee Winiarski, senior director for West Online Content Development, commented on the difficulties good advisers face when counciling strong personalities like Elizabeth. "Elizabeth was notoriously hard on advisers," Winiarski told us. "Burghley probably quit a hundred times, as he was forced to deal with Elizabeth's strong opinions coupled with habitual vacillation." Winiarski, who says she shares with Elizabeth a "sheer stubbornness and tendency to believe I'm right," seeks advisers who are not easily intimidated. "Given the hierarchical nature of most modern organizations, it is very hard to find people who are willing to tell the boss that there are other ways of looking at the world—especially in a way that allows the boss to listen without losing prestige or respect. When you find someone to work with who can maintain that level of integrity, then you have found a real partner."

Elizabeth faced difficulties on two fronts that Kim Campbell, among countless other modern leaders, have not. She was very young (only twenty-five) when she ascended the throne—and she was a woman in a world that considered *any* women unsuited to the challenges of running a nation. (Although Campbell is a woman, the status of women in late-twentieth-century Canada was significantly different than it was in sixteenth-century England!)

This meant, of course, that Elizabeth had to assemble a team that would respect her opinions and be ruled by them. Had its members not yielded to her constitutional authority she would have been forced to put her throne in their hands. Elizabeth chose to rule England. She would not serve as a puppet for those who would pull her strings. And, as she would not be a puppet, neither would she hamstring her advisers.

Once Elizabeth had chosen the players, she had to manage the team. Having selected them for their talent and diversity of viewpoint, she had the particular problem of maintaining their loyalty and best efforts on her behalf, knowing that they would often compete among themselves for her favor. She also had to overcome their inherent belief that her sex made her their inferior in political matters. This required her to establish her authority quickly. That was the right approach, according to Marleen McDaniels, chairman and CEO of Women.com Networks. "I have assumed responsibilities by taking over companies or departments in companies which suffered from suspicion and doubt. It is difficult to win over the support of people who did not sign up to be under your leadership," McDaniels told us. "I have always moved very quickly to establish my presence and leadership. I do the best I can to work with the team that I have inherited, unless they prove themselves unworthy."

Skilled as Elizabeth was in minimizing the impacts caused by male perceptions of woman's ability to rule, she faced particular difficulties in keeping the councilors from destroying each other in their attempts to influence her decisions in favor of their individual positions on issues. When things didn't go the way a particular councillor might desire, he invariably blamed it on the queen's womanly qualities, which became, in some ways, a face-saving means of dealing with personal failures of persuasion. (This seems to be a common reaction among men managed by women, as well as by many women managed by men. In particular, when men in modern western organizations are passed over in favor of a woman leader, they often find it easy to say, "it's because she's a woman," implying that the choice represented a company policy rather than a candidate's competence. This seems to serve as a personal "defense mechanism" that enables these men to think that the lack of their own promotion had nothing to do with their own lack of competency or for having had the wrong mix of competencies for the job at hand. Likewise, many talented women have grumbled but stayed on when a man has been promoted over them. In many of those cases, of course, as many court cases have shown, those promotion decisions may have been truly discriminatory; but, in cases where they were not, the private allegation of gender favoritism has served as a useful face-saver for the bypassed parties.

Although her advisers may have grumbled when the queen procrastinated on decisions and when decisions went against their personal advice, a wise *king* might well have followed Elizabeth's example in both selecting and managing *his* team! Indeed, the way Bess managed her council anticipated the latest findings on managing "teams at the top." Teamwork was not an organizational concept in the Elizabethan world, which was hierarchical by design. Teamwork, in that time, was for horses! And yet, whether called teams or not, there were examples of working groups at all levels of the hierarchy.

To understand Elizabeth's teams, it's important to understand how any team works and why some are less functional than others. That issue has been explored in depth by Kathleen M. Eisenhardt, Jean L. Kahwajy, and L. J. Bourgeois III, who studied management teams at twelve companies to learn more about the dynamics of conflict in top-management groups and its effect on corporate performance. Their report, "How Management Teams Can Have a Good Fight," first appeared in the *Harvard Business Review* of July-August 1997.

They learned that "teams with minimal interpersonal conflict were able to separate substantive issues from those based on personalities. They managed to disagree over questions of strategic significance and still get along with one another." By observing team behavior at the twelve companies, Eisenhardt and company found that the less-conflicted teams "used the same six tactics for managing interpersonal conflict." The harmonious teams:

- Worked with more, rather than less, information and debated on the basis of facts;
- Developed multiple alternatives to enrich the level of debate;
- Shared commonly agreed-upon goals;
- Injected humor into the decision-making process;
- Maintained a balanced power structure;
- Resolved issues without forcing consensus.

For political reasons specific to her time and place, Elizabeth (indeed, *any* English monarch) would have found it impossible to put together a top management group that could work harmoniously and also keep the nation together. Again, the queen's ability to adapt her leadership style to situational demands was the key to her success—and interpersonal conflicts probably aided her in her achievements. She managed in some degree to achieve each of the six points cited by Eisenhardt and her colleagues. She demanded information and encouraged debate focused on facts when facts were known. In Cecil she had an adviser who was at his best when developing the pros and cons of alternative actions. In terms of commonly agreed-upon goals, she was less successful, perhaps owing to the political considerations she was forced to consider in her appointments. There was within the cabinet, however, no question of her authority and, though advisers might disagree with specific decisions regarding succession, economics, and intervention in foreign wars, they usually found common ground in their love of England and their loyalty to Gloriana. When they did not find that ground, as Essex and Dudley failed to do, they found themselves permanently outside the queen's circle.

Eisenhardt and her coauthors found that good groups, like Elizabeth's Privy Council, require conflict. "Without conflict, groups lose their effectiveness," they wrote. "Managers often become withdrawn and only superficially harmonious. Indeed, we found that the alternative to conflict is usually not agreement but apathy and disengagement. Teams unable to foster substantive conflict ultimately achieve, on average, lower performance. Among the companies that we observed, low-conflict teams tended to forget to consider key issues or were simply unaware of important aspects of their strategic situation. They missed opportunities to question falsely limiting assumptions or to generate significantly different alternatives. Not surprisingly, their actions were often easy for competitors to anticipate."

Although the Eisenhardt, Kahwajy, and Bourgeois findings related to teams in general, special problems exist trying to enforce traditional concepts of teamwork among an organization's senior executives. Jon R. Katzenbach, a professor at Harvard Business School, has studied what he calls the "Myth of the Top Management Team."

In an article by that title in the November-December 1997 issue of the *Harvard Business Review*, Katzenbach noted that "even in the best of companies, a so-called top team seldom functions as a real team." Katzenbach explodes the fallacious thinking that leads CEOs to consider their direct reports as a "team."

"Many CEOs tend to think of their group of direct reports as a team. But shaping collective work of high value that fits the group's mix of skills is difficult. It is analogous to searching for a market after a product has been designed, rather than first identifying what the market needs and then designing the product to fill it.

"Top-level executives are chosen because their individual capabilities and experiences qualify them for extremely demanding primary responsibilities. Team challenges at the top seldom require the particular mix of skills represented by a CEO's direct reports, and such challenges do not usually take clear priority over the individual executives' formal responsibilities. In other words, it is hard to find collective work-products that justify top-level executives doing real work together."

Katzenbach concludes, "'all of a CEO's direct reports' can seldom, if ever, constitute an ongoing real team. Nor should they be trying to become one in their quest to build and maintain a high-performance enterprise. It simply does not work that way at the top."

As England's CEO, Elizabeth never thought of "all her direct reports" as a team, and, consequently, she did not expect them to "all pull together," but simply that they not pull her and the nation apart, always doing their best within their mandated areas of responsibility to preserve both queen and country.

Cindy Padnos is founder, president, and CEO of Vivant! Corporation of Oakland, Calfornia, a firm that provides an open marketplace to help companies staff projects with contractor talent by matching their needs with firms online. Vivant! has developed a unique approach to selecting its advisers. The seats of many corporate boards, particularly during their startup and early growth stages, are dominated, if not completely filled, by investors in the firm. But, as Padnos points out, "investors can add only so much, and they also typically sit on six or eight boards and are very busy." Padnos and her investor board members decided to build a different type of advisory board—one that would advise not only the CEO but also the entire management team at Vivant!.

"We asked ourselves, 'What are the gaps we want to fill? What are the knowledge and experience sets that would be great for us to have access to?' Since answering those questions, six people have been added to Vivant!'s advisory board—and the new additions have brought the company new expertise in technology, taking companies public, building Internet businesses, as well as CEO experience. We actively sought these people, found them and asked them to be on our advisory board, Padnos told us. The Vivant! management team and advisory board meet quarterly for full afternoon and evening sessions. Each member of the advisory board is "available literally day to day to take a call or e-mail from me or any member of our executive team. I did that very consciously. I don't think that I'm the only one who needs advisers. I think it's important to have a resource that members of the management team can use as a sounding board." Vivant!'s active advisers include the senior VP of sales of a major computer systems company, who serves as a sales coach, and a founder of three technology companies who advises Vivant!'s VP of engineering.

One of the best statements on team building we received came from Catherine M. Walter, a former solicitor who is now a director with the National Australia Bank in Melbourne. She said, "Where skills and styles are genuinely beyond us, we need to seek these attributes out in others. It is too easy to surround ourselves with PLMs (People Like Me) . . . The real test is to seek out in others the very skills and styles that we know we are relatively weak in and can't fully acquire. In basic terms, we need to reflect in our people selection the same tolerance of ambiguity we know we must embrace in our strategic business thinking."

Although Elizabeth believed in expertise and experience, she was not in a position (and would not have been inclined or allowed) to place "outsiders" from other companies (in her case, France and Spain) on her Privy Council. But she could and did often find outside advisers, as when she used Thomas Gresham to firm up her coinage and when she empowered Francis Drake to "advise" the less-able sailor Admiral Howard on England's naval defense. Drake, as a commoner during the Armada crisis of 1588, could not be appointed Lord Admiral; however, as the most experienced, talented, and daring seaman of his time, Drake was clearly the person to plan England's strategy. Although Howard was not bound to follow Drake's advice, he could not dismiss it out of hand and, together (even though not always in agreement) the team of admiral and his "adviser" carried the day for their queen. "Together, despite disagreement," was the premise by which Elizabeth managed not only her advisers, but England as well."

The Queen's Men

Elizabeth was surrounded by some of the most diverse and talented councillors ever to serve a monarch. In addition, she had the support of and gave support to many outside the council who played important roles in sustaining her in office. Here's a brief look at some of the key men behind Elizabeth. They comprise a "Who's Who" of the age that bears her name.

Francis Walsingham (1532–1590)

Walsingham served publicly as the queen's secretary of state and was a member of her Privy Council from 1573 until his death. In addition to his astute work as the queen's chief diplomat, he served as her spymaster, laying the groundwork for modern covert operations. He organized a network of spies that gathered intelligence from overseas merchants and undercover agents, both inside England and abroad. He spent most of Mary I's reign in self-imposed exile, mostly in Italy, where he studied law at the University of Padua. A dour, often pessimistic man,

(continues)

found it difficult to relate to Walsingham on a personal level, his intelligence efforts were the basis of her security and his loyalty was never in doubt. He uncovered several plots against the queen, including the Babington Plot, which eventually led to the execution of Mary, Queen of Scots. He also provided advance warning of the planning and launch of the Armada. Elizabeth nicknamed him her "Moor," for the darkness of his moods.

William Cecil, Lord Burghley (1520–1598)

Cecil was Bess's most trusted adviser and served her as secretary of state from her accession until 1572, when she named him Lord High Treasurer and raised him to the peerage as Lord Burghley. He continued to serve the queen until his death, at which time his son, Robert, succeeded to his role as chief adviser. Cecil had served as a chief secretary to the Duke of Somerset, regent for King Edward VI. Though a Protestant, he had supported the move to put Mary I on the throne, refusing to support succession efforts on behalf of Lady Jane Grey. Despite his support Mary declined to appoint him to her cabinet, fearing his Protestantism. He remained in Parliament, however, and served Mary's administration in a number of minor ways. Cecil was often the voice of pragmatism and moderation among the queen's advisers. He was trained to present the pros and cons of pending decisions, parsing the options carefully and presenting Elizabeth with the essential facts. Cecil coordinated the meetings of Bess's Privy Council, advised her on foreign affairs, managed parliamentary relations and supervised the Exchequer. The queen's nickname for him was "Spirit."

Robert Dudley, Earl of Leicester (1532–1588)

More than an adviser, Dudley was probably the only man Elizabeth seriously considered marrying. Dudley and Elizabeth had known one another from childhood, when both were students of the tutor Roger Ascham. Dudley headed Edward VI's Privy Council but was imprisoned by Mary I for his role in backing Jane Grey's bid for the throne, which was engineered by his father, the Duke of Northumberland. In 1559, Elizabeth named Dudley her Master of Horse, appointed him to the Privy Council, and designated him a Knight of the Garter. In 1550 Dudley married, but rumors of a relationship with the queen surfaced early in her reign and were fueled by the death of Dudley's wife, apparently by a fall down a stair, in 1560. Though cleared of any wrongdoing in the matter, the rumors were damaging and Elizabeth began distancing herself from Dudley, although she did name him Earl of Leicester in 1563. In the same year she proposed him as a suitable husband for Mary, Queen of Scots. Leicester and Cecil frequently found themselves at odds over religious and military matters. Leicester fell increasingly into disfavor and attracted the queen's fury, in particular over his secret marriage, in 1578, to Lettice Knollys, a former maid of honor to the queen. Leicester commanded two unsuccessful military expeditions to the Netherlands in the 1580s,

(continues)

during which time the queen continually questioned his judgment. To her fury, he arranged to have himself named governor-general of the Netherlands by the Dutch. He died in 1588, deeply in debt. Dudley was the stepfather of Robert Devereux, the earl of Essex (see below). Despite their differences, Elizabeth kept Leicester's last letter to her, written shortly before his death, as a keepsake and token of her love for him. Elizabeth nicknamed him her "Eyes."

Lord Charles Howard of Effingham, later Earl of Nottingham (1536–1624)

Lord Howard was Elizabeth's cousin and commander of the English fleet against the Spanish Armada. Howard was the son of Lord William Howard of Effingham and in 1575 succeeded to his title. In 1585 Elizabeth named him Lord Admiral, a post that had been held by his father, two uncles and his great-grandfather. The famous London theatrical troop, The Lord Admiral's Men, known for its production of Christopher Marlowe's plays, is named after him. A conservative commander, he was known for his willingness to listen to experienced sailors like John Hawkins and Francis Drake in planning the Armada defense.

Sir Christopher Hatton (1540–1591)

Hatton was a special favorite of the queen and, like Dudley and others, reputed to be her lover. Although looks and charm may have attracted him to Elizabeth's attention, his formidable performance in high office kept him in favor.

The queen appointed him to the Privy Council in 1577, where his advice consistently urged moderation in measures against both Catholics and Puritans. He also served in Commons, where he was considered to be the queen's spokesperson. In 1587, he was named Lord Chancellor, England's top legal post. In 1588 he was also appointed chancellor of Oxford University. The queen had several nicknames for Hatton, including "Lids" (for eyelids), "Mutton," and "Belwether."

Robert Devereux, Earl of Essex (1567–1601)

Essex was Dudley's stepson and the queen's cousin through his mother, Lettice Knollys. After Leicester's death, the queen transferred some of her affection for him to Essex, but their relationship was more characteristic of a mother's great expectations of a disappointing son than of an older woman for a young lover. In 1593 Essex was appointed to the Privy Council and named a Knight of the Garter. Essex was impetuous and ambitious and had a tendency to disobey the queen's orders. His standing with the public, as with the queen, was an on-again, off-again matter. In 1589 he incurred the queen's wrath for joining the Portugal Expedition without permission, landing not only himself but also Sir Francis Drake and other expedition leaders under a shadow. As co-leader of the successful raid on Cadiz in 1596 he became something of a military folk hero, but a year later his involvement in the unsuccessful Islands Voyage cut him down to size with both public and monarch. In 1599, he was sent to Ireland as Lord Lietenant

(continues)

and given the task of putting down the rebellion of Hugh O'Neill, Earl of Tyrone. Having dillydallied (the queen's view) and made no military progress, Essex instead signed a peace treaty with Tyrone, against the queen's instructions. In the wake of criticism and fearing he was losing favor with the queen, he assured its loss by returning to London without her permission in September 1599. She had him charged with dereliction of duty and dealing with the enemy, stripping him of all offices and his monopoly on sweet wines and throwing him in prison until August 1600. He was arrested again in February 1601 for leading an attempt to take the queen prisoner. It didn't take long for him to be tried for treason and, on February 25, 1601, he was beheaded. Elizabeth seems never to have honored him with a nickname, but did once refer to him as her "wild horse."

Sir Robert Cecil (1563–1612)

Cecil was the son of William Cecil, Lord Burghley, and primary minister of state and adviser to Elizabeth during the closing years of her reign. Though less trusted and respected by Elizabeth than was his father, the younger Cecil vied for the queen's ear with Robert Devereux , Earl of Essex, until Essex's impetuosity, failed Irish campaigns, ambition, and treachery led him to the gallows in 1601. Cecil's greatest achievement was arranging the peaceful accession to the Crown of James I upon the queen's death in 1603. He continued to serve James as secretary of state, assuring continuity in state affairs until his death.

Changing the Guard
Elizabeth's Rules of Appointment

1. Keep the cream of the crop.
2. Demand loyalty and honest advice.
3. Seek balance on all fronts so that all opinions will be put forth. (In Elizabeth's case, the balance involved age, experience, temperament, and points of view).
4. Dismiss the incompetent and those personally loyal to rivals.
5. Recognize the opposition.
6. Move slowly, but steadily, to achieve a stable transition.
7. Provide "face-saving" rationales for those dismissed.
8. Limit the number of appointees to manageable levels.
9. Clearly state your expectations.
10. Establish who is in charge.

5

Vision, Mission,
Commitment

I will be as good unto you as ever queen was to
her people . . . no will in me can lack, neither do
I trust there lack any power. And persuade
yourselves, that for the safety and quietness of you
all, I will not spare, if need be, to spend my
blood.

AFTER BEING RELEASED from the Tower of London
when evidence failed to implicate her in Wyatt's Rebellion,
an abortive attempt to oust Mary I from the throne after her
marriage to Philip the Princess Elizabeth returned to the
royal estate at Hatfield. Not long after, young Bess began
hearing disturbing reports of religious persecutions at
Smithfield, a village located on the outskirts of London.
Queen Mary's government had begun burning at the stake
Protestants it considered heretics and traitors. Though the

queen had sanctioned the burnings many felt that Philip was behind the persecutions. He had authorized mass burnings in Spain and believed that the guilt or innocence of the victims was superfluous if their deaths stifled religious and political dissent. In all, about 300 people—most of them poor, simple folk and about 60 of them women—were sent to the flames during a four-year period. Instead of striking fear in the heart of Protestants, it united them in their opposition to Mary and each victim of the burnings became a martyr that furthered the Protestant cause. The burnings were also despised by thoughtful Catholics, many of whom hated Philip as much as they loved their church. The burnings did much to unite England—but only in opposition to the onerous methods of Bloody Mary and her hated spouse.

Upon Mary's death, Elizabeth prayed that she would be a tolerant and forgiving queen—one who would end domestic bloodshed in the name of religion. The great mission of her reign became that of unifying her people politically. To that end, she would become the personification of the nation—a quasi-religious, living symbol of a state whose subjects would place their primary loyalty in the temporal power of their queen rather than sectarian religious institutions.

Elizabeth's vision of England centered on unity, but it could only be achieved if several supportive missions were first accomplished. A penniless state would not command respect; neither would a weak one. But wars cost money and money was as scarce as taxation was impossible: a heavily taxed people was likely to unite only in the negative act of seeking their queen's demise. Elizabeth had to maintain the love and respect of her people, to be perceived always as a monarch pledged to their prosperity and happiness. Although Bess made no secret of her personal desire to do great deeds that would leave a lasting mark on the nation and stand as a legacy to her reign, she vowed never to seek personal glory at her subjects' expense. When she took power, her realm's coinage was debased, recent harvests had failed, price increases had exceeded gains in wages, and foreign entanglements threatened not only peace but also caused further economic woe. Elizabeth, in the belief that rulers, including herself, had been granted power by God to serve divine needs, vowed to restore credibility to the state, quell rebellion, and give the people of England a government worthy of their loyalty. The queen needed to establish the state as the unifying force in her realm—the thing to which all must be true, regardless of their religious views. In the end, most believed in *her*.

Elizabeth never promulgated a mission statement, but she was consistent in stating her vision of England; she was eloquent in articulating her mission as its monarch; and she was tireless in dedicating herself to achieving both the vision and the mission. Had the queen been a modern executive who believed in formal vision and mission statements, hers might well have read like this:

To achieve, in my lifetime, peace abroad and economic stability at home by maintaining a balance of power among external foes and a balance of tolerance among internal political factions. We will do this by exploring and developing the potential

of the New World, avoiding costly war when possible, but letting no nation presume that we will not fully confront aggression; we will open trade with friendly nations and encourage
our best and brightest subjects to new heights of achieve-
mentsin the arts and sciences.

If you search the Internet for "mission statements," you'll
turn up more than half a million examples, as we did when
we used the AltaVista and AlltheWeb.com search engines
in April 2000. We scanned the first 500 findings on each
search service and made some interesting discoveries:

- Churches, colleges, schools, government agen-
  cies, and other not-for-profit organizations posted
  most of the statements.
- Many of the statements were posted on depart-
  mental, rather than institutional websites. (For example, we found university libraries or city building departments that posted mission statements,
  even though the universities and cities with which
  they were affiliated did not.)
- Most of the statements were from small, local
  companies rather than big-name, national and international companies.
- Many of the statements belabored the obvious ("to
  make a profit," "to serve our customers"). Others
  were merely strings of jargon and buzzwords (for
  example, "to be an outside-the-nine-dots, Seven
  Habits, 360-degree feedback, outcomes-oriented
  center devoted to transitional change and empowerment"). Most were soul deadening in their lack
  of imagery and mind numbing in their lack of

clarity. Many were written in language so vague they suggested that the company's only mission might be to hang on until another mission statement could be written.

- Some obviously had resulted from forced exercises in mission-statement writing, probably prompted by public relations crises. They seemed more like "hope" statements or "cover your rear end" statements than credos for achieving a vision. In some cases, rather than defining a mission, the statements seemed to have been crafted to define turf and make certain it was properly fenced in. These, in effect, were "antivision" statements.

After conducting the general searches, we went to the websites of about two dozen well-known companies. Most of these companies either don't have mission statements or don't post them on their websites. Surprisingly, the "no statement" companies included several of the greatest names in commerce. Nordstrom, the Seattle-based retailer known for the quality of its service and the enthusiasm of its salespeople, posts its corporate history on its website, but no mission statement. The history details the origins of many of Nordstrom's four signature business principles: quality, value, selection, and service. These four words are the basis of Nordstrom's ninety-nine-year-old tradition, but they are qualities, not a mission. The fact that Nordstrom has no formal mission statement surprised us, but we were not alone in thinking it had one. Two executives we interviewed on the topic of mission statements specified Nordstrom as having one of the best they'd ever heard. What our respondents were thinking of was Nordstrom's Employee Handbook, which is printed on one side of a single five-by-eight-inch gray notecard. It reads:

> WELCOME TO NORDSTROM
> We're glad to have you with
> our Company.
> Our number one goal is to provide
> outstanding customer service.
> Set both your personal and
> professional goals high.
> We have great confidence in your
> ability to achieve them.
> Nordstrom Rules:
> Rule #1: Use your good
> judgment in all situations.
> There will be no additional rules.
> Please feel free to ask
> your department manager,
> store manager, or division general
> manager any question
> at any time.

The "Handbook" at Nordstrom does everything a mission statement should do (and it reminded us of the sense of mission and empowerment Richard Harborne was granted upon his appointment as Elizabeth's ambassador to Turkey, discussed in our chapter on leadership). Nordstrom's handbook, like Elizabeth's commission to Harborne, is not merely a hollow statement of corporate ideals, framed and gathering dust on a wall (or posted on a website). Rather, Nordstrom's handbook states the single goal from which the unstated missions will arise and by which all actions will be determined: outstanding customer service. Recognizing that outstanding customer service can't be codified, the handbook empowers Nordstrom employees to use their own judgment in responding flexibly to the needs of Nordstrom shoppers. Significantly, the handbook does not simply abandon employees who need help with their judgment. It tells them precisely where to turn for help and thus provides the ultimate test of judgment: Is the employee capable of recognizing when he or she can benefit from more experienced counsel? Is the employee over-reliant on others to make decisions? When the employee makes a decision without consultation, does she or he usually make the right decision? At Nordstrom, four simple principles and a one-page employee handbook have carried the company from its start as a shoe store in Seattle nearly 100 years ago to its position today as one of America's most popular retailers with 106 department stores from coast to coast.

After spending time at *nordstrom.com*, we went to a different part of the retail spectrum and visited Wal-Mart, the largest and, arguably, most successful general merchandiser in history. We didn't find a "mission statement" there either; we found something better. Wal-Mart instills its mission by telling "culture stories." The company's website features four of them, titled the Sundown Rule, Everyday Low Prices, Exceeding Customer Expectations, and the "Ten-Foot" Attitude. The "Ten-Foot" Attitude, for example, explains the Wal-Mart tradition of employees greeting any customer who gets "within 10 feet of them." You can read all four stories (and learn the Wal-Mart cheer in a variety of different languages) by visiting *walmart.com*, but we'd like to share our favorite Wal-Mart culture statement here. It's called the Sundown Rule and goes like this:

> One Sunday morning, Jeff, a pharmacist at a Wal-Mart store in Harrison, Arkansas, received a call from his store. A store associate informed him that one of his pharmacy customers, a diabetic, had accidentally dropped her insulin down her garbage disposal. Knowing that a diabetic without insulin could be in grave danger, Jeff immediately rushed to the store, opened the pharmacy and filled the customer's insulin prescription. This is just one of many ways your local Wal-Mart store might honor what is known by our associates as the Sundown Rule. It's a rule we take seriously at Wal-Mart. In this busy place, where our jobs depend on one another, it's our standard to get things done today—before the sun goes down. Whether it's a request from a store across the country or a call from down the hall, every request gets same-day service. These are our working principles.
>
> The Sundown Rule was our founder, Sam Walton's twist on that old adage, "why put off until tomorrow what you can do today." It is still an important part of our Wal-Mart culture and is one reason our associates are so well known for their customer service. The observation of the Sundown Rule means we strive to answer requests by sundown on the day we receive them. It supports Mr. Sam's three basic beliefs: respect for the individual, customer service, and striving for excellence. At Wal-Mart, our associates understand that our customers live in a busy world. The Sundown Rule is just one way we try to demonstrate to our customers that we care.

Such "culture stories" are more compelling than the impotent jargon that passed for mission statements at most of the sites that turned up in our search. Wal-Mart's stories enable employees, customers, and investors to see what the mission looks like and, most important, see how the actions of individuals just like them can achieve it and benefit from it.

Before leaving the Web, we searched once more, this time for the phrase "vision statement." Here the list was much smaller (just under 50,000) when compared to the previous searches. Significantly, this search produced a higher percentage of big-name companies like Bell Atlantic and Burlington Northern and Santa Fe Railway than had the "mission statement" search. After checking out the first 200 search results it became obvious that there is a lot of confusion about the difference between a vision and a mission, and that few organizations get either kind of statement right.

What's the difference between vision and mission? Many a corporate retreat has argued that question, usually to the dismay of participants who want to get past the academic exercises and on with the program. In practice, at most companies, the distinction is not made. The words are used interchangeably—and that's too bad—for the difference between them is not just a fine point of semantics.

All organizations and their leaders need a cohesive vision and one or more supporting missions to maintain their vitality. As the Proverbist says in a verse that Elizabeth most certainly knew, "Where there is no vision the people perish." Clearly, however, some of the best organizations don't have formal vision or mission statements, although many organizations on life support turn new ones out on a regular basis. Isn't there a risk that today's mission statement will become tomorrow's death certificate? When should missions be reassessed? Only upon completion? Upon change of CEOs? Upon change in business climate? Technology? All of the above? And whereas many people cry out for uplifting visions that can be stated with the skill of a John F. Kennedy, Winston Churchill, or Elizabeth I, does a mission need to be exciting or is it enough that it be clear and necessary?

We put questions like those to the executives we interviewed and found a broad consensus on the need for a mission, but mixed reaction to the value of formal statements, which were found to be largely irrelevant, and in many cases counterproductive.

Dr. Judith Rosener, the University of California–Irvine management professor, shared with us her view that "for the most part mission statements are symbolic and don't mean anything."

"It's the difference between knowing and doing," Rosener told us." I have seen businesses all over that have great mission statements but you look at the company and they don't do any of the things the mission statement says." Mission statements, in Rosener's view, are "necessary, but not sufficient."

"I think they are frequently a symbolic substitute for action, but I think they can provide a great service for those who develop them," she argues. "If everyone is involved in developing them (which they never are) then the process in developing them is valuable because you're talking about values of the organization. Usually it's done by a few people at the top or a PR person using words that sound good. I think mission statements have to be linked with both top down and bottom up involvement. I don't see that often."

The most important element in a great mission statement, Rosener said, "is having a mechanism to see if you're achieving it." When asked to cite the best mission statement she had ever heard, Rosener responded, "The best mission statement I ever heard, isn't the hearing, it's the doing."

Mission statements are common in education, but Judith Rogala, CEO of LaPetite Academy, an 800-affiliate early childhood education organization based in a suburb of Kansas City, Missouri, says she's basically "anti" mission statement. Rogala explains her view this way: "It's not what's posted on the wall, it's the behavior."

Following a practice consistent with Elizabeth's commission to her ambassadors, Rogala aims to empower her employees and encourage them to use their judgment. "Whether it's the courier on the truck, the teacher in the classroom, or the director of the academy, I say, 'You are the president of your business.' That's how I've always managed. Make it your own. Make the decisions. Of course not everyone is on the same risk-taking level, but they are beginning to see they're not going to get beat up if they try something."

Like Elizabeth, Rogala needed to streamline her organization to achieve her goals. Within the first two months as CEO at LaPetite, she cut twenty-five positions, significantly flattening the organization. "They were absolutely in the way of people running their own business. I had 800 academies reporting to eighty-three regional directors reporting to eight directors reporting to a field officer reporting to a chief operating officer." Not any more.

Linda Bennett heads Australia's largest health insurance service with a one-line mission statement: "Improve Australia's health through payments and information." The statement is a reflection of Bennett's belief that "a mission statement should be simple to understand at all levels of the organization and be a goal all employees and clients can relate to."

Retired Air Force Brigadier General Karen Rankin is now a senior official with Johnson Controls. Johnson's mission: "To continually exceed our customer's continually increasing expectations." It captures the essence of Rankin's thought on the qualities that characterize any good mission statement. "A mission statement must succinctly express the organization's mission; its job, its raison d'être," Rankin says, "And it should enable any reader to understand who we are and what we do."

A mission statement must also provide clarity, direction, and have an element of "thinking big," according to Helen Whelan, president of MyPrimeTime.com. "Ours is about what the end run should be; the "how" and "when" are not included. It's about the Big Goal."

Betsy Reveal, who heads the United Nations Foundation, told us she's "not as enamored of mission statements as many contemporary management gurus," but adds that "the best are simple, clear, focused on outcomes and impact (not process)." And, says Reveal, they are "memorable and captivating."

Robert G. Picard, professor and director of the Turku School of Economics, Business Administration in Finland

and an expert on mission statements, recently discussed the topic before newspaper executives attending the World Congress of the International Newspaper Marketing Association (INMA). Picard noted that whereas most modern newspaper companies have mission statements, newspaper managers often fail to understand how or why such statements require action if they are to be worth more than the paper on which they are printed.

"Mission statements are really the foundations for all company plans and operations," Picard said. "They cannot be just words and they become false and meaningless unless they are followed by performance. Mission statements need to be acted upon and the statements you make must carry implications for action."

"Mission statements encompass company or organization values, principles of operations, enduring purposes of the firm or organization, and the scope of the company or organization," he said.

Picard studied newspaper mission statements and found several common elements in them. In one example, Picard presented a statement common not only to newspaper mission statements, but also to those at thousands of other companies: "We will strive to increase shareholder value."

"This means that you must make the investment of shareholders' capital more profitable, either in the short or long term," Picard told INMA. "In terms of corporate activity it means that managers must seek company growth, that the firm must make reinvestment choices to enhance value by helping the firm grow, and it means the company must seek steady financial performance by evening out earnings from quarter to quarter and year to year often through di-

versification that ameliorates economic fluctuations in geo-
graphic locations or types of media."

The desire—indeed, the need—for a mission statement
becomes most pronounced when a company's original mission no longer provides it with growth opportunities or
when companies have grown so large that many of their
employees no longer understand the "big picture" in terms
of what the company is trying to do. Employees may understand *their* jobs, but not the goals of the company. They
feel disconnected and as a result find themselves perform-
ing well at jobs that seem redundant or unnecessary. Sometimes mission statements state the wrong mission or state it
in the wrong way, problems noted by Brian Rapp, executive director of the Santa Barbara Museum of Natural History in California.

"In the museum world mission statements are changing
from being passive to active," Rapp told us. "For instance,
the old passive missions included words like 'preserve, protect, be good stewards.' The new missions talk about 'making a difference, empowering, and motivating.' We want to
show people coming into the museum what we have that
can make a difference in their lives."

"Defining an accurate, active mission statement sets the
stage for everything," Rapp said. "When the statement is
active and clear everyone gets involved in the same goals
and the job becomes more interesting. Staff members can
see the relevance of their jobs."

Rapp's mission at the Santa Barbara museum: "Turn kids
on to nature."

In England, when Elizabeth took charge, the country
was in chaos. It had passed quickly though the reigns of

several monarchs and alternated between official religions. Bloodshed, rebellion, and burnings had been the rule of the day under Mary I and, at times, it seemed the monarchy was for sale, through marriage, to her best suitor—a sale that would start again once Bess took the throne. The future was beclouded and competing visions vied for public support, but none had captured the hearts and minds of the people as a whole. The late historian Crane Brinton noted in his classic study *Ideas and Men: The Story of Western Thought* that the great mass of the common people in later Tudor England felt little tie to the monarchy, which had passed from Henry VIII to Edward VI and his regent, briefly to Lady Jane Grey, then to Mary and on to Elizabeth—all between 1547 and 1558. And, as the monarchs changed, the "official" religion changed, too. In Brinton's view, however, the Tudor population— extremists excepted—was largely apathetic to these changes. Whether the local parish church was Catholic or Anglican, most parishioners kept showing up on Sundays, modifying their public worship according to the dictates of the official church *de jour*. This adaptability prompted Brinton to note that "Masses of men can and do accommodate themselves to changes in abstract ideas, philosophies, theologies, to conflicts among ideas, in a way that the sincere and single-minded idealist cannot possibly explain except by ceasing to be an idealist about his fellow man."

Elizabeth was surrounded by single-minded idealists like Nicholas Throckmorton, Francis Walsingham, and Roger Williams, who continually urged her to force consensus by use of force; to lop off the heads of dissidents; to sow dissension among the French and Spanish; and to pour more money into battles in the Netherlands and Ireland. To resist becoming a tool of their missions, Elizabeth had to mobilize her country and strengthen her hand. She had to stir her people's faith in a common denominator other than religion. In the end she made herself the mission. In a world in which the signs outside and the practices inside churches changed with frequent regularity, Elizabeth would become the institutional constant of her nation. The result was a reign that stabilized the currency, balanced the budget, expanded England's power, and gave it, literally, a place in the New World.

You don't have to run a country to face the kind of "who cares" environment that characterized the churchgoing habits of the English people in the years prior to Elizabeth's coronation. If you've ever worked for a company where nine to five was standard operating procedure; where absenteeism abounded and was ignored; or where people spent more time planning their retirements than coming up with new ideas, you've witnessed firsthand the symptoms that should trigger an examination of mission.

In Elizabeth's day, of course, no one had ever heard of a mission statement. Missions were for missionaries. The fondness for mission statements in modern corporations became popular in the 1970s and was inspired by President Kennedy's early 1960s call for America to send a man to the Moon and safely return him to Earth by the end of that decade. Kennedy's call to action has often been used as an example of perhaps the best mission statement ever written. It had the advantage of being limited to a single, highly measurable goal—a specific goal within the administration's greater, unstated vision of a New Camelot. One of the traps organizations fall into when trying to write their mission statements is that they try to do too much. Different divisions of a company may have different missions and different product lines may have different missions within divisions. The vision of a department may call for it to "serve our coworkers and other departments as if they are valued customers." That may be part of a vision but it doesn't have that "man on the moon" specificity. A Kennedy-like mission statement would call for the department "to complete installation of a fully integrated cross-departmental customer database within two years."

If they are not continually revised, vision statements can actually blind organizations to opportunities. Likewise, if a company fulfills its mission without having a new mission in place, it will likely find itself dealing with apathy and declining performance.

A *Few Effective Mission Statements*

COSTCO

To continually provide our members with quality goods and services at the lowest possible prices. In order to achieve our mission we will conduct our business with the following five responsibilities in mind: obey the law, take care of our members, take care of our employees, respect our vendors, reward our shareholders.

STARBUCKS

To establish Starbucks as the premier purveyor of the finest coffee in the world while maintaining our uncompromising principles as we grow. The following six guiding principles will help us measure the appropriateness of our decisions.

- Provide a great work environment and treat each other with respect and dignity.
- Embrace diversity as an essential component in the way we do business.
- Apply the highest standards of excellence to the purchasing, roasting, and fresh delivery of our coffee.
- Develop enthusiastically satisfied customers all of the time.
- Contribute positively to our communities and our environment.
- Recognize that profitability is essential to our future success.

FORD FOUNDATION

The Ford Foundation is a *resource* for *innovative people and institutions* worldwide.
Our goals are to:

- Strengthen democratic values
- Reduce poverty and injustice
- Promote international cooperation

- Advance human achievement.
- This has been our purpose for almost half a century.

Comment: *This is more a description of the organization, rather than a vision of what it will achieve or a measurable statement of what it hopes to do. Clearly, the Ford Foundation has a clearer sense of what it's about than the statement indicates. We believe that if the foundation were approached for a grant to "reduce injustice" it might well ask for specifics from the grant writer. By how much? With what approach? Will your approach be targeted or general?*

BELL ATLANTIC

To be the customer's first choice for communication and information services in every market we serve, domestic and international.

Comment: *It's short, it covers all aspects of the company's many lines of business, it's customer-focused, and it's measurable.*

BURLINGTON NORTHERN AND SANTA FE RAILWAY

Our vision is to realize the tremendous potential of the Burlington Northern and Santa Fe Railway by providing transportation services that consistently meet our customers' expectations. We will know we have succeeded when: Our customers find it easy to do business with us, receive 100% on-time, damage-free service, accurate and timely information regarding their shipment, and the best value for their transportation dollar. Our employees work in a safe environment free of accidents and injuries, are focused on continuous improvement, share the opportunity for personal and professional growth that is available to all members of our diverse workforce, and take pride in their association with BNSF.

Our owners earn financial returns that exceed other railroads and the general market as a result of BNSF's superior revenue growth, an operating ratio in the low 70s, and a return on invested capital which is greater than our cost of capital. The communities we serve benefit from our sensitivity to their interests and to the environment in general, our adherence to the highest legal and ethical standards, and the participation of our company and our employees in community activities.

Comment: *The main statement may be a bit unclear; but the "we will know we have succeeded" language makes the statement real. It is sprinkled with strong, direct, and specific language: "free of accidents and injuries" and "100 percent on-time, damage-free service." Those are measurable and meaningful goals.*

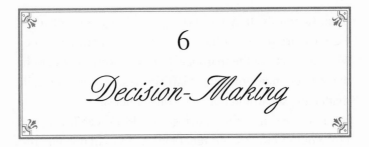

6

Decision-Making

The word "must" is not to be used to princes.

ELIZABETH HAD WITNESSED firsthand the perils of rushing into action and of allowing circumstances to force hasty decision-making. She had seen the gruesome results of precipitous decision making: the heads of rebels staked on the streets of London.

In January 1554, England and Spain signed a marriage treaty that would wed the English queen, Mary I, to the most powerful man in Europe, Philip of Spain. Mary hoped to produce a male Catholic heir for the throne, and Philip found the marriage an easy way to bring England into his orbit, knowing that, as Mary's consort, he could bend the malleable queen to his will. (She might be queen, but she would be Philip's wife, and wives—even royal ones—were expected to obey their husbands in all things.) Opposition to the marriage was strong. Although Mary's councilors wanted the queen married, they had hoped she would marry an Englishman. Certainly, they had not wanted her to choose a foreigner more powerful than herself. Parliament petitioned Mary to abandon the marriage, but the queen would not be denied her choice of mate. Marriage, she said, was a private matter and she would not marry one of her subjects. When it became clear that the marriage would proceed, England broke out in protests and rebellion. A group of noblemen—both Protestant and Catholic—joined in a conspiracy to remove Mary from the throne and put the twenty-one-year-old Elizabeth upon it. The uprising was to be launched from four different locations in mid-March, but Mary's government learned of the plan. Knowing this, the conspirators decided to launch their assault prematurely rather than wait for another opportunity at surprise. As a result, only one of the forces, 4,000 men led by the Catholic knight Sir Thomas Wyatt, actually took the field. Marching on London, his forces were defeated and Wyatt was arrested, convicted of treason, and beheaded. Elizabeth, implicated in the uprising merely on grounds that she had most to gain from its success, was escorted to London under guard and placed under house arrest at the queen's estate at Woodstock while Mary's prosecutors sought evidence that would link the young princess to the conspirators. Suffering from migraine and nephritis, Elizabeth was carried through gates and streets lined with the quartered bodies and spiked heads of Wyatt's men—grim testimony to the foolhardiness of moving too quickly, of ignoring data.

Elizabeth has been described by most of her biographers as a person who had difficulty making decisions. Her advisers were often frustrated by the queen's reluctance to act immediately on their recommendations and her delay in signing important papers and, sometimes, her changes of mind. Views of the queen as indecisive are invariably based on the recollections of the frustrated, rather than the frustrator. One has to ask, in considering Elizabeth's inaction, whether it was she who unduly delayed key decisions or her advisers who unduly sought them prematurely? Did the queen's delay serve England's interest and her own, frustrating an adviser's suit for a quick decision that served only himself? Was what appeared as "vacillation" to her advisers instead a wise tactic for allowing Elizabeth to maximize her options?

Marilee Winiarski, senior director of West Online Content Development in Eagan, Minnesota, is a longtime student of Elizabeth's life and has given much thought to the traditional view that Elizabeth was indecisive. "To some extent, I think Elizabeth's hesitation in making decisions is misunderstood." Winiarski told us. "It is generally characterized as fear and vacillation. In the Net world of today, when the common view is that any action is better than no action, postponing decision making is difficult to defend. But I don't think Elizabeth was ever really indecisive. She knew her mind, and she knew what she wanted. She knew she didn't want to marry. She knew she didn't want to take her country to war. She knew she didn't want to execute Mary, Queen of Scots, she knew she didn't want to name her successor. If she appeared indecisive about any of these matters, it was because she knew that these were politically unpopular positions. She believed firmly that she knew what was right, but politically she had no choice but to play for time . . . and hope that circumstances would change."

Winiarski noted that "there is risk in waiting, and there is risk in moving. For her, "the deciding point had to be whether you can make incremental steps along your decision path which allow you to uncover more of the future as you go, so you can adjust. Executing Mary, Queen of Scots, was not something Elizabeth could undo once done. But Elizabeth managed to stall the decision, moving forward incrementally, for a period of twenty years, gathering evidence against Mary, capturing her, trying her, and then allowing her execution. But the decision was made only after the proof of Mary's guilt was overwhelming and only when England was strong enough to bear the brunt of the foreseeable reaction—the Spanish Armada. If that Armada had showed up in 1568 rather than 1588, her country might not have withstood the onslaught.

"My natural inclination in decision-making," Winiarski told us, "is to want to have all the facts, which you can never have. So I have to fight against the tendency to wait too long to decide. I recently held off a reorganization of my staff to address changing work flows because a bigger reorganization was 'imminent' and I wanted to reduce disruption to the workforce. But unfortunately the larger reorganization has been delayed for five months, and my staff has had difficulty coping with the work flow. I would have been smarter to go ahead or at least make changes in the one place in my organization most directly affected— which I finally did informally. When I can break up a decision into smaller pieces and move one at a time, I tend to feel more in control of the situation."

There are dozens, if not hundreds of models for decision-making, but most boil down to five steps:

- Gather the facts;
- Analyze the facts;
- Seek the opinions of others;
- Weigh the merits and likely outcomes of alternative actions;
- Make the decision most likely to produce the best outcome.

In addition to these techniques of formal analysis, many decision experts advise factoring in an intuitive gut check that answers the question, "Does it feel right?"

The ancient Greek historian Herodotus gave one of the earliest descriptions of this decision-making process. Herodotus wrote that the ancient Persians, when facing a major battle decision, would meet in council to methodically review their options. They studied reports on terrain, the balance of opposing forces, the equipment of both camps, and the past battles of enemy generals. After reaching a decision in the most sober and left-brained fashion, they would proceed to the gut check. Their means of doing this was to get stupifyingly drunk and again talk over their plans. Upon reaching the same decision, both drunk and sober, they knew they had a good plan and marched confidently into battle. Using this technique, they dominated most of the known world for decades.

Given her knowledge of Greek, it's likely Elizabeth stumbled across Herodotus's *History* in her youth. But whether she did or not, Bess seems to have understood Persian wisdom; namely, that the key to successful decision making is to make sure any venture you pursue resonates positively in both head and heart; that it makes sense both analytically *and* intuitively.

When Elizabeth seemed to vacillate, it was likely because the analytical and intuitive aspects of a pending decision were not in sync in terms of the action itself or its timing. (Her means of exploring the intuitive aspect of her decisions is unknown to us, but being notoriously abstemious, she certainly she didn't use alcohol.) It's likely that meditation, distraction through dancing or sport, or a good night's sleep enabled her intuitive side to come to the fore.

Betsy Johnson is a former helicopter company president and aviation administrator who, at the time this book went to press was running unopposed for an open seat in the Oregon legislature. She spoke to us about the need for patience and data-sufficiency in making decisions. "[Sometimes] externalities require a quick decision," Johnson told us. "There are other things that . . . profit from thoughtful reflection. Too often I have fired off a letter or have been tempted to tell somebody off, but the thought occurs to me that if I wait just a second, maybe this is a teaching moment. Maybe there's something I'm not seeing." Whether a decision should be made or postponed depends entirely on the nature of the decision and the facts at hand. Johnson says, "I ask myself how much do I know about the operative circumstances? I can't know everything; I'm willing to take a leap. I am informed to a certain point. I can't know every exigency, and I make a call. There's a boldness in doing this that I think is a trait in successful entrepreneurs."

Linda Bennett, who heads Australia's primary health insurance provider, has a checklist for deciding when to make a decision. She says:

- Postpone when there are too many differing views on how or with what to proceed. Give space for more data collection or for people to change their initial stand.
- Probably the most common hasty decisions are staff related because we are sensitive to people's needs and their desires. These decisions in haste can go very wrong.
- The decision on a promotion for a staff member still in the process of developing new skills is best postponed until they have an opportunity to demonstrate them with confidence.

Sara King, director of open enrollment programs at the Center for Creative Leadership in Greensboro, North Carolina, noted the importance of delaying decisions when facts are lacking or when they fail to produce a decision that feels right intuitively. "You never have *all* the data, but when you have a decision that impacts a wide variety of people and you don't have enough data, then I'm hesitant."

King was describing the problem of "data sufficiency," a concept so important that it forms a major unit in the Graduate Management Admissions Test (GMAT), the examination most students must take as part of the admissions process for the nation's business schools. Examinees are presented with a problem in math or logic and given three pieces of information that can help them solve the problem. They are then asked to determine, not the solution, but whether the information they were given was A) not enough to find the solution B) just enough to find the solution or, C) more than was needed to find the solution. It's a tough test, partly because it's structured differently from the other sections of the exam; partly because most high schools and colleges focus on getting the right answer, not getting it most efficiently; and partly because many of the questions require a knowledge of geometric formulas test takers may not have used in years. Nonetheless, the Data Sufficiency section of the GMAT exists for good reason: Gathering information takes time and money. Gather more than you need and you're wasting time and money, and wasting time and money is antithetical to efficient business practice.

Amal Johnson, principal at Weiss, Peck & Greer Venture Partners in San Francisco, notes that timing is critical, particularly in today's investment-banking world—and delay is often a tactical consideration. "[The world of venture capital] is about postponing the decision for as much as you can so you can think about it," Johnson said. "In the investment world . . . making no decision is better than making the wrong decision. You take your time to think about things until the last minute, which could be five minutes after you meet the entrepreneur or five weeks. It depends on the nature of the deal."

Karen Rankin, the retired Air Force brigadier general, noted the importance both of "sleeping on decisions" and making sure they pass the "feels right" test, particularly in personnel matters. "Anytime a decision can impact an individual's life or career, a decision should be 'slept on.'"

Although consciously "sleeping on decisions," can be helpful, putting them off when they need to be made is another matter. Betty Hollander, chair and CEO of the Omega Group, Inc., in Stamford, Connecticut, told us, "In the normal course of any day, there are always minor pressures to make a decision." With those, she said, "it is easy to 'take a breath' and respond later." However, said Hollander, "procrastinating or putting decisions off is extremely unhealthy for a business." Why? Because "colleagues, whether inside the company or outside the company, judge a leader by her ability to assess conditions and respond."

Entrepreneur Sandy Gooch told us that the pressure and temptation to get things done quickly is often counterproductive. Citing an example from her first startup, Gooch said "when I first developed the partnership in Mrs. Gooch's (Natural Food Stores), I was too hasty in setting up the legal aspects and the allocation of the stock. Giving away too many shares of stock made it difficult regarding 'control' and 'power.' I find it is wise to think through a platform, or concept, and how it may work rather than just going and doing it then having to fix or discard it."

Michelle McCormick, principal of MMC Communications in Sacramento, California, told us "It's best to postpone a decision anytime all the potential ramifications of an action haven't been considered, or if there is missing information. It's easy for a group to get on an emotional roll, and want to decide upon a specific action." In a statement

that could have been made by Lord Burghley himself, Mc-
Cormick said, "as a counselor, it's often my role to point
out all the consequences, or the facts we haven't gathered
which may lead to undesirable consequences. At the same
time, there definitely comes a time for action, and it can
also be my role to urge a client to move forward."

McCormick's thoughts were echoed by Rachel Owens,
who runs her own insurance services practice in Laguna
Hills, California. Owens told us, "If you feel you do not
have enough information in order to weigh the pros and
cons of an action it is best to postpone. But you must also
set limits for the gathering of the information and a time
frame in which to make a decision." And, she said point-
edly, "inaction is also a decision."

There are three areas, in particular, that frustrated Elizabeth's advisers, who characterized them as examples of "a
woman's" indecisiveness: the matter of Mary, Queen of
Scots; the matter of Elizabeth's marital status; and, in the
absence of a marriage, the naming of a successor. The
queen eventually made clear decisions in all three cases:
Mary was beheaded, Elizabeth chose not to wed, and she
named James VI of Scotland as her heir. The frustration for
her advisers, suitors, and Parliament was that the quickest
of these decisions—Mary's beheading—took nearly twenty
years to be reached. It was not what Bill Gates would call
"business at the speed of thought." Of course, things *did*
move at a much slower pace in the sixteenth century, but
Elizabeth was a master at protracting the decision-making
process when it suited her to do so—and, in the three cases
cited, it seems to have been the best policy.

Take, for example, the queen's so-called indecisiveness in the matter of Mary, Queen of Scots. The Scots queen was the darling of Elizabeth's opponents, being both Catholic and having a strong claim on the throne as a direct descendant of Henry VII's daughter (and Henry VIII's sister) Margaret. As such, she enjoyed the same status with Catholic rebels that Elizabeth had enjoyed with Protestant leaders like Nicholas Throckmorton, one of Wyatt's partners who barely escaped execution. Having herself been suspected of a role in Wyatt's attempts to put her on the throne, Elizabeth was likely to feel sympathy for Mary, as a person who might well be innocent of plotting with those who tied their political ambitions to her accession. Elizabeth had been in the same position herself and always asserted that she was innocent of any wrongdoing. If she had been innocent, wasn't it likely that Mary could be, too? And, as we have noted elsewhere, Elizabeth was conservative and believed in the established order of government and succession. If she were to kill Mary, she would be setting a precedent that might eventually lead to her own beheading. Finally, Elizabeth felt there might be other, less draconian, methods of neutralizing Mary as a force of opposition. She had even tried to marry the Scots queen off to Dudley—an improbable event, but one that, if secured, would have put the queen in the "yoke" with a fiery Protestant who, as Mary's husband, would have the authority of a husband at that time to rule his wife's actions. Also, if Elizabeth acted precipitously in ordering Mary's execution, she would touch off a war with Spain and perhaps with France as well. Wars would cost money and lives, and the gross expenditure of either would threaten Elizabeth's popularity and spur rebellion within her own kingdom. Finally, and not insignificantly, although Elizabeth could be cruel of necessity, she was not cruel by nature and was hesitant to act to take any life unless circumstances demanded it of her. For all of these reasons, the queen was slow to approve the execution of her cousin and acceded to her death only after receiving overwhelming evidence of Mary's direct involvement in the ill-fated Babington Plot of 1586, which aimed at assassinating Elizabeth herself.

Clear proof was a standard for Elizabeth in matters in which decisions were irreversible — executions being the primary example. She had to serve as ultimate judge in other executions during her reign, most notably those of the traitors Norfolk and Essex. Although she acted rather quickly in ordering Essex's execution where the evidence was clear and there were virtually no foreign-policy implications, she acted slowly in the case of Norfolk, where the evidence was clear, but the foreign-policy implications were great. Norfolk, the only duke in the realm, is usually described as a popular man, whose affability and religious beliefs made him a dupe for the machinations of others. Rather than a leader, he was a follower. Unfortunately, in 1570, the duke joined in the scheme of a London-based Florentine banker and freelance foreign agent named Ridolfi. Ridolfi, who excelled in telling his employers (including Pope Pius V) what they wanted to hear, hatched a plot whereby Elizabeth would be dethroned and Mary, Queen of Scots put in power. (Actually, at this time, Mary wasn't even on the throne of Scotland, having abdicated in the wake of a scandal. Elizabeth, ironically, was considering whether it might not be in England's interest, with certain restrictions, to have Mary restored to her former position.) Ridolfi recruited Norfolk to lead troops against Elizabeth. The Italian also sent a lot of letters to Rome, various foreign ambassadors, Norfolk, and other hoped-for conspirators. When some of these letters were intercepted, Burghley set to work getting them deciphered and eventually turned up Norfolk's name along with months of evidence concerning Ridolfi's plans and other efforts to put Mary on Elizabeth's throne. After a lengthy trial at which reams of evidence were presented, Norfolk was found guilty and sentenced to death—an act that required the queen's authorization. She balked. She had not previously sent any noblemen to the chopping block—let along a popular one. Elizabeth had made a mission of avoiding the internecine bloodshed that characterized her predecessor's reign. And, of course, there were policy implications abroad. If the queen failed to sign the death warrant she would be perceived as weak; if she signed it, she might further the efforts of rebels backed by foreign powers. Her advisers urged an immediate signature, but Elizabeth, knowing that once a head is lopped off it cannot be lopped on again, wanted time to think things over. While she was thinking, two ruffians made an inept attempt to rescue Norfolk by attempting to assassinate not only Elizabeth, but Burghley as well. This increased pressure upon Bess to sign the warrant, but again she deferred. She finally signed the warrant in early February, only to countermand it before it could be carried out. The same thing happened again in April. Finally, in June, faced with adamant cries from Parliament that Norfolk be executed, Elizabeth signed the final decree.

Although she appears on the surface to have vacillated in Norfolk's death, Elizabeth was, in fact, moving a number of other decisions forward and consolidating the support needed to carry them out. For example, the Spanish ambassador de Quadra, who was implicated in the Ridolfi matter, was sent packing. The queen also changed her policy toward Mary, Queen of Scots. Having previously considered backing Mary's restoration—a move that would have strengthened Mary's chances for succession to the English throne with Elizabeth's backing—she dropped all efforts on Mary's behalf. The Ridolfi plot had provided significant, if not conclusive, proof of Mary's involvement in attempts against Bess. By postponing the decision to execute Norfolk, Elizabeth fueled the fury of Parliament against Mary and her supporters and allowed the public time to understand the duke's complicity in the plot. By the time Norfolk's head rolled, his popularity had waned, and he died as surrogate for Parliament's real target: Mary herself. In postponing Norfolk's execution and making Parliament force the action, Elizabeth was able to maintain her image as a clement and nonviolent monarch, one able to send troublemakers out of England, so they couldn't stir the waters of rebellion in the wake of Norfolk's death. She had allowed the "court of public opinion" to catch up with the legal court action and build a consensus that Norfolk's execution was proper; and, significantly, she had adopted a new policy toward Mary, which it was best to have in place and understood before taking an action certain to upset Mary and her partisans.

The second area in which Elizabeth was criticized for not making decisions involved the attempts to find her a husband. Here the problem was not so much that she was indecisive, but that her private decision *not* to marry was unacceptable to her advisers. To hold them at bay and hold the country together she allowed herself to be seriously courted by fourteen candidates, ranging from Robert Dudley to King Philip and various foreign princes. In some cases she was almost to the altar before finding a logical reason to call off the nuptials. This was particularly frustrating to Burghley, who often engaged in an early form of S.W.O.T. analysis, carefully drawing up lists of the strengths, weaknesses, opportunities, and threats posed by the queen's suitors and presenting them to Elizabeth for review. In hindsight it seems that what appeared to Burghley and others as "a woman's indecisiveness" was merely a mask for the decision Bess had made to remain married only to her people. That she chose not to be candid and go public with this decision for many years should not be held against her as a sign that she couldn't make up her mind— she simply chose, for good reason, not to reveal that she had done so.

The marriage question was closely tied to the third area cited as a sign of Elizabeth's indecisiveness—the demand that she name a successor. She cited many good reasons for not doing so, but never once implied that she was avoiding the decision. She told Parliament, in a stinging speech, that she was not about to name a successor who would be subjected to the same threats and dangers she had been subjected to as a princess. Nor would she undermine her own authority by naming an heir who could be drawn into attempts to unseat her. This was prudence, not indecision. Her long reign gave Elizabeth the opportunity to weigh the strengths and weaknesses of many proposed candidates and test their mettle. It also enabled her to lay the groundwork for succession by signing treaties and agreements like the Treaty of Edinburgh that would strengthen the eventual successor's acceptability. In the end, although the younger Cecil maneuvered behind her back to prepare for the transfer of power to Scotland's King James VI (later James I of England), Elizabeth indicated that she knew what was going on and must tacitly have approved of Cecil's back-door efforts, which she eventually sanctioned on her deathbed. The result was nearly perfect: The son of Mary, Queen of Scots, sworn to uphold the primacy of the Church of England, ascended to the throne with the blessing of the queen who had executed his mother, uniting England and Scotland in a reign that preserved most of Elizabeth's councilors in power and extended her own accomplishments.

Betsy Reveal, director of the United Nations Foundation, says she favors decisiveness, but notes from personal experience the type of problems that can result when actions are taken before the groundwork for understanding them is laid. "In my own career I have certainly made personnel decisions that were too hasty, both in regards to myself and others," Reveal told us. When Reveal was senior financial officer for the city of Philadelphia, she had to deal with a major fiscal crisis and chose to commit to paying debt-holders before employees as a means of protecting the city's long-term creditworthiness. In hindsight, she says, the decision "might have stuck better if I had taken more time to lay the groundwork for it." Reveal told us that "decisions which will put human beings in harm's way need more

Elizabeth's Guide to Decision-Making

Decide not to decide if:

- You need more facts.
- You need to lay the public relations groundwork for the decision.
- You need to buy time so you can plan the management of outcomes that will result from your decision.
- Others are rushing you and speed doesn't suit your purpose. (Corollary for those who would rush the boss: The word "must" is unlikely to carry your case.)

Decide slowly when:

- Lives are being affected
- When the decision will be irreversible.

Make the decision when:

- The facts have been determined.
- The likely outcomes have been determined and are acceptable.

careful thought—but not necessarily more time—than ones that don't, and decisions that are irrevocable do, as well."

Although none of the executives we spoke with advocated avoiding decisions, they noted both the perils of acting too quickly and without adequate information, as well as the pitfalls of acting under emotional stress.

Lillian Vernon, the direct-mail legend, stressed the importance of data. "First, I need to have all the facts in front of me so I can carefully analyze them in order to make a sound business decision," Vernon told us. "If I have an ounce of doubt and instinctively feel that a decision is wrong, despite advice from others, or I feel the timing of a decision isn't right, under no circumstance do I move forward. During a rapid surge of growth in the early 1980s, we grew our business too quickly without the proper systems and people in place. I learned that too much growth can be as risky and harmful for a company as too little."

Stephanie Teer, director of the mentoring business program at California State University–Long Beach, says she's found "it's best to postpone a decision when I'm too emotional—either negative or positive. I like to calm all those emotions and mix in some element of logic and reasoning." Teer says she's sometimes made too-hasty decisions when dealing with students who may not have fulfilled their commitments or responsibilities to the program. "I was too emotional when dealing with them and I felt like a mother lecturing at them, as opposed to a director who was providing them with a learning experience," she said.

In the final analysis, Elizabeth's apparent vacillations and about-faces were part of the process that led her, in the face of continual pressure intended to force decisions, to make mostly good ones, each in its proper time and each assured to match her goals of limiting bloodshed, balancing England's budget and securing the best possible outcome in terms of preserving her legacy.

7

Vast Intellect

. . . this day I have been forced to scour up my
rusty old Latin.

ELIZABETH I USED every intellectual tool she pos-
sessed to persuade, impress, cajole, intimidate, and outrea-
son those who opposed her and would undermine the interests of England. She did not suffer fools gladly and
sometimes wielded her intelligence with fool-withering effect. In 1597, for example, Paulus Jaline, the new and inex-
perienced Polish ambassador to England, something of a
popinjay, was allowed an audience with Elizabeth to present what the queen believed to be a complimentary message from Poland's king. Jaline arrived at court in full am-
bassadorial regalia, kissed the queen's hand with aplomb,
then stepped back ten feet, struck a pompous pose, and
launched into a formal diatribe in Latin. Jaline berated the
queen, arguing that English sea actions against Spain were
jeopardizing the interests of Polish merchants. While the

entire assembly of Elizabeth's ministers listened aghast, the ambassador threatened that his master would punish Elizabeth if she did not comply with Poland's demands that England cease its actions immediately. Court custom called for the queen to respond to foreign ambassadors through her ministers, but Bess was not one to stand on ceremony while diplomats minced words. Suited by both genius and temperament to take matters into her own hands, the queen leaped from her throne, thrust aside her Lord Chancellor, and broke out, extempore, in a vicious rebuke of the Polish envoy.

Speaking in flawless Latin, Bess blasted Jaline's impudence. "Never in my life have I heard such an oration! I marvel at so great and such unaccustomed boldness in a public assembly. Neither do I think, if your King were present, that you would say so much." She then questioned the upbringing and wisdom of any king who would send such a rude message—or so rude an ambassador. And she implied that, were it not for his office and his inexperience, she would have the ambassador horse-whipped for his audacity. "In the meantime," she concluded, "farewell, and be quiet!"

As soon as the admonished Jaline left the room, the queen broke into self-delighted laughter. "God's death, my Lords!" she said, "This day I have been forced to scour up my rusty old Latin!" At age sixty-four, and long past her daily Latin studies, Gloriana had spoken clearly, vigorously, and perfectly in the only language certain to be understood in both word and nuance by the upstart ambassador.

Mentally vigorous throughout her life, Elizabeth's intellectual accomplishments rivaled those of the leading scholars of her age. But, unlike most scholars, Elizabeth was able to apply her intellectual skills directly to matters of state. As a princess, her fine, well-exercised mind enabled her to outsmart those who sought to deny her the throne. Once she was crowned, her brains helped her thwart efforts to usurp her—and kept her in power for nearly forty-five years.

Just how smart was Elizabeth? There were no formal measures of intelligence in the sixteenth century, but we can judge her mental powers from anecdotal evidence provided by tutors and historians, as well as by her writings and speeches. Gloriana was, foremost, a remarkable linguist. While still a princess, at age fourteen Elizabeth could speak English, French, Latin, Greek, Spanish, Flemish, Italian—and a bit of Welsh! Throughout her life she kept fluent in these languages, and her fluency was often rewarded. The incident involving the Polish ambassador was not the first in which Elizabeth was "forced to scour up her rusty old Latin." Years before she had drawn on it to debate points of theology with scholars and churchmen at Oxford, where she quoted church documents in Latin—and scripture in New Testament Greek! Anyone who debated with Elizabeth quickly discovered that she was not only well informed but also able to express her thoughts clearly in whatever language best suited her needs and those of her audience.

Unlike many polyglots, Elizabeth was also a master of her native language. She wrote exemplary letters and poems in English. Because words were important to her, she developed an elegant style of penmanship with which to put them in writing, and she honed her oratorical skills to make sure her words were well spoken.

Sir Roger Ascham, Elizabeth's esteemed tutor, once described her intellectual accomplishments this way:

> The Lady Elizabeth has completed her sixteenth year; and so much solidity of understanding, such courtesy united with dignity, have never been observed at so early an age. She has the most ardent love of true religion and the best kind of literature . . . no apprehension can be quicker than hers, no memory more retentive. French and Italian she speaks like English; Latin with fluency, propriety and judgment. She also spoke Greek with me frequently, willingly and moderately well. Nothing can be more elegant than her handwriting, whether in the Greek or the Roman character. In music she is very skillful, but does not greatly delight. She read with me almost the whole of Cicero, and a great part of Livy. . . . In every kind of writing she easily detected an ill-adapted or far-fetched expression.

In addition to languages, music, and religion, Elizabeth's youthful studies included the principles of architecture and astronomy. Among her pastimes, she enjoyed playing chess and cards, as well as riding, walking, and attending the theater and bear-baiting contests.

The queen's wide-ranging interests and diligent studies no doubt contributed to her ability to stay sharp as she aged so that, until her last hours, at the age of seventy, she remained mentally agile. She had to. The sixteenth century was arguably the world's first Information Age, characterized by the discovery of new worlds, the widespread dissemination of challenging new ideas, and an explosion of scientific advances.

Elizabeth faced a formidable task when it came to keeping abreast of developments in this period of transformational change. In our own time we have come to expect exponential increases in knowledge, but that was not the case in Elizabeth's era. The ideas emerging in the sixteenth century were truly revolutionary; they did not so much extend prevailing ideas, as overthrow them. The proliferation of knowledge and its rapid dissemination produced culture shock, creating an environment from which new economic systems, new types of government, new churches, and new world orders would spring. For example:

- Books were being printed for laymen, not just clerics and scholars—and they were being printed in common languages, not just Latin. More books in more languages meant more ideas in the heads of more people than at any previous time in history. Vernacular Bibles stirred religious ferment as lay Christians were able to form their own opinions about the meaning of texts rather than having to rely on priests to translate and interpret them. The political manifestations of religious rivalry caused England to change its official religion four times in the decade preceding Elizabeth's coronation!

- The world itself seemed to be changing. European explorers discovered new lands and peoples in the Western Hemisphere. A new type of map— the Mercator Projection of 1568—not only depicted the New World, but also showed the Old World in a new way.

- Even as new countries were being placed on new globes, Copernican views were placing Earth in a new location. Copernicus argued that Earth was not the center of the universe, nor even its own solar system, but merely one of several planets circling the Sun.

- While astronomers and churchmen argued about the planet we live *on*, the anatomical explorations of Vesalius changed views about the bodies we live *in*. With new medical understanding came new treatments for injury and illness.

- Regardless of one's worldview, new inventions enabled the world to be more precisely measured and understood. Peter Henle of Nuremberg invented the watch in 1509; in 1546, Georgias Agricola created the modern system for classifying and studying minerals; Galileo perfected the thermometer in 1593, and the Gregorian calendar was instituted in Rome in 1582 (although England stubbornly refused to recognize it for many years to come). In 1590, Galileo overturned centuries of Aristotelian theory with publication of his *Law of Falling Bodies*. And in 1600 William Gilberd, one of Elizabeth's most trusted advisers (and an ancestor of Pam Gilberd's husband), launched the study of electricity and magnetism.

- New tastes swept the Old World. Tobacco was brought from the New World quickly became a fashionable drug of choice. Coffee, introduced in 1517, had begun to stimulate the minds and disturb the sleep of Europe. (Coffeehouses, the Elizabethan equivalent of Starbucks, started making their appearance in London.)

- Changes in taste extended to the arts as well. Thomas Tallis was composing some of the most complex vocal music ever written (before or since); William Shakespeare and Christopher Marlowe were writing plays that would be treasured by readers and audiences for centuries to come.

- The unprecedented abundance of New World gold was transforming economies and fueling the growth of capitalism, which was still in its infancy.

In trying to keep abreast of such sweeping changes, Elizabeth was handicapped in ways we are not. She had no *New York Times, Wall Street Journal,* or *Economist* to draw on. She had no Internet. No CNN. No telephones. No faxes. Nonetheless, she was always up-to-date on all things going on around her.

Though times have changed, Elizabeth's methods of gathering information and keeping her skills sharp remain valid nearly 400 years after her death. The queen's use of multitasking, delegation, and filtering techniques enabled her to stay on top of the flood of new information and maintain her mental agility.

Here's a look at how Elizabeth used each technique, along with some examples of ways modern executives use the technique to stay sharp and avoid information overload:

Multitasking.   Elizabeth never heard the word "multi-tasking" (and would no doubt have considered it an "ill-adapted" and barbarous expression); nonetheless, Bess was a consummate practitioner of doing several things at once. One of her favorite "tricks" was to read while taking her daily walk. In our own age, this type of multitasking is so commonly practiced that the term has become a buzz-word. We listen to books on tape while we jog, work out, or commute; we clear e-mail from our computer screens while listening to voice-mail messages; cell phones accom-pany us everywhere; and, if we are drivers in Los Angeles, we have proven that we can talk on the phone, eat break-fast, and shave or apply makeup while waiting in traffic. Elizabeth did not have as many enabling technologies as we do for multitasking, but she seems to have recognized that the ultimate benefit of doing several things at once is not that of saving time, but rather of creating synergy from varied, simultaneous activity. That benefit can be particu-larly powerful when it springs from simultaneous develop-ment of body and mind. That's why many successful mod-ern executives apply mind-body multitasking with a vengeance. For example, Audrey Rice Oliver, president and CEO of Integrated Business Solutions, goes to her gym every morning at five o'clock to work out and watch the news. Oliver is a disciplined pursuer of information, setting aside an hour every morning before she goes to the office to catch up on reports, then devoting an hour in the evening to simultaneously catching up on general reading and reviewing previously taped TV broadcasts in which she has an interest.

Oliver believes in keeping the mind, body, and spirit healthy. Just as Elizabeth did, Oliver exercises all of them regularly as a means of keeping her mind focused and clear of distractions. "When you're too busy focusing on negative thoughts," she says, "you can't get out of the quagmire [that prevents you from being] creative."

Julie Mower Payne, sole proprietor of Creative Services (and self-professed whiz at *Trivial Pursuit*), says she's found synergies between the time she spends helping her son with his homework or assembling a puzzle with her six-year-old daughter, and the information demands of her job. "Too often we forget to turn the prism to get different angles of light," Payne says. "My kids always keep me on my toes to see things from a different angle, or to get to the root of the matter."

Filtering. Betsy Bernard is the executive vice president for National Mass Markets at Qwest, a company at the forefront of the fast-changing telecommunications and information industry. She has to deal with an extraordinary amount of fast-breaking technological and consumer information. Bernard's secret for handling the data: filtering. "The challenge is to zero in on the facts and data that are on point," Bernard says. "You can lose a lot of time poring through information that isn't relevant to the matter at hand." Faced with mounds of data, Bernard asks herself a simple question: Is this the right data? "Often, people get sidetracked with peripheral issues or they're swayed by data that isn't exactly on point. If I'm making decision about a product launch, I want to see numbers about how receptive the marketplace is likely to be, not just data about how great the product performs—the information has to match up with what's at stake. I think it's important for the logic of a leader's decision to be very clear—and having strong, relevant data helps provide that clarity."

Queen Bess couldn't agree more. She routinely pored over mounds of briefings from her spies, advisers, and envoys, testing each piece of data, questioning first its accuracy and then its relevance.

Carolyn Elman, executive director of the American Business Women's Association, believes leaders often find themselves drowning in an ocean of data when called upon to make decisions. When Elman herself wants to avoid unnecessary haste or delay in making a decision, she asks, "Can I comfortably act on this situation with the information I have now?'" If the answer is yes, she acts on it. "Sometimes, however, I'll decide not to do something because I don't have time to research it and don't want to make the decision based on the information I have."

Working to make sure she has enough data to make a decision, Elman also tries to ask for no more than she needs. Getting more than you need to solve a problem can waste time and money—and often muddies the waters of decision making, Elman says. "The key rule when gathering information is to get just the right amount of the right information needed to solve the problem. No more, no less."

Myrna Nickelsen, CEO of *NextMonet.com*, filters information by trying to get it from the most authoritative sources—both formal and informal. "I keep up with current information through trade and general business publications," Nickelsen says. She also stresses the importance of relationships in obtaining sound information. Those relationships may come from networking with other heads of business, bonding with her staff, or keeping in touch with old friends. "I do my own reading, but I also rely heavily on staff who read different publications," say Nickelsen. "We cut out articles, forward e-mails, etc. Fortunately, I've honed my ability to synthesize information quickly — which, ultimately, is what a CEO must be able to do."

Delegating. In an age of no Internet, no daily newspapers, and no broadcast news, Elizabeth had to rely on private and governmental sources, including her spy networks, to gather the news she relied on in making decisions. Some of her advisers were prone to color information to suit their ends; others were tempted to avoid conflicts by telling their volatile queen only what they thought she wanted to hear. She once told a French ambassador that she was "always careful to discriminate between those who advise me from affection for my service and welfare of my subjects, and those who advise me for other reasons."

In an effort to assure that she received the best possible information, Elizabeth required intellectual honesty from her advisers. In her making her first major appointment, for example, she told William Cecil (later Lord Burghley) that she trusted he would "not be corrupted with any matter of gifts, and that you will be faithful to the state; and that, without respect to my private will, you will give me that counsel which you think best."

Having a staff that can be counted on to research and advise honestly is the key to successful delegation of information-gathering, according to Carolyn Elman. Elman continually asks herself, "Am I going to the right source, asking the right person for the information I need?"

In delegating research, Elman says leaders must "ask themselves if they are prepared to accept information that doesn't support their preconceptions about an outcome." When she faces such findings, Elman says, she first examines the data more closely, recognizing that doing so requires intellectual honesty and flexibility. "Leaders must be able to accept facts as they are, not as they want them to be. If leaders aren't ready to change their views given new sets of facts, there's no use getting the facts in the first place."

Like Elman, Elizabeth was receptive to facts that challenged her preconceptions — even when her initial reaction to bad news indicated she was not! The queen's advisers often criticized her (usually not to her face) for postponing decisions while awaiting further verification of information she found distressing. Once the facts had been tested, however, Elizabeth seldom ignored them. For example, in the events leading to the execution of Mary, Queen of Scots, Bess required absolute proof of Mary's personal knowledge of and involvement in plots to seize the English throne. That proof came when Sir Francis Walsingham's code breakers succeeded in translating letters Mary had received and written in a secret code. The letters proved Mary's involvement in the attempt to overthrow Elizabeth. But the queen questioned the source of the data, demanding to know both how it had been obtained and who had done the codebreaking. Her advisers believed Bess was determined to deny the evidence in order to avoid issuing the death sentence. In fact, Elizabeth was anxious to avoid becoming a pawn of the Mary-phobic Puritans, whose staunchest adherents included Walsingham and several of his spies. As the evidence unfolded and her questions were answered to her satisfaction, Elizabeth abandoned her stated desire and belief that the Queen of Scots was not a direct party to the plots. Faced with solid information, she accepted it—and Mary was beheaded for treason.

Throughout the delegation process, honesty is critical to both the delegator and the information gatherer. Qwest's Bernard puts it this way: "People want honesty in their leaders—I think most employees have good intuition about who they can trust and who they can't. It's critical for me to be able to say that I've looked at a situation from every possible angle, and made a decision that's the best possible under the circumstances. To get to that point, I have to be able to accept facts as they are, not as I might want them to be. Even if I have a preconception about an issue, I have to be honest enough and flexible enough to base my opinion on the available information. That's really the only way to do it."

In our interviews with modern executives, we found several common—and very Elizabethan—attributes concerning their attitudes toward knowledge. The executives were all lifelong learners. Each recognized the importance of having solid information in usable form. Each believed in fact-based decision making and leadership. Each had thought seriously about the process of gathering and using information. All of the executives had developed systems and relationships for gathering information that were adapted to their specific requirements in terms of time, data quantity, and data quality. The consistency of responses among the interviewees underscored the managerial precociousness of Elizabeth's emphasis on fact-based decision making.

In a twenty-first century dominated by the fact-based style Elizabeth modeled 400 years ago, the ultimate managerial sin may be ignorance. Micki Napp, national marketing executive for IBM, puts it this way: "If you're not current, your credibility suffers. Your effectiveness as a leader is impaired. If people question your credibility, then you have to regain their confidence."

Elizabeth was born with a good mind, was well trained in its use, and was diligent in its maintenance. In an age when the average life expectancy was less than forty years, the queen not only lived long, but also remained intellectually and physically fit until her seventieth and final year. Indeed, in September 1602—only six months before she died—a visitor described her as capering about her garden like an eighteen-year-old! At times people wondered if she might not be immortal. The queen had, after all, thwarted numerous attempts on her life, evaded outbreaks of bubonic plague, and survived a near-death bout with smallpox. Although she lived long and well, Elizabeth left us no secrets concerning her health and longevity. She simply engaged in healthy practices of the type doctors have recommended for centuries. She rode or walked almost daily throughout her life (at age sixty-nine, for example, she astounded her retainers by taking a vigorous ten-mile ride on a spirited horse and later going hunting!). She was abstemious in her habits, drinking little and eating lightly. She kept her spirits up by surrounding herself with young people and often joined them in dancing and debate. She maintained her extraordinary reading regimen, and attended sports and cultural events regularly. Perhaps most important, she found ways to use on a near-daily basis knowledge she had acquired in her youth.

The queen's extraordinary early education may explain why Elizabeth was nearly as acute at seventy as she was at seventeen. Recent research indicates that the volume and complexity of knowledge one acquires prior to age twelve helps keep the mind sharp as one ages. Here's an analogy to help you understand why:

Imagine your brain as a wilderness that has just been opened to settlement. Imagine bits of information in the form of new towns springing up in the wilderness. Imagine yourself as a road builder. As new towns are formed, you build roads to connect them. Now consider two scenarios. In the first, the wilderness goes largely unexplored and only two small towns are settled. You build a two-lane blacktop to connect them and the settlers happily travel back and forth. Then a flood washes out the road, leaving both towns isolated. Now consider the second scenario: The wilderness explodes with towns—hundreds of them. Each town wants to communicate with as many of the others as possible. They set up sports leagues, trade fairs, and tourist facilities. You become a very busy road builder—and the wilderness blooms. Before long you've built a network of highways that make it possible for residents of any town to reach any other town easily. There are dozens of intersections and junctions—you've even built roads between roads—and there are many ways by which to reach each town. As a result, when a road washes out, it's easy to detour travelers to several alternative routes. It's almost impos-

Language Lessons

Elizabeth's mastery of languages was a powerful factor in controlling her cabinet and in establishing direct communication with ambassadors to her court. Many of the executives we interviewed told us that their knowledge of languages had played an essential role in advancing their careers or enhancing their effectiveness in their current positions.

Cindy Padnos, founder, president and CEO of Vivant! Corporation, told us how, in a previous position, her knowledge of French landed her a key role on a team negotiating with the French government to obtain preferred rates and tax preferences for a cruise-ship manufacturer. "I knew nothing about the travel industry but . . . they needed to get some government tax preferences in order to build these things when they were starting up the company. Because I spoke French . . . I flew over to France and made a presentation." That was a case of having the right language skills and being in the right place to use them at the right time.

Sister Karen M. Kennelly, CSE, uses her Spanish skills routinely in many aspects of her job as president of Mount Saint Mary's College in Los Angeles. "During my early years at the college," Kennelly told us, "I often directed a welcome to parents of new students in Spanish as well as English during fall orientation sessions at our Doheny campus. There the student body tends to be about three-fourths Hispanic; most students are the first in their family to attend college. Often parents do not speak or understand English, especially the mothers. Hearing a welcome in their own language helped them feel at home and lessened their fears about what it would mean to have a daughter attending college.

"Being able to exchange casual conversation from day to day with our many Spanish-speaking employees has also been a valuable asset. It builds morale and makes for a personal connection with employees who otherwise might feel quite remote from college administration. Being able to converse in Spanish with candidates for faculty and administrative positions provides an excellent reality check when fluency in Spanish is one of our criteria for hiring.

"I also believe my speaking Spanish gives the college greater credibility in the eyes of foundations and corporations when we seek their support for projects such as our Center for Cultural Fluency as well as for faculty and curricular development projects relating to access and diversity."

Many of the executives we spoke with who lacked foreign language skills said they wished they had developed them. For example, Naomi Bloom, sole proprietor of the Bloom and Wallace human resources consultancy in Fort Myers, Florida, noted: "As my work experience has gotten broader I have learned that there are no educated Europeans who don't speak two, three, four languages and it gives them a tremendous advantage in doing cross-cultural business." That's an advantage Elizabeth had from her early years and used to her benefit throughout her reign.

sible for a town to be isolated, and when new towns are settled, it's easy to incorporate them into the system.

Now imagine the towns as brain cells. Think of the highways as dendrites and axons, the connectors along which brain traffic moves from cell to cell. And think of "complex knowledge" as a road-building machine powered by youthful energy. Get the picture? As your brain develops, it activates its cells and the links among them. Signals pass from cell to cell through the dendrites and axons. Your brain network will make more connections or fewer connections depending on the volume and complexity of your studies. No matter how many connections you build when you're young, they will deteriorate if you don't use them as you age. In terms of brainpower, it appears that people who acquire the most knowledge early in life are better able to acquire new knowledge throughout their lives than are people who did not stretch their minds when they were young. (Don't despair if you didn't stretch your brain in childhood and now wish you had. Research indicates that it is never too late to build new information highways—only that it becomes more difficult as intellectually passive years accumulate.)

When it came to brain building, Elizabeth was a master engineer. There was virtually no aspect of Elizabethan life with which she was not familiar and no area of knowledge that eluded her interest. Her mind, full of information and connections, stayed keen throughout her life. She seems ideally suited to have ruled England during its Renaissance. The value she placed on fact-based decision making and the techniques she used for gathering and sifting information were innovative in her time and remain relevant to executives striving to keep pace with twenty-first-century developments in our later information age.

8
Style

> Bacon, how can the magistrate maintain his
> authority, if the man be despised [for his dress]?

IN DECEMBER 1549, the Princess Elizabeth, laboring
under vicious rumors that she had had an affair with her recently executed uncle, the traitor Thomas Seymour, traveled to the court of her brother, Edward VI, where she was
received with great pomp and ceremony in an effort to restore her image and maintain her status as a possible successor to the throne. She chose for the occasion to appear in
simple attire, without jewelry or makeup. A tall, striking figure with translucent skin and flowing red hair, she struck
awe among the assembled courtiers, whose doubts about
her character were overcome by her chaste appearance.

Here was no vixen, but rather a sober, thoughtful, lady-
like, simple young woman—an angel whose lack of adorn-
ment stood in stark contrast to the frivolous vanities of the
young women who populated the court. Young Bess wore

her hair long and free, rather than curled and double-curled in the manner of the day. Her appearance was visual proof that she had scorned the excesses of her father. The staid churchman, John Aylmer, wrote of her that "the King, her father, left her rich clothes and jewels, and I know it to be true that in seven years after his death she never, in all that time, looked upon that rich attire and precious jewels but once, and that against her will; and that there never came gold or stone upon her head."

On the occasion of her return to court, Elizabeth's regal bearing, modest appearance, and the austerity of her dress made it impossible for any but the most cynical observers to believe that she had played the wanton lover of her promiscuous uncle and had borne his child. Who could possibly oppose her on grounds of unseemly behavior?

Throughout her life, Elizabeth was conscious of personal style in everything she did. Bess paid careful attention not only to what she said but how she said it; not only to what she wore but how she wore it. Prior to her accession, she often chose, as described above, a maidenly, understated mode of dress to underscore her youth and inexperience, thereby mitigating the fears of opponents to her succession. Upon becoming queen, however, Elizabeth adopted more formidable and expensive attire to enhance her stature and authority as Gloriana. As she became older, Bess worked diligently to appear as young and energetic as possible, not only adopting youthful attire but also surrounding herself with young people, often dancing with them and exerting herself vigorously in riding and hunting forays, even as she approached the age of seventy.

Modern observers have positively characterized Bess's image consciousness as a sign of her shrewdness and charisma. They have also described it negatively as duplicitous and a mark of vanity to the point of narcissism (a sin for which a true princess may be allowed a measure of forgiveness).

Attentive to her own style of dress, Elizabeth also demanded a sense of style from those around her. She once asked Francis Bacon, in insisting on the importance of the mien and appearance of an official, "How can the magistrate maintain his authority, if the man [for his dress] be despised?" Indeed, she required those who served her to dress as impressively as their rank allowed. In our own time, only the fashion-conscious Washington Camelot created by Jacqueline Kennedy has come close to matching the interest in style, manners, and culture that Elizabeth established in the age that bears her name.

The queen's concerns in matters of dress and appearance were not superficial, but rather part of the carefully engineered image she wished to create for England both at home and abroad. She could, arguably, best keep suitors at bay by attracting as many as possible. She was more likely to attract more suitors by being physically, as well as politically, attractive. Cultivating her beauty and remaining notoriously flirtatious throughout her life, Bess guarded her reputation as a hard-to-win, if not inaccessible, virgin wedded to her realm. Her decision to remain unmarried was more useful to her politically if she could foster the idea that she was eminently marriageable should the right suitor turn up. The more perfect she could make herself seem, the less suitable seemed the various suitors proposed for her. But the challenge of winning an attractive, intelligent, fun-loving, powerful, and picky queen only fueled the desire of suitors, providing further opportunity to play one against the other for England's benefit.

Elizabeth's concern for proper dress was as strongly imposed on the men around her as on the women. In her court, clothes could quite literally make the man. No slobs were allowed and one of the best ways for a man to attract favorable attention was to show up for his audience well attired. Biographer Anne Somerset has noted that "Elizabeth indeed felt so strongly about what men about her wore that in 1594 she put all her courtiers to considerable expense by issuing an order through the Lord Chamberlain that no one would be admitted to her presence wearing a cloak that came below the knees. 'It cometh in a good hour for tailors and mercers and drapers, for all men are settled into the long cloaks,' commented one aggrieved gentleman." The implication is strong that Elizabeth's emphasis on style may well have been, as Somerset suggests, not only a matter "of royal caprice," but also a matter of bolstering a weak sector of the English economy!

What were the hallmarks of Elizabeth's personal style? She was intelligent (and flaunted it!); she was witty and indulged in broad, sometimes wicked humor; she carefully guarded her personal honor and defended it against all attempted scandal; she was outspoken when it suited her needs; she was flirtatious; she delighted in keeping people guessing, not only about her personal relationships, but also her views. Her favorite motto was said to be "video et taceo" ("I see and am silent").

In his biography of Elizabeth, historian Christopher Hibbert relates a telling story about the queen:

> . . . when Lady Mary Howard, a young lady whom Essex greatly admired, appeared at court with a sumptuous velvet dress embroidered with pearls, upon which others bestowed the most fulsome compliments, the Queen called her up and asked if she could borrow it. She then put it on herself; but, as she was taller than Lady Mary, it did not fit her. Was it too short for her? she asked Lady Mary, who had to agree that it was. "Why then, if it become not me as being too short," said the Queen, "I am minded it shall never become thee, as being too fine. So it fitteth neither well."

The queen returned the dress to its owner, who never again wore it in her presence.

This incident has been interpreted as a sign of the queen's vanity—perhaps prompted by a jealous concern over Essex's attraction to Lady Howard—but it is equally likely that the queen was merely enforcing one of her basic rules: that dress should suit, but not exceed rank and, as a consequence, the queen must never be outshone in a way that could diminish the image of power attached to the throne nor her self-chosen role as style setter.

Throughout our interviews on executive style for modern managers, the need for a sense of humor was cited as an important attribute—and it was one for which Elizabeth is well known through both her public and private communications. Her humor was usually based on word play, but she was not beyond practical jokes. In June 1577, for example, when Dudley, the Earl of Leicester—known for his hearty appetite—was staying with the Earl of Shrewsbury, she sent a playful communication to the earl's steward prescribing the diet Leicester should be fed during their visit. It called for a meager regimen of two ounces of meat and a single sip of wine a day, except on festival days when "as is meet for a man of his qualities, you shall enlarge his diet and allow unto him for his dinner the shoulder of a wren, and for his supper a leg of the same, besides his ordinary ounces." History does not record Leicester's reaction to the joke, although he returned no thinner from his journey. In official matters, her humor was often characterized by classic put-downs. At the age of sixty-three, when the Bishop of St. David's preached before her during Lent, he took occasion to remind her by various calculations that her end was not far off. The queen, though not amused, told the bishop, "You might have kept the arithmetic to yourself!" And, upon receiving a message from her spies that she had angered the king of France, she used her wit to convey her desires saying, "I see the King of France is bursting with rage, and I do not want him to burst any more." Many of Elizabeth's witticisms and humorous jibes may have resonated more strongly with their hearers as her power increased. Lanny Martin, a former attorney who now serves as CEO of NL Industries, a leading producer of titanium, noted this phenomenon when he told us, "the biggest difference between being a practicing lawyer and a CEO is that my jokes became funnier as a CEO."

The queen's sense of humor could sometimes be as coarse as her manner could be informal. Her speech was punctuated with oaths, "God's Death!" and "Jesus!" being among the most common. These confounded both Catholics and Protestants and caused both sides to be as concerned that Bess had no religion as that her religion was not theirs. From Bess's point of view, however, such displays served her well: If, in fact, she left the impression that she was unredeemed in her speech, both factions could pray for her salvation—and perhaps eventually win her soul.

It is difficult to imagine that these displays were not studied. Elizabeth was, after all, one of the most precise and thoughtful monarchs in history when it came to her use of language, both written and spoken. If she sometimes employed raw language and used coarse humor, it was no doubt to produce a desired effect on her audience, either as a way of piercing their presumption or demonstrating her alignment with the common folk of her realm.

One of the best-known anecdotes about Elizabeth's informality and coarseness involves a courtier, who in bowing before the queen suffered an unfortunate bout of flatulence. He was so embarrassed to have broken wind before Bess that he placed himself in self-imposed exile for seven years. Upon his return, he was granted an audience of reprieve before Gloriana, who received him with the words "Alas, My Lord, we have forgot the Fart!"—no doubt causing those present to break into laughter at the poor fellow's expense.

Such incidents served notice on Elizabeth's advisers, foes, and allies that she was not bound by the strictures of conduct placed on women of her time. She was their queen (or, as she preferred to style herself, their "prince") and could speak as she pleased. If she spoke forthrightly, it was more likely her male advisers would be at ease around her, rather than couching their views in genteel language. Her advisers must see her as their sovereign, not as a woman to be "protected" from the harsh realities of diplomacy. Language was a means to that end.

The first obstacle Elizabeth faced upon assuming the reins of government was that of establishing that she intended to rule, not merely preside. To do that she had to maintain discipline in a court that was notoriously unruly. And she had to overcome male stereotypes, at first, of her youth and, throughout her reign, of her gender.

Biographer J. E. Neale has noted that, "However they disguised their belief, statesmen [in the sixteenth century] held government to be a mystery revealed only to men." Elizabeth had to challenge that belief at every step. Elizabeth could not afford to surrender ultimate decision-making power to her advisers without permanently losing the ability to influence decisions. She recognized that she would be doomed were she ever to acquiesce to the prevailing views men had of women as gentle creatures, not suited to rule. To counter such impressions, when Elizabeth spoke, she spoke firmly. "[She] gives her orders and has her way as absolutely as her father did," wrote Count Feria, the Spanish ambassador to England.

Elizabeth was particularly adept at using the talents she had been blessed with. Her ease with many languages enabled her to conduct conversations directly with foreign ambassadors, virtually none of whom spoke English—it was simply not a language of diplomacy in her time. In questioning her advisers, she pushed for facts and opinions to help her form her own views, rather than simply asking what the advisers thought she should do. To avoid being overwhelmed by her all-male cabinet, she most often met with her councilors individually, establishing a one-on-one equality, woman to man, rather than calling large councils in which she would be the only woman present. That practice also enabled her, when necessary, to "divide and rule" her fractious Privy Council.

The lessons of personal style to be learned from Elizabeth lie not in the specifics of the style she used, but in the recognition that matters of dress, speech, and manner are essential traits for any leader, although they may vary for different leadership situations. Elizabeth's need for flexibility made inconsistency a constant of her managerial style.

Most executives become aware, at some point in their careers, of their need to be perceived in particular ways—and many have seen the need to change their image with the times. This concept applies routinely in modern political campaigns, during which some candidates (George W. Bush comes to mind) usually are seen wearing suits on the campaign trail, whereas others (Al Gore) choose to dress more casually. The clothes make a statement as to the style of the leader and the audiences within the electorate with which they are trying to identify and from which they seek support. The same is true in modern organizations that may maintain traditional dress codes as a way of underscoring their longevity or adopt casual dress modes as a means of underscoring youth, creativity, a focus on essentials, or egalitarianism in the workplace.

Former Gannett Company chairman Al Neuharth for years wore signature attire consisting of an elegant black, Italian-cut suit and *always* a white shirt: a power look that said, in effect, "I'm all business."

Consumer advocate and Green Party presidential candidate Ralph Nader seems always to be wearing simple suits with conservative shirt-and-tie combinations that experts say lend his challenges to corporate behavior credibility and undermine efforts to depict him as a radical.

Mohandas Gandhi wore suits in his early years as a civil rights lawyer in South Africa, but later favored the attire of a mendicant when he challenged British rule in India. Winston Churchill once described Gandhi as "a fakir in a loin-cloth," but Gandhi won the hearts of the world and the support of all India when he matched his attire to that worn by the people he most cared for.

The importance of personal appearance in establishing power within a business culture was cited by several of the modern executives we interviewed. Carole Hyatt, president of Hyatt Associates, Inc. of New York said, "Appearance is an enormous factor. Not that we have to look like men, but we have to fit into that culture. You don't wear jeans to Wall Street, but you do to a startup. It's a matter of the culture and what are they are used to accepting."

Hyatt said she wears expensive clothes when she appears as a speaker because she wants to epitomize the conventional norm of success. "I am successful and I want to exude success and part of that is the costume I choose," Hyatt told us. "I pay a lot of money for designer clothes so that when I walk into a room there is no question that I am monied, I am successful. It's an impression." Hyatt tells a story that is a modern version of Elizabeth's comments to Bacon concerning the disheveled magistrate:

"I ran a research company for many years and I had a wonderfully smart woman who was a slob. She was the worst dresser in the world. I talked to her about this and she said, 'Look, this is the way I'm going to dress.' I said, 'Fine, you can do that but you have to be twice as smart, your reports have to be twice as good. You can look any way you want but you better be twice what anyone else is in order to pull that off.' She was willing to do that. She wasn't willing to conform. She could be a maverick because she was smarter than anyone else was. But she worked twice as hard."

Always a style maven, Elizabeth used dress and makeup as a way of reinforcing her image as the Virgin Queen. Her signature white makeup—which became the fashion of her age—was symbolic of the purity she sought to portray to her people. In the movie *Elizabeth*—a film that despite its historical inaccuracies still contains good management lessons based on the myth of Gloriana—we see the queen adopt the forbidding countenance created by this makeup in the wake of her accession. Her change of countenance underscores her power—she remakes herself physically as a sign that she is not an ingenue. She has become Gloriana, the dedicated Dread Queen of a powerful realm. Times had changed, Bess's role had changed, so she underwent a makeover to reflect those changes. The concept of "management makeovers" was not unknown in Elizabeth's time. Indeed, her illustrious predecessor King Henry V, the subject of Shakespeare's finest historical trilogy, had modeled it for her. As the young Prince Hal, Henry was a hellion—a hard-drinking, brawling delinquent who hung out with doss-house regulars like Sir John Falstaff, with whom he had occasionally helped relieve unsuspecting victims of their purses. As Shakespeare would have it, young Hal was an unpromising candidate to become king, let alone one of the most distinguished kings in English history. Upon the death of his father, Henry IV, however, the prince had greatness thrust upon him, and he rose to the occasion. He cast aside his riotous lifestyle, abandoning Falstaff and his gang, to take the reins of government firmly in hand. Just as Hal made himself over and quickly evolved from bad boy to good king, Elizabeth, nearly 100 years later, made herself over, evolving from solitary and studious young girl into the formidable Gloriana of legend. Although Shakespeare wrote his *Henry* saga years after Elizabeth's coronation, it is significant that this most theatrical of queens nurtured the cultural environment in which Shakespeare's theater prospered. She, as much as he, understood that "all the world's a stage."

It is also significant that both Hal and young Bess incorporated name changes in their transitions from ruled to ruler. He became Henry; she became Gloriana. Sometimes a name change results, not from a desire to leave the past behind, but from a desire to seize the future. Lillian Vernon, the catalog legend, provides an example from her own life:

"I am proof there are advantages to changing your image at some point in your career to achieve more success in business," Vernon told us. " I named my business Lillian Vernon forty-five years ago as a link to the founding of my company in Mount Vernon, New York. As my business grew, I realized my customers equated me with my company name, so I legally changed my name [to Vernon]. My choice was a wise one."

Iris Goldfein, vice chairman of National Human Resources, PriceWaterhouseCoopers, Chicago, notes the importance of managerial makeovers in today's business world:

"The ability to actually remake yourself is a fundamental competency," Goldfein told us. But successful makeovers involve far more than cosmetic change. In Goldfein's case, they involved changes in skills and approaches. "I had a point in my career that I remember, where it was so numbing for me," Goldfein said. "I looked in the mirror and I would say a dinosaur looked back. I felt that the skills that I had that were once valuable were no longer valued in a very changeable market place. And though I never wanted to leave my job, I wanted to know that I could. I was losing my confidence that I would be desirable to others. Maybe you make your own breaks, but the first time I had the opportunity to remake myself, I was a little cowardly and got pushed into it. It was the best thing that ever happened to me. I was to take on a client where I felt my particular skill set didn't match. It turned out to be the client of my life. I learned new skills, rebuilt my confidence."

Sara King, director of Open Enrollment Programs, Center for Creative Leadership in Greensboro, North Carolina, argues that for women leaders, in particular, style can be critical to success. "I think of how it relates to the individual. That is a considerable topic in our organization for several reasons. One, we are a cross between an academic and corporate environment. Because of those blends there is tension. We have those who work in an academic environment where dress is a little more casual. There is the other part that deal with clients outside and meet with clients who dress more formally. If I were going to stereotype the individual that moves up in the organization, individuals who pay attention to their style and image portray a sense of self, pride in how they look. They are perceived as being more committed, passionate about work and more professional."

Our interviewees were nearly unanimous in their view that one's image—personal or corporate—must create a impression that is both true to oneself and consistent with the expectations of employer, client, or consumer. Flori Roberts, founder of two specialty cosmetics firms, Smart-Cover and Flori Robert Cosmetics, cited this as a particular strength of Elizabeth. "That's one of the things I love about her. In the movie [*Elizabeth*], I loved the moment when she said, 'I am Gloriana. I am married to my people.' "In effect, Roberts said, Elizabeth was adding, "And this is the way I need to look to project that image. I can't be worldly. I have to be otherworldly. I can be that big."

Robin Holt, now a career consultant with Charles Schwab, told a story that underscored the importance of first impressions of the type so important, not only at Elizabeth's court, but in any business situation. Before joining Schwab, Holt worked in a career development office where everyone dressed "very businesslike to give an image of confidence to our clients." But when she walked into Charles Schwab on her first day of work, she was "so unbelievably overdressed . . . it was embarrassing.

"First impression is so important," Holt said. "I knew right away I had made a mistake and I felt funny about it. I dressed just like they did from then on. More casual pants, denim blouse or sweater sets. No more suits and silk blouses. It only happened once. This is their technology enterprise, but all of Schwab is very casual.

"This is something I try to communicate with people as this is an issue that comes all the time about how can I fit into the new working world, the dotcom world, being over forty or fifty. . . . You have to see how people dress. How you look makes a difference. You have to get that kind of credibility. It sounds shallow but it's the truth."

Sometimes, however, one's personal image is so strong, even if it doesn't fit with the current fashion, that change can be perceived as phony and have counterproductive results—even for politicians. Betsy Johnson, a former aviation executive now running unopposed for a seat in the Oregon legislature, has faced this issue head-on. "I am short. I'm overweight. I speak in a commanding voice. I dress somewhat unconventionally. I don't do that intentionally. It's the way things turned out. There's an upside and a downside to that. . . . Sometimes politicians try to create a persona for themselves, but I just elected to remain who I am. I don't need to reinvent myself because I'm running for elective office. If you like it, vote for me. If you don't, don't . . . I'm fifty years old. I've gotten where I have by behaving and acting and thinking in a certain way. Some people have found that to be an attractive or a winning combination. At age fifty, this old dog isn't going to learn a lot of new tricks."

As Elizabeth knew, style is not only a matter of how one speaks and dresses, but also how one behaves. In today's workplace the question of dress and behavior has become a question of particular concern to women, as pointed out in a front-page article in the February 7, 2000, edition of the *Wall Street Journal*. Writing on changing workplace behaviors, reporter Ellen Joan Pollock noted that "when an earlier generation of women started work 25 or 30 years ago, they found their best strategy lay in pretending their home lives did not exist and in covering up their sexuality. Remember those awful suits and silly bow ties? Their daughters are joining a very different work world. There are plenty of other talented, able women around. Young people work around the clock and have little interest in erecting barriers between their social and work lives. Women are far more relaxed. They are wearing tank tops to interviews and Capri pants around the office. They are also less inhibited about using the personal tools at their disposal to get ahead professionally."

The Pollock article was printed just about the time the hit movie *Erin Brockovich* was released to theaters, setting off a round of commentary concerning appropriate dress and behavior by women in the modern workplace. In the movie, based on the true life story of a California legal aide, Roberts wears provocative and revealing clothing and uses her considerable physical attractions and sexy personality to gain access to important information from men, who consistently drool at the chance to help her. After the film's release, high-school and college women soon began adopting Brockovich's style and articles proliferated in the media about the social impacts on business, the women's movement, and appropriate workplace attire and ethics.

No doubt, Erin Brockovich would have been exiled from Elizabeth's court, where the men had to be handsome and well dressed, but women who attracted too much male attention were often barred because Elizabeth wanted her servants to project a maidenliness that matched her own.

Patricia Ireland, president of the National Organization for Women, discussed the Brockovich Syndrome with us: "Of course, every woman must decide for herself how to dress at work," Ireland said. "But she ought to be fully aware of the possible consequences of how she presents herself."

Elizabeth understood, as few monarchs before her, that she not only had to match her style of leadership to the situation at hand, but also to make sure that her manner of exercising that style was shored up at all levels in terms of her appearance, her tone of voice, her choice of words, and the timing and setting of her action. That attention to detail of presentation—to form, as well as content—was essential to establishing her authority as a matter of presence, not simply rank.

Judith Rogala noted in our interview with her that all "leadership is situational. You have to draw from male and female attributes every day to be a successful leader. You have to go in some days and be tough. You have to put on a game face. That's what's situational about it. Still you have your core of beliefs that people know they can count on."

Elizabeth's makeovers seldom belied faith in her core beliefs—nor in her ability to be seen as a complete *leader* whose personal attributes were in keeping with her public persona as a complete *person*. Throughout her life she wrote the script that enabled her to adapt her costume, her makeup, and her lines to the demands of her role.

9
Gender Politics

I know I have the body of a weak and feeble
woman, but I have the heart and stomach of a
King—and of a King of England, too!

ELIZABETH'S FORMAL CORONATION took place on January
15, 1559, a Sunday. The day before was marked by the coronation procession, a daylong spectacle during which the
queen moved through London's streets amid swarms of
well-wishers who weathered a bit of snow to catch a
glimpse of their new ruler. Bedecked in jewels and cloth of
gold and borne on a litter trimmed in gold brocade, Elizabeth was paraded from the Tower to Westminster Abbey.
Along the way, she was greeted with cheers and received
good wishes from the thousands who lined her circuitous
route. As the procession moved forward at a stately pace, it
stopped periodically to view a series of five elaborate
"pageants," prepared by London's authorities to demonstrate the city's faith in its new monarch. Each of these

staged homages to the queen featured loud, celebratory music, along with artistic displays replete with Latin verses of praise. As the procession stopped a child—usually a young boy—would deliver a message to Elizabeth that helped explain the significance of the display. The first show, at Gracechurch, displayed Unity and Concord and was arranged in three tiers, one showing Henry VII and his queen; the second, Henry VIII and Anne Boleyn (hardly a marriage of concord!); and, topmost, Elizabeth herself— representing the hoped-for unity that would emerge from the discord of the past. The second pageant, in Cornhill, featured a small girl who represented Elizabeth. She sat on a seat supported by four people representing Virtues (including Pure Religion) treading on the Vices of the country (including Superstition and Ignorance). At Cheapside, the queen was greeted by the particularly merry third pageant, where the Lord Mayor presented her with a gift of a thousand marks in gold. The fourth pageant featured the theme of Time. The scenario presented two hills, one green and fertile; the other withered and dead. Between them was a cave from which emerged Time, leading his daughter Truth—a surrogate for Elizabeth—by the hand. Truth held a copy of the English Bible. The narrating youth explained that the Bible provided the guidance needed to bring England into a flourishing state and enable it to leave behind the wastelands of the previous reign. Truth then presented the Bible to the queen. The fifth and final pageant recognized and leant support to Elizabeth on the matter that raised, perhaps, the most difficult problem she would face: confidence in her gender. The pageant, at Fleet Street, paid tribute to her sex and the formidable tasks she faced. The scene depicted Deborah, the Old Testament prophet, "the Judge and restorer of the House of Israel." It was perhaps, the most important sentiment expressed on that day of days because it addressed the major question that would haunt the early days of Elizabeth's reign. In the wake of Bloody Mary's reign—England's first experience of womanly rule (and a most unhappy one)—Elizabeth not only would have to restore confidence in the monarchy, but also show that Mary's sex had not been the cause of England's sorrows.

It is impossible to ignore Elizabeth's gender in assessing her achievements as a major world leader. Her predecessor had brought out the worst in religious bigots of all persuasions and aroused, particularly among Protestants, a fury that combined their loathing of the former queen's religious views with a general fear and dislike of women. Not least among these foes of woman's rule was the fiery Protestant leader and Scots rebel John Knox. Only months before Mary's death, Knox wrote an infamous tract titled *First Blast of the Trumpet Against the Monstrous Regiment of Women*, one of the most misogynistic broadsides ever penned. Among other sentiments, Knox argued that "It is more than a monster in nature that a woman should reign and bear empire among men." He ranted that woman were by nature weak, feeble, fragile, foolish, and impatient and the "gate of the Devil" It was unnatural, he went on, that the foolish should govern the wise, the lesser rule the greater, and, therefore, it would be an affront to God and a perversion for women to reign over men, thereby justifying their being deposed, by whatever means, from any throne. This "Knoxious" nonsense had been drafted as a blatant piece of anti-Marian propaganda and followed a previous publication that had all but called for Mary's assassination. The timing of Knox's broadside could not have been worse. Ironically for Knox, Elizabeth—the great Protestant hope—came to power only months after his tract was printed. Upon Elizabeth's accession to the throne, an observer noted that Knox's *Trumpet* had been "blown out of season." Protestant leaders disowned the work. For them, it was enough that a virtuous Deborah had replaced a villainous Jezebel. Elizabeth might be a woman, but she was theirs, a restorer of all they wanted set right. By whatever path Knox reconciled his views of women with his desire for a Protestant ally on the English throne, Elizabeth would continue to despise him throughout her reign and his name was not allowed even to be mentioned at court.

Biographer J. E. Neale has noted that Elizabeth was "not likely to be disturbed by theories about the legitimacy of feminine rule. Her problem was not the theory, but the mentality behind it and the practical difficulties that faced a Queen." Neale argues, in fact, that many of the men closest to Elizabeth had less faith in their "Deborah" than did the misogynistic Knox. They were, however, more reasonable and better skilled in the art of disguising their belief that government was the business of men. They were also motivated in their view, not by religious fervor, but by possible fear of displacement. After all, if a woman could rule, would male counsel be heeded—or needed? Even a loyal councilor like Cecil, who knew well the queen's temperament and power of mind, had difficulty accepting the validity of his experience of her. More than two years into Bess's rule, Cecil chastised a foreign representative for taking up a matter of diplomacy directly with the queen. He told the representative that "a matter of such weight" was too much for "a woman's knowledge." Cecil no doubt knew that no matter was too weighty for the mind of the genius for whom he worked. It is likely that his comments were designed to make sure that he was not circumvented nor his role as gatekeeper abrogated by those who may have found him a superfluous middleman.

And yet Elizabeth had to sometimes take matters into her own hands, lest she wind up placing the reins of government permanently in the hands of her retainers. As we discussed earlier, Elizabeth structured her meetings to make sure the men around her did not overpower her. And her use of her foreign-language prowess not only gave her the opportunity to go around her advisers, but also to directly demonstrate her skills at language and diplomacy to foreign ambassadors. Both of these traits would have assisted any leader, but they were especially important to one who had to overcome the gender politics facing Elizabeth.

Although Elizabeth sometimes chose to emphasize her womanly qualities, particularly when she needed to arouse the male protective instincts of her soldiers or when keeping suitors at bay, she routinely referred to her position in male terms. She thought of herself, ex cathedra, as "a Prince," consciously using this term to establish equality with her male counterparts. Her word was "the word of a Prince," her practices were the "acts of a Prince," and, she told a diplomat that "the word 'must' is not be used with a Prince." In all cases, she was referring to herself—signaling clearly that she was not only constitutionally empowered, but also that she did not doubt it and would brook no doubt in others.

Elizabeth also took steps to turn the perceived liability of her gender into an asset. She did this through the balancing act that characterized her private and public behavior.

Elizabeth lived in three worlds. First was the world of her Withdrawing Chambers, or private quarters, where only her servants, personal friends, and invited guests were allowed. Here she had a modicum of privacy, though attempts to invade it were common. (When her beloved Robert Dudley, Earl of Leicester, berated first a minor official and then the queen herself for denying his manservant admission to her quarters, Elizabeth cut him down to size with the words, "I will have here but one mistress and no master!") In her quarters women caretakers, chosen carefully for their loyalty and discretion, surrounded the queen. The second world was that of her Privy Council. Access here was limited. The queen was in the company of her closest official advisers and their subordinates. She could speak her mind and deal plainly with them, but she had always to underscore her role as their ruler, not their pawn. Finally, there was the Presence Chamber to which access was easy. Here the queen was on display, granting audiences and greeting well-wishers. Virtually all members of the royal staff of 1,500 had access here and Elizabeth's actions had to be taken with the understanding that private, discrete discussion was impossible in this setting.

As a young, unmarried woman, Elizabeth had to foster a reputation for personal honor and yet maintain a court that was considered splendid, vigorous, and "exciting" enough to attract the trained men necessary to staff it for success. And she needed splendor to impress foreign visitors. If they perceived the court as lackluster or impoverished, they would perceive her as weak and embeggered. On the other hand, if the Court were too excessive in its splendor, it would be seen as a sign of female profligacy. In steering her course through these waters, Elizabeth made sure that any attacks on her personal honor, particularly sexual rumors, were quickly answered and quashed. In matters of spending, she seems to have modeled the behavior that Shakespeare later captured in one of his plays, "costly thy habit as thy purse can buy; rich, not gaudy." The court, historically, had been designed for kings whose splendor and largesse had earned them great respect. If Elizabeth were to join the ranks of the great, she would have to command the same kind of respect her male predecessors had enjoyed. She was able, through her charm, her intelligence, her proper attention to the splendor of her Court, and her personal magnanimity, to blend the affection of courtiers for worthy sovereigns with affection of men for mothers, wives, daughters and—yes, mistresses. The confusion Elizabeth created in the minds of the men around her, created, in Neale's words, "a fine but artificial comedy of young men—and old men—in love."

In establishing her authority, Elizabeth was not shy about using that affection to her advantage—flattering, cajoling, and, yes, flirting—to impose her will and get her way.

Finally, Elizabeth was able to overcome gender politics with emotional intelligence. She had a well-developed sensitivity when it came to reading other people combined with intelligent charm and an excellent sense of humor. She had affectionate nicknames for most of her councilors: Dudley she called "Her Eyes," Christopher Hatton her "Lids" (for eyelids). Sir Walter Raleigh was "Water," Burghley her "Spirit," and Sir Francis Walsingham her "Moor." These nicknames and the letters acknowledging their contributions to her reign were signs of the comradeship which endeared monarch to subject. She could joke with her men; she knew them well; she cared for them. She knew them and valued them for the traits they most wanted to be valued for.

Elizabeth lived in times different from our own, but the difficulties she faced in earning the trust and confidence of the all-male group she managed still characterize many professions and industries, according to the women executives we interviewed.

The interviewees had each used with success one or more of the techniques Elizabeth had modeled 400 years ago.

"Until female executives gain a respected business reputation in their given field, they face Elizabeth's dilemma over her cabinet every time a new situation is encountered," says business strategist Lynn Manning Ross, author of *BusinessPlan.com.*

Diane Sena, managing director of Monterey Bay Aquarium in California, spent years in the airlines business. She has often been described as an executive "equally respected by both men and women." Sena says many women executives make an early choice that limits them later on in their careers. "A lot of women early on seemed go one way or another," Sena told us. "They [either] wore the suits

Elizabeth's Lessons in
Overcoming Gender Politics

1. Play to your skill strengths (speak a foreign language like a diplomat).
2. Focus on the job.
3. Structure your meetings to avoid being outmanned (or, if you're a man, out-womanned).
4. Graciousness and charm are universally appealing, regardless of gender.
5. Separate yourself (as man or woman) from your position (be a prince.)
6. No one will play on your team if you don't act the winner.
7. Be feared or loved, but always be respected.

with the little ties or . . . they kissed up to [male] egos." Although Elizabeth managed to play things both ways, as the situation demanded, Sena thinks there's another way. "Maybe where I was different was that I focus on the similarities of men and women. [I emphasized that] we're all here to get this done. For instance, [I would say] 'I don't know how to do this, I've never run an airport. But I've got this job, you've got that job, wouldn't it be neat if we could do something great together? We're all here because we want to be part of something we're proud of, so what can we do together.' I didn't work hard to make men to feel comfortable—or work hard to make them feel uncomfortable."

Sena is a particular believer in the power of humor in winning the respect of male counterparts. We could almost hear Elizabeth cackling in her grave when Sena told us this story about how she overcame male doubts about her abilities to do a job:

Sena was sent to a major West Coast airport as manager of "station operations and customers services" for one of America's largest airline companies. "I was twenty-five years old. I was the youngest employee at the station and I was in charge. A lot of my struggles along the way had as much to do with my age as my gender. I thought I could deal with resistance. I showed up for the 6 A.M. briefing [in Customer Service], but no one would look at me. No eye contact. I realized I was talking to myself.

"Then I went down to the nerve center—Operations guys with crew cuts. When I went down to introduce myself I thought they were going to fall over when they saw me. They were in shock. It was even worse than I had imagined it would be. The manager stood up when he saw me and asked, 'You are the new manager?'

"I said, 'That's the rumor.'

"He said, 'Hope you don't take this the wrong way, but looks like one little wisp of wind would knock you right over.'

"'That's good,' I said, 'I've been trying to lose some weight. So what do you guys do down here?'

"He said, 'I hope you don't take this the wrong way, but we're used to the days when an older man is the boss whom we can respect.'

"I said, 'Really?'

"He said, 'Yeah.'

"'This is going to be a big problem.'

"'Yeah.'

"'Because, you know, I don't think I'll ever be an older man.'

"A couple of them cracked up and that was it. I thought, 'OK, Diane, you're going to eat this elephant one bite at a time.' I stayed down there all day and sat down with each of them. I told them I knew nothing of operations from this point of view, just from the airplane. They started getting excited about explaining what they do.

"I decided I was not leaving that room without some human connections, from some of them. I wanted them to know that I really did care about what they do. That's all. If I could accomplish those two things I would be happy.

"Little by little we all made progress. One year later when I was leaving they all put in their transfer request to go with me.

"One of them poked his head in my office and said, 'I have only one thing to say to you and if you ever repeat this I'll kill you. You're the best goddamn boss I've had in twenty-five years!'"

When Sena was managing airports, a group formed at United Airlines called WHAM (Women for High Achievement). "The acronym itself bothered me," she recalls. "Of course the men immediately renamed it to mean 'We Hate All Men.' I never related to the women who were crusading. You can't argue with results. I focus on competence and want to be with people who want to share in that."

Amal Johnson, principal with Weiss, Peck and Greer Venture Partners in San Francisco, took a different approach—demonstrating the tougher side of Elizabethan ways—to prevent gender politics from getting in her way.

"The first time I became a branch manager for IBM in Oakland, California was in 1986. My administrative manager . . . walked into my office and said, 'Amal, I have something to talk to you about one on one.' I said, 'Fine.' He closed the door and said, 'I can tell you with confidence that the team here does not want to work for you.' I'll never forget that meeting. I looked at him and said, 'Great, I would not expect that they would want to work for a person they don't feel comfortable with or respect. No problem. Tell them that I would be delighted to find job opportunities for them anywhere they want to go. Let them put their names down, where they want to go, and I'll facilitate that for them.'

Three months later the manager was gone. The staff hadn't had a problem accepting Johnson, the manager had.

Laura Barron, who runs a training consultancy based in Knoxville, Tennessee, told of her experience in being accepted in an all-male environment. The secret, in her case, was to develop one relationship, build on it, and find a unique contribution she could make that would be valued by the group as a whole. Here's how Barron told the story:

> I was on an all-male team for three years. It was in a large corporation in the Facilities Services [department]: maintenance, print shop, and cars. We were in four different cities. . . . My VP and peers were almost all engineers, or had a very technical background. They had been on the team longer than I had.

I found that to get their respect starting out I had to be pretty aloof. I'm very extroverted and they were not. . . . I had to calm myself down, present my views with facts and figures so they could hear it. I changed my communication to suit their needs or I wasn't going to be heard. [It wasn't a matter of their goodwill, just of different styles of learning.] I had to prove myself in that first year to gain their respect.

What was helpful in that situation was that the VP and I were very similar in Myers-Briggs. We were both very intuitive. Which means we're out there on creativity and vision. My peers were not. My VP had a huge vision . . . but when he talked about it my peers didn't get it . . . he talked in pictures and big visions and they were very detail oriented. He didn't take [his vision down] to that level. He expected them to [do that, but] they . . . expected the VP to be very specific as to how to do it.

After we had been working together, they realized that I was grasping it. They started coming to me to explain what the VP wanted. I became the interpreter. That gave me a lot more credibility and more informal personal power with them.

Barron's story has a counterpart in Elizabeth's. Although Elizabeth had to struggle with an all-male group of advisers, they also had to struggle with her. And they frequently complained that they were baffled by her moods, her changes of mind, and the positions she would take on key issues. Elizabeth was the equivalent of Barron's visionary VP, whereas Burghley was in the interpreter role that Barron adopted. Burghley was the conduit through which the problems separating an all-male team and its female leader were resolved. Barron, as the lone woman in the group, became the conduit through which men with different problem-solving approaches communicated. In both cases, the interpreter became the nexus of the team's success.

Although Elizabeth's techniques have applications in the modern workplace, they must be applied with a recognition of some differences. For example, Elizabeth was the lone woman in a virtually all-male power structure. There were no female role models in England's royal past (she certainly couldn't model herself after Mary I!) and there were no female policy advisers. Virtually all institutions were not simply male dominated; they were male only. Even in the theater, men played all the female roles. Also, there were no women's organizations (except for nunneries) to provide support for women. Although some women ran inns, taverns, and doss-houses, there were few women-owned companies in the modern sense, let alone women managers to run male-owned firms. A woman-to-woman network of sorts connected educated women including Elizabeth, Catherine de Medici, and Mary, Queen of Scots, through correspondence—but the correspondence that has come down to us indicates that these women communicated as "princes" and seem never to have discussed issues of gender and power.

In Elizabethan England there was simply no sense of competition among women and men in the workplace. In manual and household work, women did one thing, men did another. In wealthier households, a woman's supervisory duties were confined to instructions to household servants. All other managerial duties were usually in male hands. In this male-dominated world of business and politics, Elizabeth's choices in dealing with men were arguably easier than those faced by modern women in mixed-gender environments. She did not have to choose between a "male" or "female" style of management, as articulated by various commentators on leadership style. She rather had to invent a way to best preserve her image as a woman while getting the powerful men around her to respect her mastery of their traditional skills. In the end, she achieved that with a style that might best be described as "managerial androgyny."

The twenty-first-century workplace has become increasingly a place of gender equality, but there remain many male-dominated industries in which women do not win ready acceptance. Carole Hyatt, president of Hyatt Associates of New York, described to us the problems women face in such environments.

"If it's a male-dominated industry with great status involved [men] aren't going to give it up easily," she said. "They believe they deserve their place, that their stature is God given." Hyatt says a woman can overcome bias in such an industry only on the basis of ability and performance. "First she has to be able to bring in the client. . . . Those who can sell, those who can bring in [business], those who can get in to the decision maker, those who appear to have more status and more power and be well connected will be admired by a team. Those who look like they aren't going to make the team rise are going to lose."

Hyatt says any style can work. "I've watched really macho women and very feminine women become very successful. It's the power you exude, the stance you take, it's the ability to make definitive relationships—client, CEO, board."

The presence of many women-owned, women-managed, and women-dominated businesses means that gender politics cuts both ways today. Cheryl McLaughlin, owner of MP Sciences, a high-performance research, training, and consulting firm in Danville, California, has worked as a coach and trainer of professional athletes—many of them men. One of her messages to women who would lead is that they must take themselves seriously, if they want to be taken seriously by others and by men, in particular. Like Elizabeth, McLaughlin has not had any doubts about her abilities. "I knew I could coach effectively whether I was a woman or a man," she told us. "[So] I had to present myself not only as a professional, but [as someone who could] teach them things they didn't know. I have worked with the Phoenix Suns and many male pro athletes. When I first walk in they look at me as if to say, 'What can *You* tell *Me*?' The key has always been teaching them something about their performance that really speaks to them, that gives them something they didn't know before. The other piece to this puzzle is to be persistent. People will eventually believe you if you have something to offer [and are persistent in letting them know it]."

Carushka Jarecka, owner of Carushka, Inc., the pioneering Van Nuys, California maker of bodywear apparel for athletes, dancers, and fitness aficionados, started up her business in 1979. Of all the executives we interviewed, her story captured best the flexibility, humor, and androgyny of Elizabeth's successful techniques for battling gender politics. "My first five years I went into 'battle' against the [then] 'male-dominated' banking establishment (only they didn't know [I'd declared war]!)," says Jarecka. "First, I completely changed my appearance from a natural blonde to short, dark auburn hair and tailored pastel suits (a strong feminine look). Second, I hired the top and most chauvinistic accounting firm to lead the way. Men love to help the "weaker sex," which I played into for five or six years and still use only when absolutely necessary. But, after twenty-one years, my track record speaks for itself." Today Carushka, Inc., sends its catalogs to more than a million customers.

Elizabeth, who kept trim enough throughout her life to wear Carushka Bodywear, never failed to portray herself as "a weak and feeble" woman when doing so would stir the protective instincts of her soldiers to her defense; but she also made her peace with other chauvinistic males, as needed, to limit the harm they could cause and maximize the good she could derive from them.

Elizabeth had no intention of surrendering her powers, or acquiescing to sixteenth-century male views of women's capabilities. She longed "to do some act that would make her fame spread abroad in her lifetime, and after, occasion memorial for ever." By overcoming gender politics through her wise management of those around her in ways that preserved her ability to do her job, she accomplished far more than a single act of greatness—she made an age.

10

Competitive Intelligence

Princes have big ears which hear far and near.

A REMARKABLE PORTRAIT of Elizabeth now hangs in Hatfield House, the royal estate where Elizabeth learned she would be queen. Probably painted in the queen's early middle age by the court painter Isaac Oliver, the picture is a masterpiece of symbolism and mystery. In this Rainbow Portrait, the queen's face stares from the canvas, her eyes wide, as if they are taking in the whole world. Her expression is calm, indicating perhaps that she will remain levelheaded in dealing with what she sees.

It is not Elizabeth's face, however, but rather her attire that captures our attention. She wears a luxurious yellowish-red dress embroidered with depictions of eyes and ears! They are all different and each seems aimed in a different direction and seems to be focused at a different range. The symbolism is obvious: the queen sees and hears all! A serpent—symbolic of wisdom—adorns the sleeve of her dress, indicating that the queen knows how to wisely use her knowledge and, perhaps, like a serpent, strike with deadly force when facts indicate the necessity of doing so. In her right hand, Elizabeth holds a rainbow, above which is written the legend "non sine nole Iris," which means "there can be no rainbow without the Sun," a reminder that the queen's radiance creates a covenant of protection for her subjects—protection, no doubt, enabled by her ability to see all, hear all, and act in accordance with the knowledge attained through her eyes and ears.

If the queen is the sun, the Rainbow Portrait shows her surrounded by shadow. She is a shining light of intelligence in a world of darkness, penetrable only by the rays of Gloriana's majesty and the acuteness of the sense organs that adorn her costume—and, in different form, populated her court. Elizabeth understood the value of knowing what her enemies—domestic or foreign—were up to; and she developed, through Burghley, Dudley, and Walsingham, the world's first intelligence service, a vast network of reporters and spies who kept her abreast of all developments that might require the serpent to bare its fangs.

Competition is often perceived narrowly in terms of head-to-head conflict in which one party must win and the other must unequivocally lose. Business people know intuitively that this is seldom the case. In some instances, all parties can win; in other cases, through onerous compromises, all parties can lose. Competition is usually a matter, not of victory in a zero-sum game, but continuing growth in which all ships rise with the tide of a growing market. Competition is also more than a matter of battling for market share, customers and profits. It may involve competing for grants, for the services of good employees, for the attention of the media. Sometimes, as in a sports competition, one's opponent is easily identified; in other cases, as in competition for media attention, competitors are difficult to identify and may change minutes before a broadcast is aired or a newspaper goes to press. In this situation, one's press release may be bumped from a newspaper's business section or off the six o'clock news, not by a competitor's publicity, but by an editor's belief that a story unrelated to either of your businesses will be of greater interest to readers or viewers.

Professor Michael Porter of Harvard Business School has made a life's study of competition and the forces that impact the ability to compete. His now classic "Five Forces Theory" of competition, first articulated more than twenty years ago, revolutionized the field of competitive analysis and stands as a monument to Porter's acumen. In his book *Competitive Strategy*, Porter demonstrates that competitive analysis requires a company to look, not only at threats posed by its direct competitors, but also at four other factors that limit competitive options. Porter argues that competitive analysis must not only consider the impacts of one's obvious and direct competitors, but must also examine the possible entry of new players into the market and the possibility that a substitute product or service will threaten the viability of one's product or service. He notes, too, that suppliers can take action that weaken a company's competitive position. And he shows how the ability to compete can be changed by the behavior of buyers.

Elizabeth did not have Porter available as a Privy Councilor, but her actions indicate she intuitively understood the impacts of the five forces on her ability to compete not only *with* France and Spain, but also *for* the hearts and minds of her people. Here's a look at how Elizabeth, armed with Porter's concepts, might have analyzed the competitive situation in the early years of her reign:

1. *Direct Competitors.*   These are competitors that do what you do, much the way you do it. This is true whether you raise money for a heart-research charity, make automobiles, publish magazines, offer business advisory services, run a hardware store, or franchise fast-food outlets. Your competitors may differentiate themselves from you in small ways, but basically, they do what you do with similar products and services.

Elizabeth's most troublesome direct competitors were France and Spain. France and England competed over territory, notably the city of Calais and the question of who should rule Scotland. The French were particularly anxious to hold onto Calais, which they had reclaimed under the reign of Mary I. England, on the other hand, was particularly anxious to drive the French from Scotland, where their presence had been especially troublesome after the Scots' King James V married Mary de Guise, a member of the militant and nefarious de Guise family that plotted for three generations to bring not only Scotland, but England itself under French control. Even more threatening to English interests was Spain, whose forces under Philip II served as the military arm of the Vatican. Spain sought to control England for many reasons, including a desire to strengthen its position against France, a desire to suppress Protestant "heresies," and a desire to maximize its holdings in the New World. All three powers, along with Portugal, battled for New World supremacy and New World gold, and the elimination of any competitor meant more prosperity for the remaining players. And these competitors also battled in other arenas—most notably the Netherlands—to strengthen their positions in the larger battle for "market dominance."

Identifying her direct competitors was easy for Elizabeth, but other competitive forces were at work—as they are in any competitive situation.

2. New Entrants. These are companies that could do what you do, but haven't yet established themselves in the field. Ideally you and your direct competitors have erected barriers to entry that make it difficult for upstarts to come in and steal your business. If you're a car company, newspaper, or steel mill, your investments in plants, presses, or pot lines may discourage new entrants from setting up against you. Long-term contracts with your major customers also represent a barrier to entry—making it difficult for a newcomer to start a relationship with your "locked up" customers. Elizabeth could not afford to dismiss the threat of New Entrants—it could be argued, in fact, that England itself was a New Entrant, not because it hadn't been around, but because it had been seen as the prize for Spain and France rather than a significant challenger to their hegemony. Still, if there were going to be new players in the market—China, perhaps, or the tribes of North America, or religious dissidents in the Netherlands—Elizabeth might be able to use them as allies in her battles with Spain and France.

3. Substitution.   These are companies that meet the same need your product or service fills, but do it in a totally different way. For example, when air travel became commercially viable, it took dollars away from passenger railroads; photocopying substituted for carbon paper; computers substituted for typewriters; and, today, Internet and direct-mail shopping substitutes for in-store purchasing. Several substitutions were at work in the sixteenth century. National languages were replacing Latin as the "lingua franca" of commerce, diplomacy, and science; Protestantism was substituting for Catholicism as the ruling religious philosophy in Northern Europe; technology was replacing human labor in key industrial sectors like textile manufacturing; and democratic institutions, particularly in the Netherlands, were challenging political concepts like the divine right of monarchs. These new ways of doing things were mutually supportive, creating a competitive environment in which "business as usual" could not be counted on as the path to continued success. By recognizing the significance of these substitutions, Elizabeth was able to compete more effectively for the volunteered loyalties of her subjects, whereas her competitors continued to rely on the ways of the past to support their entrenched power.

4. Buyer Actions.   The action of buyers can affect you in several ways. For example, if you're a consumer marketer and tastes change, your buyers may desert you. Perhaps they've become convinced that small cars are unsafe, unsexy, and really need more passenger room. If you want to keep buyers' dollars coming your way, you may need to come out with a sports utility vehicle. In hard times, buyers may become more resistant to your vehicle's price, forcing you to trim your margins, offer bigger discounts, or reduce quality and features. If you are in the business of selling advertising to car dealers and their sales or margins drop, they'll demand more bang for their advertising buck. You may have to lower your rates or offer value-added incentives so you can keep their spending levels consistent. Elizabeth, of course, was not selling cars or advertising; she was selling herself. Her buyers were advisers and subjects whose acceptance of her as their ruler was critical to her success. She responded to pressure from these "buyers" throughout her reign. If her advisers had difficulty swallowing the idea of a woman ruler, she would become a demigod; if the people would not accept exorbitant taxes and "bad money" she would fight to keep taxes low and issue only quality coinage.

5. *Supplier Actions.* If you run an airline and the price of fuel goes up, your margin is likely to go down. Certainly, you could raise your fares, but how much can you raise them before passengers decide to forgo a vacation or business trip, thereby reducing your revenues or sales volume? In Elizabeth's case, if the interest rates on her loans from the bankers in Antwerp were too burdensome, her ability to balance her budget, keep taxes at acceptable levels, and maintain an adequate navy were diminished. That, in turn, might strengthen the competitive position of her direct competitors. Likewise, if the share of booty she granted to Drake and other privateers, or the profits she allowed merchants she had blessed with monopolies was deemed inadequate to reward them for their risks, she was likely to find her own revenues reduced. Elizabeth keenly understood that the rewards she would accrue from good supplier relationships were based in large part on the benefits vendors received by doing business with her.

When a supplier's actions raise your costs disproportionate to those of your competitors, your ability to compete—particularly on price—is impaired. When this happens, your buyers may look for new ways of doing business (turning to substitutions), or simply convert their allegiance to a direct competitor or new entrant that offers a better deal.

The key to using Porter's Five Forces depends first on getting the facts and then assessing which forces present the greatest threats and opportunities to both you and your competitors. In using your findings, you are trying to learn not just what is going on in the present, but also how current actions will affect the future.

Eva Maddox is president and chief creative strategist for Eva Maddox Associates, Inc., a Chicago-based interior design firm with an international reputation for innovative design solutions for healthcare, retail, and commercial environments. Her firm is particularly impacted by changes in taste, style, and technology—the actions of her buyers and suppliers. "Change is a constant in my organization and we thrive on the speculating about the *future* implications of actions today," Maddox told us. "I am an avid researcher of trends and their implications for business, society, and design and am a member of the World Future

Society. In 1999, I initiated a course in Future Studies ... to study the impact of trends and countertrends in healthcare and wellness, government, religion, culture, technology, communications, politics, education, and ethics on design. Our team at Eva Maddox Associates has managed the work schedule to teach design through distance learning at the University of North Carolina. These activities, in addition to the usual professional meetings, lectures, symposia, and conferences, are critical to achieve innovation in our creative work."

In assessing current and future impacts on business, competitors may find that change in a particular Porter force will affect them equally, in which case the competitive impacts of the force may be neutral. Often, however, forces that affect direct competitors equally make all of them less effective against substitutions. Take, for example, competition in industries that are strongly impacted by a vendor force: the price of paper. These industries include direct mailers and the publishers of newspapers, books, and magazines. Among companies of equal size and buying power an increase in the cost of paper will impact all equally. Each will pay more for their basic commodity and each will continue to be cost-advantaged in terms of smaller competitors who receive less benefit from large-volume purchases. More efficient producers will continue to enjoy the same relative advantage they have enjoyed against less-efficient producers. And if readers must have the information published by these firms, they will likely pay the higher prices. This assumes, however, that there are no alternatives to ink-on-paper as a means of conveying content. If, however, alternatives do exist, all direct paper-and-ink competitors will be disadvantaged in dealing with the competitive threats posed by substitutive competitors. Instead of paying higher prices for books, magazines, and newspapers forced by the higher cost of paper, buyers may start getting their news and advertising over the Internet or television and radio. Buyers might decide to read newspapers at work; drop their Book Club memberships and spend more time at the library; or buy books, magazines, and newspapers with less frequency or only after they are remaindered. In these cases each direct competitor may maintain his share of the print market, but the market itself may shrink as buyers shift some of their dollars to nonprint sources of information or reduce their overall information consumption.

Imagine you are Elizabeth and you are faced, as she was, with a situation in which all five forces are at work: The Treaty of Edinburgh. Applying Porter's theory to the competitive situation surrounding the treaty we came up with the following analysis:

The direct competitors are the usual suspects: England, France, and, lurking in the background, Spain.

The new entrants are Scottish nationalists, who want their own government and all foreign troops off their soil.

The Substitution Force is Protestantism.

The buyers are the English people who strongly desire an end to bloodshed, reduced taxation, and some clarifications regarding the claim to the English throne of Mary, Queen of Scots. (If these goals are not achieved, Elizabeth is likely to face additional unrest at home and the defection of her followers' affections).

The vendors are, among others, continental bankers who see the conflict as a bottomless pit from which they may never recover their loans to the combatants. As a consequence, these bankers are reluctant to throw more money down a rathole. To cover their risks, they are raising interest rates, making it more difficult for France and England to gain a competitive advantage through increased expenditures on arms.

Elizabeth and her councilors, having analyzed the situation, knew what they had to achieve, leaving as a major question when it might be best to force negotiation of a treaty. Always adept at timing, Elizabeth acted promptly when circumstances handed her the opportunity. In May 1560, the English army soundly defeated the French in the battle of Leith; in June 1560, Mary de Guise, regent of Scotland and puppet of France, died, setting off a succession crisis in Scotland, and, by June, England was in firm control of the seas. France's bankers were nervous and the Scots were ready to embrace Protestantism as part of the price for freedom.

The treaty was concluded in July 1560 and the outcome was to have positive repercussions for England for decades to come. Under the treaty's terms, both England and France agreed to pull their forces from Scotland and keep them out. This ended a costly battle for both countries, as well as ending a civil war between Scottish Protestants and their Catholic counterparts over who should serve as regent following the death of Mary of Guise. The French also agreed that no French subject would hold any position of power in Scotland and that France would no longer interfere in Scottish affairs. The Treaty also required Mary, Queen of Scots, to drop the English coat of arms from her ensigns. The agreement set up a Protestant Scottish Parliament, which would name five members to a ruling council of twelve, the others to be named by Queen Mary. Neither Mary nor Elizabeth was happy with the outcome, which Mary refused to approve because it did not recognize her as heir to the English throne. Nonetheless, the treaty was observed by all parties and was officially ratified years later after Mary was ousted from the Scots' throne. England and France were free for a time to focus their foreign-affairs efforts on Spain which, though not a party to the treaty, had to consider the ramifications of Scotland emerging as a Protestant power, as well as Mary's weakened claim to the English throne. Spain also had to be concerned because peace enhanced the ability of both its English and French competitors to start paying down and restructuring their wartime debt.

The ability of Elizabeth's negotiators to analyze competitive factors and successfully negotiate the treaty required them to have strong knowledge of the facts behind the forces at work. And in terms of gathering competitive intelligence, Elizabeth's team was unsurpassed.

Elizabeth's "eyes and ears"—Burghley, Dudley, and Walsingham—didn't have CNN, MS-NBC, the Associated Press, or thousands of reporters working for hundreds of newspapers to provide them with information. That's why they had to develop their own information-gathering networks in the countries they needed to monitor. They worked with merchants, travelers, students, bankers, and others to gather the type of mundane information modern businesses take for granted: How's the weather in Paris? How's the economy in Cadiz? What's the buzz in Venice, Antwerp, or Constantinople? What did Philip say about

France? How's the pope reacting to German Lutherans? Today we get such reports on a twenty-four-hour, seven days a week basis. Average citizens in 2000 have more information at their fingertips at any moment than did all the monarchs and intelligence services in the world during Elizabeth's time! Unfortunately, many organizations derive only limited advantage from the extraordinary intelligence services at their disposal. Francis Walsingham once said, "knowledge is never too dear," which explains why he used so much of his own and Elizabeth's money to purchase it. We, however, are fortunate in being able to obtain far more of the type of knowledge for which Walsingham paid dearly—and it is yours for a pittance, in an instant, on the Internet.

Lacking a spy network as extensive as that employed by Burghley—who operated it without legal restriction—what are the best ways for modern organizations to monitor the actions of their competitors and analyze the competitive forces likely to affect their operations? When we put that question to the modern executives we interviewed, one answer came back time and again: Use media, particularly the Internet.

The executives we interviewed use the Internet as a competitive intelligence tool in different and, in some cases, highly creative ways. They employ it to monitor direct competitors' websites where they find information on competitors' new products, prices, staff changes, client lists, sales pitches, and positioning statements. They use it to monitor technological developments, social trends, and buyer behavior. They use it to monitor vendor announcements that might signal forthcoming price increases, research efforts, and new product offerings. They use it to send signals to customers and competitors about their own planned price and product changes. They use it as a research tool to survey customer needs and satisfaction and provide a convenient means of obtaining customer feedback. They use it both to preempt competitors and to prevent their own preemption. Many were aware of the Internet's positive and negative capabilities as a source of "misinformation," and, significantly, of "disinformation."

BizRate.com and *amazon.com* are both great Web sources of "competitive intelligence"—even though that is not the primary purpose of either site. *BizRate.com* describes itself as "the only resource continuously collecting direct feedback from millions of actual customers as they buy." The company also says it is "unlike any other search engine, portal or price-bot" and does not allow stores "to pay for listing or placement in our site. . . . Instead, we generate our revenues by helping consumers buy online and by helping stores study and better understand how to serve the needs of consumers buying online." The company explains that it makes its money from selling aggregated market research and from processing fees derived from sales that pass through its "People's Portal."

BizRate.com lists about a dozen main categories of online stores and several sub-categories under each. For example, if you are interested in determining how typical your experience was with a specific gourmet food service, you would go to *BizRate's* Food category and the Gourmet subcategory. You'd then find about sixty-four online sites rated on ten key characteristics, including the one consumers find most important—on-time delivery. The services are ranked best to worst using a five-star rating system, but you can also see how many of them rank on individual service factors as well. These factors include price, product selection, product description, ease of ordering, and a rating for the website itself, among others. You can even call up profiles that provide a narrative description of the company's strengths and weaknesses as reported by customers. Fascinating and helpful as this type of information is for consumers (and the companies themselves, who benefit from the feedback), it can also be a useful source of competitive information. Let's say you are the CEO of Company Y and you compete with Company X in the gourmet food category. Your *BizRate.com* overall rating is three stars, whereas your competitor earns four. You are dissatisfied with your rating and want to improve perceptions of your online sales operations. Examining the individual ratings, you find that your competitor outranks you in terms of offering lower prices and better customer support. So that's where you put your money first, setting aside a little to make further improvements in your product selection.

Amazon.com also functions as an intelligence resource, primarily for the book-publishing industry, but also for monitoring social trends (for example, what's the hot new self-help topic? What books are businesspeople reading? Are *Dilbert* books outselling *Chicken Soup* books? What's the hottest type of diet in America?). *Amazon's* regular rankings of book sales are watched eagerly by publishers and authors, not only to see what's hot, but also to assess likely overall sales of a competitor's books. The same is true for *amazon's* rankings of videos and CDs.

Of course, just as you can mine websites for useful information, you can bet your competitors will be doing so too. Lynda McDermott, president of EquiPro International, Ltd., the New York–based consulting firm, put it this way: "Until the Web I wasn't that concerned about competition, I tried to be in touch with trends. . . . But once [I got] on the Internet and before I had a website, I found my competitors' [sites]. I've gone on to the Web because I feel now that is a way I will be compared more directly and I can compare more directly. . . . It flattens the playing field in a both positive and negative way. . . . With the Web my site is accessible to them as theirs is to us."

The double-edged sword of web research means you have to think twice about what you put on your site, carefully considering the balance between the benefits you gain from having consumers view it and the advantages and disadvantages of making it available to your competitors. Think, too, about the information competitors can gather about you from neutral sites like *BizRate.com* and *amazon.com*. If you are sliding, they'll know it—just as they'll know if you're gaining ground.

The executives we interviewed were keenly aware that intelligence gathered from the Internet must often be supplemented and sometimes verified by "HumInt," the term professional spies use for "human intelligence"—information gathered directly by people from people.

Industrial espionage is a particular problem for the high-tech, biotech, defense, and telecommunications industries, where competition is particularly intense. Most of it is legal. A company's detectives (often but not always employees) sift through garbage, chat up a competitor's employees at trade shows, and befriend disgruntled workers, among other techniques in their attempts to learn about new products that may be in the works, changes in management structures, new pricing structures, and bidding procedures. To counter such tactics, many companies have engaged counterespionage experts to spot and plug information leaks and to train staff so they'll know when they are being pumped for competitive information. They may ban using e-mail, cell phones, and unsecured phone lines for conveying sensitive information and they make constant use of document shredders.

The cloak-and-dagger aspects of competitive intelligence struck many of the executives we talked to as unnecessary, even paranoid; but others assured us that it was one of the necessary realities of modern business. Micki Napp, National Marketing Representative for IBM, told us that for technology companies, in particular, "the changes in our competitors' and our own products happen so quickly, that by the time you would check a published resource [at] the library or check patents . . . [the information you obtain] is too late to be useful."

Napp told us that useful information, in technology fields, has to be obtained as quickly as possible, in real time and, in most cases, that means the information has to come from professional contacts with peers and associates. "You have to be careful you aren't doing it in illegitimate or illegal ways," Napp cautioned. Napp described a typical situation in which she might try to obtain information within ethical confines. " I would talk to someone [who wasn't under] a confidentiality agreement," Napp said. "Typically I would be calling a good friend, and the

"Knowledge Is Never Too Dear"

The Secret Service of Sir Francis Walsingham

Early in Elizabeth's reign, spying was financed, as were so many government needs, by the private wealth of the queen's courtiers. Burghley and Dudley both maintained their own small but effective spy networks within Britain, paying for the information they received out of their own pockets. When Elizabeth nicknamed Dudley her "Eyes" it's probable that she was recognizing his role in bringing her useful competitive information. Sometimes she even used a cipher (OO) when referring to Dudley, indicating her own penchant for spycraft.

Lord Burghley's undercover agents in Catholic circles reported to him concerning plots against the queen. These agents served Burghley and the queen well, especially after Pope Pius V excommunicated her in 1570, an act that was interpreted by radical English Catholics as giving them license to kill Elizabeth. Burghley's agents helped discover, among other conspiracies, the Ridolfi plot (described pre-

last thing I would want to do is put a good friend in an uncomfortable position. Sometimes I would call even within a company, not necessarily a competitor, and say, 'I would really like to know about blah, blah, blah, can you talk about it?' Sometimes they'd say yes and sometimes they'd say no."

Napp emphasized that "the big point is that in the field of technology, you can't wait until things get published. It's old news by then." The only way to get current news is a matter of "who you know—the old networking thing," viously) when they produced the letters and cracked the code that led to the Duke of Norfolk's execution in 1572. Burghley's chief agent in the Ridolfi affair was Francis Walsingham who, the year following Norfolk's execution, was named secretary of state as Burghley moved on to the Exchequer.

Walsingham took over some of Burghley's agents, but was not content with the limited size and scope of operations that depended on private funding. Walsingham was also plagued throughout his career with debts; he couldn't afford the secret service he had, let alone the one he needed. Elizabeth, however, could not afford to operate without strong intelligence. It was a matter of life and death — her own! Walsingham eventually persuaded the queen to part with some dollars to subsidize his services on her behalf. By 1582, he was receiving about £750 a year (about $600,000 today) which grew to £2,000 pounds (now about $1.6 million) by 1586. After obtaining the state subsidy Walsingham established the first true intelligence

(continues)

Napp told us. "The way information moves around these days, everybody knows everything. Or they can, if they put their minds to it."

Betsy Reveal, head of the United Nations Foundation, also emphasized the importance of not limiting one's questions to one's peers. In addition to extensive reading and Web-surfing, Reveal spends time "talking to people in all walks of life and at all levels of the organization so I can best 'triangulate' what's going on and where the broader community's head is." Reveal told us that "intelligence agency. Walsingham's network functioned both domesti-cally and abroad, as both FBI and CIA (or, for British read-ers, MI5 and MI6). His agents also served as a secret police and were willing and able (and all but licensed) to kill any-one seeking to take the queen's life. The agents engaged in all aspects of intelligence work. In the absence of media, much of their work was devoted merely to picking up re-ports of public actions, royal proclamations, and economic news in the foreign cities in which they were stationed. But Walsingham's agents infiltrated groups of Catholic expatri-ates living in France, Spain, and elsewhere. The playwright Christopher Marlowe, for example, was recruited while a student at Cambridge and sent to a Catholic seminary in Rheims, where he served as Walsingham's eyes and ears. Some of these infiltrators also served as agent provocateurs, sometimes acting as catalysts or even launching the types of conspiracies Walsingham was expected to prevent. They also were adept at sowing misinformation.

Walsingham's critics accused him of exaggerating and fabricating evidence not only to be used against those he arrested, but also to convince the queen of the value of his services and the need to fund them. The queen, however, seemed aware of both Walsingham's personal stratagems and of the tendency of any intelligence service to dwell on bad news. If the mandate of a service is to report matters that might threaten a nation's peace or its queen's life, the

gathering is a full-time endeavor and should happen in the taxi, at the dry cleaners', in the lunch room, as well as the board room."

As a final note on competitive intelligence, remember that no fact is useful unless you put it to work.

service will dig out and present any and all information that poses a threat—and will grade its own performance on the number of possible threats it can turn up. Left unchecked, conspiracies can easily be found where they do not exist and, in extreme cases, they can be created by the presence of an agent provocateur. Also, there was, in Walsingham's case, a direct relationship between the number of alarming reports received and the number of agents in the field. The more agents, the more reports. Clearly, if agents were being paid to report disturbing developments, they'd better find some—and, minor as the threats might be, it literally paid to overstate them. The tendency to exaggerate the number and significance of anti-Elizabeth plots created a near paranoid sense of alarm among her security forces. If, however, the service's focus had been on "good news" and the identification of loyalists, rather than dissidents, the queen might have been lulled into relaxing her vigilance.

We've profiled Walsingham in a previous chapter, but there is a particular aspect of his relationship to the queen that bears mention here: Elizabeth didn't like him. She may even have feared him. But she respected his skills and kept him around. She also kept him in check and weighed carefully his reports on conspiracy, filtering out his self-interest and the tendency of his self-interested intelligence operatives to exaggerate.

Michael Barach, CEO of *MotherNature.com*, does just that. Barach keeps up on competitive forces the way most of the leaders we spoke with do: He reads a wide range of business and industry press; openly exchanges insights and ideas with other business leaders within his industry; seeks direct communication from customers "as a way of keeping intuitive"; and he asks people at all levels for feedback. But Barach told us of a simple question he routinely asks that not only gives him access to what those around him have learned but also tests its relevance. The question: "What have you learned lately about this business and how to make it better?" Barach's question focuses the benefits of gathered intelligence and forces the question of how best to use what one has learned—just as Elizabeth knew that ultimately, all intelligence had to be placed in its correct context for action.

Bess was a chess player and understood that simply knowing how the pieces moved was not the same as having a strategy to coordinate their movement and achieve victory in the game. Just as a good chess player moves his pieces as part of a plan, you must use facts to achieve your business goals. Elizabeth and her chief spy, Sir Francis, did that time and again.

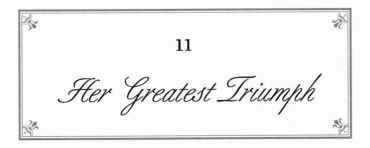

11

Her Greatest Triumph

And therefore I am come amongst you as you see
at this time not for my recreation and disport, but
being resolved in the midst and heat of the battle
to live or die amongst you all; to lay down for
God and for my kingdom and for my people my
honour and my blood even in the dust.

BY SUMMER OF 1588, the long and not-so-cold war between Spain and England had reached the boiling point.
Revolt in the Netherlands had smoldered for more than a
decade. Despite continual encouragement of the Dutch
States-General by Elizabeth's agents, the Netherlands fell in
1584 and the nation was occupied by forces led by Duke of
Parma, husband of King Philip's half-sister and the principal
behind the assassination of the Netherlands' Protestant
leader, William of Orange. The assassination had caused
England to formally, if reluctantly, enter the Lowlands fray
by supplying troops and money to aid the Dutch. The inter-

vention angered Philip but when, shortly afterward, Elizabeth finally allowed the execution of Mary, Queen of Scots, the Spanish king decided that enough was enough!

Fed up with the problems caused him by English upstarts and their "heretic queen" Philip opted for a bold and final solution: he would invade the British Isles and put them under the Spanish Imperial banner. The dream he had long hoped to fulfill by diplomacy, marriage, or subterfuge would now have to be achieved through overt aggression. Philip assembled the largest invasion fleet in the history of the world. Despite various setbacks (his chosen commander died only weeks before the planned launch), Spain's Great Armada set forth from its harbor in Cadiz, sailing up the Atlantic Coast with the intent of defeating the English at sea, then landing thousands of troops on English shores, seizing the government, and "freeing" the nation from Elizabeth's rule for all time.

Thanks to her able spies, Elizabeth had long anticipated the likelihood of such a move and she had developed a plan to quickly mobilize a defense. To outward appearance, all odds seemed to favor Philip: his navy was enormous and experienced; he had large numbers of ground troops not only aboard his ships but ready for transshipment to England from the nearby Netherlands; and, significantly, he "knew" that God was on his side.

Initially delayed by weather, the Armada reached the mouth of the English Channel on July 29. It was an awesome sight! How could Elizabeth's England possibly survive an onslaught of such magnitude? Yet survive it did. Within days, the Armada was in disarray, destroyed by a combination of strategic cunning, tactical innovation, and luck that testified to Elizabeth's skills as a leader and her acumen in capitalizing on the hubris of her ambition-blinded opponent.

———

England's successful defense against invasion by the Spanish Armada captures as no other event in Elizabeth's reign the effectiveness of her management skills, all of which were brought to bear in producing a major English victory and preventing the "hostile takeover" effort that had put her tiny island nation on the acquisition list of Spain, Inc.

As a metaphor for modern business warfare, the Battle of the Spanish Armada illustrates how grand strategies can be carried out in ways that multiply chances for success. It also illustrates, in Spain's case, how events can be mismanaged to assure failure. The lessons to be drawn from this legendary military campaign can be specifically applied to a broad range of modern business situations. When the lessons have been ignored, companies have suffered the same kind of crushing defeat Philip suffered at the hands of Elizabeth's navy.

"The Case of the Spanish Armada" presents a classic comparison of the defeat suffered by leaders like Philip—those locked into old ways of thinking—and the victory of leaders who, like Elizabeth, understand the power of technology, innovation, and empowerment.

The Armada campaign's lessons will make most sense if we reestablish the metaphor from which they will be derived. Consider this case not as a matter of "kings and wars," but as a story about big companies versus small companies, about management, leadership, and the winning of hearts, minds, and market share. It's a story of teams and their management, of motivation and morale building, of listening to advice and acting on it when it makes sense; of taking advantage of technology and not being afraid to use it. It's common for management texts to analyze business situations in military terms, but here we will turn the tables and analyze a military action using the language of modern management. And we'll provide some examples of modern-day companies whose CEOs might have salvaged victory from defeat if they had thought about "Philip's Folly."

There is no magic in identifying the key factors in developing and managing a successful business strategy. The *magic* lies in the skill with which the lessons are applied and the recognition that inattention to *any* key factor can lead to massive failure.

In previous chapters, we have detailed Elizabeth's strengths as a decision maker, communicator, visionary, delegator, and information gatherer. She recognized:

- The need for a clear mission;
- The need for good intelligence about one's competition;
- The need to understand the technological environment in which one operates;
- The need for clear and frequent communications;
- The need to build and maintain morale among those charged with carrying out a campaign;
- The need to recruit the right team for the job; and
- The need to have a backup plan if things go wrong.

When these factors are in place, success is probable; when they are lacking, disaster is the likely result. In the case of the Armada, the *biggest* and *most powerful* organization in the sixteenth-century world failed to satisfy *all* of these needs simultaneously—whereas its underdog opponent succeeded on every point.

Here's how the story unfolds: The year is 1588. The place: The Imperial Court of Spain, where we join King Philip in his palace, the Escorial. Philip, as you know, heads the largest empire in the history of the world. He is the corporate CEO of Spain, Inc., a diversified multinational corporate Goliath. Philip's holdings include Spain, control of much of Europe, and ownership of most of the Western Hemisphere. His treasure-laden galleons are regularly landing in Spain's ports, carrying gold from the New World—gold Philip needs because his expenses are great. He is, in fact, the only true superpower on the globe. The king not only controls the physical world, but also defends a spiritual one. His legions are the military arm of Roman Catholicism and he himself is the chief defender of papal authority.

For years Philip has been concerned over the presence of a radical but successful new competitor. This upstart, as you know by now, is England. Its CEO is Elizabeth I. England has only begun to challenge Spain's supremacy at sea and in the New World, but the country is disrupting Spain's shipping lanes . . . and it operates under a philosophy that is alien to Philip. The English queen, daughter of King Henry VIII, is a Protestant. The whole damn country just doesn't play by the comfortable rules that have kept Spain in command. Worse, in Philip's view, is the fact that he was married to England's previous queen and had been on the verge of merging the two countries but Queen Mary died before she could produce a son Philip could nurture to CEOdom. If only he could have concluded the desired takeover peacefully! He even wooed its sassy, heretical new queen, Elizabeth, who rejected him outright and has taunted him since with that embarrassing rejection.

The king has long been patient with Elizabeth, but her impudence has, at last, exceeded his tolerance. Philip concludes that to further Spain's interests, he must force the upstart out of business—and he has come up with a divinely inspired means of doing just that. Convinced that the English are Catholics at heart and that they will welcome liberation from their "oppressive" Protestant queen, he has decided to attack England with the largest fleet assembled in all of history–the Great Invincible Armada. The Armada consists of 130 ships–large ships, carrying a total of 8,000 sailors, nearly 19,000 soldiers, 2,100 oarsmen, 728 servants, 238 unattached officers, 167 gunners, 146 gentlemen, 180 priests, 62 medical orderlies, 6 surgeons and 6 physicians.

The king, a poor delegator, has personally determined the rations to be allotted to each man. He has also personally appointed all commanders of the fleet, told them their mission, drawn their maps—even drawn up rules of moral conduct for the soldiers and sailors. He has left no stone unturned—and he has chosen to turn virtually each stone himself!

Philip's confidence is high. His Armada will face the forces of a much smaller country—a country whose navy is comprised primarily of undisciplined pirates. And God, he believes, is certain to be on his side because England is led by a woman . . . and a heretic! Philip knows that those who, like Spain, are in control have many advantages that assure they will stay on top! In modern business parlance, we call those advantages "barriers to entry" and they consist of all the things that make it difficult for a small competitor to succeed against market leaders. For businesses, these advantages typically include reputation and brand-power; distribution networks; market dominance; infrastructure; capital; alliances; size and skill of sales force; and experience.

To outward appearances, the formation and launch of the Spanish Armada is flawless. Everything has been planned down to the smallest detail. All arrows point in favor of Spain, Inc.—as presumably they should for a market leader.

The position in which Spain found itself in July 1588 was not unlike that held by IBM in the late 1970s. "Big Blue" virtually controlled the computing industry and had established a reputation for invulnerability to effective competition. Although a few other and much smaller companies made computers, IBM was the clear market leader. It had more sales offices, more employees, better-paid employees, more manufacturing facilities, more name recognition, more stockholders (all happy ones), and, most importantly, it had implanted a "worldview" in the minds of consumers that said large-scale computing required large, powerful, centralized processors run by experts, most of whom had been trained on IBM equipment and who had been indoctrinated with IBM's view of what computing was about. IBM also had a reputation for backing its products to the full and for this it charged large amounts of money and enjoyed huge margins, which it could reinvest in fostering its image as the reliable market leader, keeping its shareholders and employees happy, and discouraging would-be competitors from challenging its position by creating the myth that it was invulnerable. In survey after survey, IBM was named by employees and potential employees to be the best place to work.Within a decade, however, IBM was forced to downsize by more than 80,000 employees, restructure its organization from top to bottom, watch as its profit margins slipped and its stockholders' returns declined, shift its product focus, and change its fundamental philosophy based on centralized computing. Most of its perceived assets had been converted to liabilities by the rise of a new philosophy, built around customer empowerment, of nontechnical, personal computing led by Apple Computer and its founders Steven Wozniak and Steve Jobs.

The "Apple Revolution" was only the first of several changes that left IBM reeling in the wake of the "democratization of computing." Its first line of defense was to dismiss personal computing as a phenomenon for hobbyists, rather than to shift its own computing philosophy. When Apple began making inroads in graphic arts and business markets, IBM touted its reliability as a company as a means of justifying its higher-priced and overpowered equipment—far more powerful that many small businesses needed and more expensive than they could afford. IBM emphasized customer service in terms of its ability to back its products, rather than reengineering its products to meet new demands from customers.

Just as hubris had made IBM slow to respond to the changes afoot, an undue reliance on techniques of the past impeded its ability to make changes even after its top management accepted the notion that change was required. IBM had obligations to all of those employees and stockholders. Its managers were trained—well trained, in fact—in all aspects of managing an established company, but few had entrepreneurial experience. IBM was skilled in maintenance of the existing order. As the market leader, IBM had little interest in change because change would have to come at its own expense.

In the early stages of its transitions, IBM's responses to the changing computing environment were not dissimilar to those of Philip in battling Elizabeth. IBM's initial "big idea" was to marshal all forces to defeat the upstarts. In IBM's case, this involved major public-relations and selling efforts to convince would-be buyers that Apple was unreliable, that it would fail, that its machines were not sophisticated enough for business use, that its corporate philosophy was "radical," that its resources were limited, that it knew little about customer service.

These "big ideas" failed to stem defections from IBM's traditional base of customers. Apple was cheaper, easier to use, adequate for most small business applications, offered superior graphic arts capability, provided friendly, twenty-four-hour-a-day, seven days a week customer support and was radical only in that it was not IBM!

IBM was hamstrung, like Philip's empire, by its sheer size, which required layers of middle management and slowed market response time. Marie Cumminsky, now vice president for Technology with PepsiCo, has responsibility for the technology infrastructure across all PepsiCo divisions. She joined PepsiCo Business Solutions Group in

October 1998. Previously Cumminsky held leadership roles with Perot Systems and as a senior technical consultant and account executive for IBM. Cumminsky recalled her experiences with IBM, noting in particular the problems the company faced fighting its own structure. "The PC was in high demand, customers were getting into it, but as customers wanted to customize or wanted to get some specific product enhancement, IBM was divided into different departments. The PC company had a piece of it . . . [but] in order to get the software to run correctly you needed to work directly with another company of IBM's. In order to get another piece of it done you had to go to another company of IBM's. It was too hard to do business.

"My job at that time as an account exec was to represent one-stop shopping for the customer," Cumminsky told us. But the "one-stop" goal was not easily attained. Cumminsky recalled that she "had to link up with five or six different organizations in order to be heard, in order to get your priority on the table. . . . The development cycles were long. Sometimes they were out of sync. If the software was available by a certain day, the hardware that was required to run that software was not available. The cycle time was the biggest thing we had trouble with. . . . If you look at the whole chain of events that had to occur before one of their products could go out to market, compared to the Apples or any other company, IBM had a lot more hand-offs and sign-offs across that chain."

As with Philip's Spain, IBM had trouble realizing that its glory days might be behind it. "You get very comfortable with becoming very successful," Cumminsky told us. "Therefore you don't have to act on your own internal processes as hard. You're comfortable the way you are. You look at Dell today and then look at IBM as far as being able to get the whole retail market. With Dell you can order directly. Dell changed the whole way desktops are now being delivered. It's amazing. Now it's another scramble. There are the Dells, the Gateways—and IBM—having to act differently now. I think that threw Compaq for a loop too. With the Internet coming in, I think every company is going to be faced with a complete new way of having to do business now. The IBMs of the '80s are now the companies of the 2000s that are looking at e-commerce and business-to-business commerce and saying 'OK, how are we going to go to business now?' They have to be a lot faster now, and a lot humbler. . . . They have to be willing to learn."

As every schoolchild knows (or should), England (with help from the weather) repelled the Spaniards and Philip's Armada suffered disastrous defeat. Much of his fleet was eventually wrecked on the west coast of Ireland. England entered a period of expansion, soon acquiring an empire that would far surpass Spain's, and Spain entered a long period of decline, eventually losing virtually all of its once-vast overseas empire.

Let's look, in management terms, at lessons Philip should have learned before he challenged Elizabeth on her own turf:

1. Bigger Is Not Better.   Philip's basic strategy was grand, but not very creative: "Let's put together history's largest fleet." His strategy assumed that size matters, that bigger is better—and that Elizabeth would cower at his magnificent show of force. But Elizabeth, Admiral Howard, and Drake proved that in naval warfare, "bigger" can be a liability. Philip failed to recognize that England and its capable seamen were changing the nature of naval warfare. The king had planned his campaign based on classic lines. He had invested enormous amounts to build large ships that could dominate traditional battles. In 1588, a traditional battle was one in which huge ships, filled with soldiers, closed on an enemy vessel and pounded it with powerful, short-range cannon (the cannon were too inaccurate to use at long range). The attacker would then sail up against its victim, use grappling hooks to tie the ships together, board the captive ship, and engage in hand-to-hand fighting with enemy soldiers. Philip's navy was designed for this kind of battle, in which the navy was primarily a means of delivering soldiers to battle areas, putting them either on shore or on an enemy ship. England didn't do that. They sailed in much smaller ships that carried few soldiers but were equipped with accurate, long-range guns. Consequently, the English were not interested in boarding Philip's galleons—they were happy to sink them from afar. Being smaller, the English ships were far more maneuverable than Spain's cumbersome troop carriers. Howard, Drake, and company could literally sail rings around Philip's galleons.

At the same time IBM was battling changes in the corporate battlefield, another U.S. giant, General Motors, was facing a similar fight against Japanese automakers like Toyota and Honda, who were capitalizing on consumers' demands for smaller cars of first-rate quality. A senior GM division executive described the situation GM faced and noted how the company has since changed its ways. The story is particularly relevant to the Armada story because it shows how operating with a "big concept" can blind a company to the need for ongoing change in the "small picture."

"The old GM management philosophy always tried to find the 'big hit,' the one thing that could boost productivity, the 'silver bullet' that could make a difference to the bottom line, but in reality it could be fifty smaller things that need changing," the GM executive told us. "Toyota's management philosophy was looking at the little things to lead to the big picture."

The manager described a time when GM's "big idea" was that of increased automation. In the 1980s, before GM began benchmarking, it built huge warehousing facilities, very automated, to solve productivity and quality problems relating to human error. Every warehouse was run differently. Even the arrangement of products was different at each location. When GM started going to benchmarking sessions with competitors, it found that the competitors talked only about procedures. According to the executive, that caused GM to realize it had to look at details, not the big picture. That required a major corporate change and GM made it. "The biggest lesson we learned," he said, "was the need to understand and document processes first, then automate.

"Before the benchmark sessions, plant managers had often visited competitor's plants, but they went in with blinders on," we were told. "Since GM had led the market for so many years, they never felt the need to look or listen to others or change. When managers visited places they saw only what they wanted to see." Since adopting solid benchmarking programs, GM has improved its productivity by establishing "new template" facilities that are smaller (no more than 200 people) and it has looked at "people and process issues" that were ignored in big warehouses.

"The new GM business philosophy is smaller, flexible, lean, fast," he said. "The new template facilities, now six of them, use a standard operating system that is centralized — a 'McDonald's' format where each facility is set up and run the same way."

Although they had never heard of benchmarking, Elizabeth, Drake, Admiral Howard, and John Hawkins had intuitively arrived at the decision that the "new General Motors" philosophy of "smaller, flexible, lean, and fast" was the only way to beat Philip, who was operating along the lines of the "bigger is better" philosophy of the "old GM."

2. You Must Have an End Game.   Having put together the largest attack fleet known to humankind, Philip didn't really know what he wanted to do with it. Although he planned most details of the voyage — including many petty ones — he never got around to telling his commanders or troops what he wanted them to do after they got to England. Apparently, with God's help, the Armada would defeat the English army and capture or kill the queen. The king's commanders weren't sure if, prior to landing, they were expected to engage the English navy, and no one knew what they were supposed to do in the wake of a victory. In short, the Armada lacked a complete mission statement. Instead of employing a Kennedyesque Moon mission statement with a definite "go there, do this, and return safely by a certain date," Philip's statement might well have been "gather the ships, sail away, do your best, and we'll figure the rest out later." In reality, he didn't even say that much.

3. *Bad Data Will Sink You Every Time.* Philip might not have sent the ships at all had he received proper intelligence about affairs in England. The king had a weakness for favoring spies who confirmed his own preconceptions. Since the king believed England was waiting to be liberated and would welcome his fleet, he was delighted when his intelligence service presented him with supporting evidence, however slender. Philip was particularly fond of reports from a man named Mendoza, his agent in Paris. Mendoza invariably reported that England was ready to explode into rebellion in an effort to free itself from Elizabeth's Protestant rule. Mendoza was not fabricating these reports—he was merely passing along what he was told by his sources. But Mendoza's paid informants told *him* exactly what *he* wanted to hear—they knew he'd pay handsomely for information indicating England was vulnerable. Mendoza's other informants—English Catholics living in exile— had a vested self-interest in feeding exaggerated reports of English unrest to Mendoza. Their religious zeal having led them to treason, these "sources" couldn't return home until Elizabeth was off the throne, and Spain was their best hope for achieving her demise. Philip himself had no way of checking what Mendoza told him. In fact, the very few Englishmen Philip knew, as well as those who wrote to him, were all equally outcast from their country. Perhaps, no monarch about to launch a war was ever so mistaken about his enemies. Philip was led to believe the Protestants of England were a small minority that oppressed a large majority of Catholics who were itching to revolt at first sight of the Armada. And, in the most tragic misapprehension of all, Philip believed to the point of delusion that England—whose Protestants and Catholics had united in opposition, years before, to his marriage to Mary I—would now welcome him as a conquering hero!

4. *Get Together.* Unlike Elizabeth, who often hesitated to put anything in writing, Philip believed in management by memo. He tended to avoid direct contact with subordinates, even in time of war and even with his key lieutenants. The principle Spanish military leaders in the Armada campaign were the Marquis of Santa Cruz, who commanded the fleet until he died two months before the launch; the Duke of Parma, who commanded the army; and Don Bernardino de Mendoza, the chief of intelligence. Santa Cruz was in Lisbon, Parma in the Netherlands, and Mendoza in Paris. Each sent frequent and long dispatches to the king and he to them, but throughout the months of preparation for the Armada's launch the four of them never met. There was never a conference, never a council of war. The king, immovable in the palace, never saw his Armada, his army, or his commanders—and the commanders never saw each other!

According to one observer, "the intrinsic reason why the Armada failed [was] the king's belief that he could organize a huge operation of war without leaving his study, without consulting anyone, without any human advice, without allowing his commanders to discuss it."

5. *You Need "Know-People," Not "Yes-Men."* Philip liked "yes-men." During the planning stage for the Armada, Philip often handed down detailed instructions as royal edict. Sometimes these reflected egregious ignorance of basic seamanship. Admiral Santa Cruz, an elderly man who had spent a lifetime on the seas, would try to gently educate Philip on the fine points of sailing and ship's practice, but Philip would not be corrected. Instead he became perturbed with his "fussy" admiral.

When Santa Cruz died, two months before launch, Philip promptly replaced him with the Duke of Medina-Sidonia, a man sure to do exactly what the king wanted because, unlike Santa Cruz, he had never held a naval command and therefore had no grounds for questioning orders from Philip (who had never worked on a ship!).

6. *Inspire If You Can, but Never Deflate.* Unlike Elizabeth, the king was not a student of men and motivation. He was far more concerned about the morals of his troops than he was about their morale. Indeed, he killed morale by insisting on strong punishment for minor offenses of swearing, gambling, and fighting. His rules for his soldiers read like a guide for conduct at a Sunday-school picnic. Unlike Elizabeth, who went out among her troops and delivered an uplifting speech, Philip stayed in his palace and waited for news of his certain victory. Philip felt he didn't need to motivate his troops. He *assumed* they were motivated and that they shared his goals. If they weren't motivated and didn't share his goals, he believed his on-board priests could motivate them in his place.

Philip's plight is a metaphor for modern managers. Although he was a bad manager, particularly in his handling of the Armada, he was also a clearly successful monarch. His company was No. 1! If you think of Philip's Armada plan as an attempt to gain market share for his empire and his church, you'll quickly see that the situation was not unlike modern efforts by competing phone book publishers to drive each other from a market. Not unlike Xerox versus Savin and Ricoh. Or IBM versus Apple. Or Detroit versus the Japanese automakers. Or Proctor & Gamble versus Wilson Harrell's Formula 409. In each of these cases, great existing enterprises lost market share to upstart companies because of flaws in *executing* grand market strategies and because of a Philip-like arrogance that assumed those on top can stay on top even in the face of changing market demands, customer attitudes, and technology.

A few years ago, Proctor & Gamble identified an upstart competitor in the field of household cleaners. The product was called Formula 409, and a small Connecticut company owned by an Englishman named Wilson Harrell made it. It was so successful—like Elizabeth's England—that it drew attention from P&G. Now Proctor & Gamble didn't send out ships, but it did launch a major campaign built around its normal method of operation: that is, establish a new product, sell it to retailers who already handle P&G's other products, and advertise heavily enough to ensure capturing a large market share.

In this case, to protect its own advantage, Proctor & Gamble would have to snare as much of the new spray cleaner market as possible by coming up with a competing product. In 1967, it began test-marketing a spray liquid cleaner called Cinch.

In their book *Life and Death on the Corporate Battlefield*, authors Paul Solman and Thomas Friedman tell the rest of the story: 409's Harrell learned that Proctor & Gamble was planning a market test in Denver. It was important information, and Harrell didn't waste it. He pulled his product out of the Denver market. As a result, P&G's Cinch sold like hotcakes. During the test, P&G decided to roll out the product nationally. But while Proctor & Gamble planned, Harrell engaged in guerrilla warfare. He packaged a gallon and a half of Formula 409 in a special package and sold it for $1.48. Now the secret here is that a gallon and a half is a year's supply of Formula 409. And at $1.48, everyone bought a year's supply. Of course, by the time Cinch hit the market, no one needed it. It was subsequently pulled from the market. Proctor & Gamble lost millions. Harrell had won the day.

Like Philip II, Proctor & Gamble based decisions on poor intelligence that led them to the wrong conclusions. In both cases, the result was failure. There is, however, another story about P&G, which shows that—unlike Philip—P&G learns from its mistakes. It also illustrates a certain kind of business karma in the sense that what comes around goes around. Charles L. Decker, the former P&G executive who has written a book on the company's many successful campaigns, shared another story about P&G in which one of its competitors failed when it took the wrong action based on its own limited competitive intelligence. According to Decker, P&G developed a toilet-bowl cleaner based on new technology and put it into the test market. It worked great. A competitor decided— perhaps on the basis of the Wilson Harrell's success—to preempt the P&G product. Decker told us the competitor copied everything P&G had done: the color, the packaging, "they even put on a number that made it look official because there was a number on the P&G label." Decker said, "they copied everything they possibly could then rolled it out nationally to preempt Proctor & Gamble." There was one problem, however: "The only thing they didn't get right was the formula. So it flopped!" Decker uses the example in his book to point out one of P&G's strengths. "It's a cultural thing," he said. "P&G believes in true fundamental product performance, whereas not all competitors do. Competitors think it's all marketing, smoke, and mirrors."

Perhaps Philip thought that Elizabeth's navy was all "marketing, smoke, and mirrors." Like P&G's competitor, he learned otherwise. Fundamental product performance, based on innovation, was just one of Elizabeth's secrets that led to the Armada's defeat.

Elizabeth had another "secret" on her side in the Armada defense. Not only was she "Apple to the core" and a forerunner of the "new GM," but, unlike the stodgy and reclusive Philip, she knew how to motivate people! Instead of dictating morals and meals, she sought opinions from her advisers then urged them to use their best judgments. Instead of hiding in her palace like Philip, she went down to the docks at Tilbury and delivered a stirring message to her troops. Instead of planning every move herself, she coordinated with her loyal and able military experts—and later gave them credit for England's victory.

Elizabeth and Philip present a magnificent study in contrasting management and leadership styles:

- Elizabeth was charismatic and a master delegator; Philip was a lackluster micromanager;

Elizabeth's Speech to the Troops at Tilbury

Elizabeth's mastery of the spoken word never shone more clearly than when she addressed her ground troops at Tilbury during the Armada campaign. The speech pulled out all stops in its appeals to the soldiers to do their best for God, queen, and country. One of the finest motivational speeches in history, it has been used on countless occasions since 1588 to call forth the patriotism of the English people in time of war.

"My loving people, we have been persuaded by some that are careful of our safety to take heed how we commit our self to armed multitudes for fear of treachery, but I assure you, I do not desire to live to distrust my faithful and loving people. Let Tyrants fear, I have always so behaved myself that under God I have placed my chiefest strength and safeguard in the loyal hearts and good will of my subjects. And therefore I am come amongst you as you see at this time not for my recreation and disport, but being resolved in the midst and heat of the battle to live or die

(continues)

- Elizabeth was vivacious and liked to ask questions; Philip was dour and preferred to dictate instructions;
- She understood vision and mission; he understood tradition and administration.
- Elizabeth surrounded herself with some of the most courageous and brilliant minds of all time; Philip surrounded himself with unimaginative toadies;

amongst you all; to lay down for God and for my kingdom and for my people my honour and my blood even in the dust. I know I have the body of a weak and feeble woman but I have the heart and stomach of a King, and a King of England too, and think foul scorn that Parma or Spain or any Prince of Europe should dare invade the borders of my Realm to which rather than any dishonour shall grow by me, I myself will take up arms, I myself will be your General, Judge and Rewarder for every one of your virtues in the field. I know already for your forwardness you have deserved rewards and crowns and we do assure you in the word of a Prince, they shall be duly paid you.

In the meantime my Lieutenant-General shall be in my stead, than whom never Prince commanded a more Noble or worthy subject, not doubting but by your obedience to my General, by your Concord in the Camp and your valour in the field we shall shortly have a famous victory over those enemies of God, of my Kingdom and of my People."

- She was a pragmatist, easily adapting her methods to capitalize on opportunities; he was a fanatical idealist who let his view of how things ought to be blind him to the realities of how things were;
- She worked to build the future, whereas he focused on protecting the status quo.
- She ruled, while he only presided.
- He had faith that God was on his side, and she had faith that God was on her side. The difference was that she had faith in her people as well.

Elizabeth herself best stated the net result of these differences. In a letter to James VI of Scotland, sent just after she had learned of the Armada's defeat, she wrote: "For my part, I doubt no whit that all this tyrannical, proud and brainsick attempt will be the beginning, though not the end, of the ruin of that King, that most unkingly, even in the midst of treating peace, begins this wrongful war. He hath procured my greatest glory that meant my sorriest wrack."

Beyond its interest to military scholars, the Armada is a classic metaphor for studying management style and approaches. As a business metaphor, the battle tells us that any business plan—any marketing plan—any well-run enterprise—must have a clear mission. A team must carry out the mission, working together, in constant communication. The team must contain the right mix of talents. Directions must be explicit. Contingencies must be allowed for. Line workers must be inspired. The competitor must be understood. And you must understand the technological environment in which you do business and use new technology and new techniques to their fullest to create battles you can win.

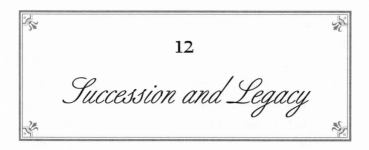

12

Succession and Legacy

[It is my hope] to do some act that will make my
fame spread abroad in my lifetime, and after [to]
occasion memorial forever.

MARCH 23, 1603. The queen is dying. The Archbishop
of Canterbury has been called to pray by her side and her
courtiers await word of her passing. Only six months before
she had gone on a vigorous ride of ten miles astride her
horse, then returned to join in dancing. Now there was no
joy in her. The closing year of her reign had not been a
happy one. As she faded away, England had faded with her,
beset with ongoing strife in Ireland, rising prices, failed harvests, and deepening poverty. To stave off the effects of difficult economic times she had achieved passage of the Poor
Laws to protect debtors from their creditors and, though
these helped, they had not been enough. Behind her
back—though she was fully aware of his maneuverings, her
chief adviser, Robert Cecil, had been carrying on a secret

correspondence with Scotland's King James VI, preparing the way for James to ascend the English throne upon the queen's death. It was the inevitable and best choice and was achieved with her concurrence, but the self-serving and unnecessary subterfuge of the younger Cecil was no doubt painful to her—his father would have been less devious!

But now the queen must die—and it was time; time to leave behind her the intrigues of the court, the machinations of her enemies, the sorrow of her youth, the joy of her great achievements. And she could die, too, knowing that the throne would be in good hands and the succession battles and questions finally resolved as James, estranged son of Mary, Queen of Scots, would unite England and Scotland under one rule. She had laid the groundwork, forty-three years before, by achieving the Treaty of Edinburgh, but she would not live to see that her patience and wisdom in grooming James, rather than naming him as her heir, would be considered perhaps her greatest accomplishment.

She died in the early hours of March 24, leaving behind a legacy of great achievement that would "occasion memorial forever."

The issue of who would succeed her on the throne was raised immediately upon Elizabeth's own accession to it. Her advisers had a clear succession plan in mind: the queen would marry and bear an heir, preferably male. Of course, this had been the plan of Mary I's advisers—and it had failed miserably. Mary chose Philip II for a husband, sending England into rebellion, and she had died heirless.

The issue of who Elizabeth's successor would be intensi-
fied as Bess aged and as, year after year, she rejected suitor
after suitor. Once the Queen passed beyond her childbearing years, the concerns remained, although the queen had
by then so consolidated her power that few dared question
her further in the matter.

Elizabeth cited several good reasons for not naming her
choice of successor until absolutely necessary. First, she
said, she could not be expected to name a successor and
build up his hopes of kingship as long as the possibility existed that she might bear an heir. Second, having herself
been put forth as the heir presumptive to Bloody Mary,
Bess did not want to place anyone in the dangerous position she had occupied—a situation in which her life was
threatened, her reputation maligned, her position exploited without her permission, and her concurrence in
plots against Mary continually solicited. Elizabeth also argued that naming a successor would only alienate those
who had not been selected, in which case she risked arous-
ing the enmity of those who were passed over. Likewise, as
long as the succession question was open, she kept everyone in hope—and that hope meant all candidates were
more likely to maintain civil relations with Elizabeth and
avoid alienating her affection. And, the queen argued, she
would not undermine her own authority by having advisers
continually going behind her back as a means of ingratiat-
ing themselves with the future monarch.

The shortlist of the queen's potential successors included
several candidates who had been named in Henry VIII's
will as being in the line to succeed. Henry's will had
named eight people in all: Edward I had reigned and died;

Mary I had reigned and died; Jane Grey reigned briefly and was beheaded; Frances and Eleanor Brandon (daughters of Henry's sister) had died. Elizabeth herself was on the throne. That left only two of Henry's "qualifiers" still in line to succeed Bess: Catherine and Mary Grey, Jane's sisters. In the interim, however, Frances Brandon's daughter, Margaret Clifford, had come into the line of succession upon the death of her mother. The Grey women and Clifford, however, were not the only succession candidates because there were questions as to whether Henry's will was binding on Elizabeth. The leading candidate, specifically excluded in Henry's will, was Mary, Queen of Scots. Mary's claim was questioned by many on grounds that she had been born in France and was therefore a foreigner, barred from holding land in England. She was also, of course, a Catholic, which made her a problematical succession choice for Elizabeth and her advisers. Nonetheless, Mary's lineage seemed to qualify her for the English throne (she was the granddaughter of Henry's sister Margaret and Scotland's King James IV). Mary was not unqualified by talent and she seemed, at least in the early years of Elizabeth's reign, to be the queen's preferred succession candidate. Elizabeth's presumptive heir, however, was Catherine, the elder of the two surviving sisters of Jane Grey. Elizabeth was not fond of either of them, not least because of their association with rebellion in the matter of Lady Jane's abortive attempt to take the throne following Edward VI's death. A distant claimant, backed by Dudley but not named in Henry's will, was Henry Hastings, the Earl of Huntingdon. Dudley liked him and, as the only male candidate in the bunch, Huntingdon had his partisans at

Court despite the weakness of his claim and his apparent lack of interest in being king. There were several other claimants and all of their claims had problems. Questions of bastardy, treasonous ancestry, and the provisions of Henry's will marred one or another of the claims. Matters first came to a head in 1562 when Elizabeth contracted smallpox and it was generally presumed she would die from the disease. Her councilors, faced with the need for an immediate succession plan, narrowed the shortlist to Catherine Grey and Hastings. But with what she thought would be her dying breath, the queen threw the council a curve: She said she wanted Dudley to succeed her. He could not be king but could rule the country as its Lord Protector. And to clear him of the taint of adultery, she declared that she and Dudley had never had sexual relations.

Of course, Elizabeth recovered from smallpox and as she and her reign grew older many of the potential successors died, marriage and childbearing became out of the question, and there were less than a handful of "family" members left to take over the business. Elizabeth wanted a successor who would continue to rule in her tradition, preserving her memory and legacy. The strongest surviving claimant, by both birth and qualification, was Mary's son, King James VI of Scotland, and it was to him that the throne was passed.

Succession is a question for all organizations and one that inevitably must be dealt with by business owners, CEOs, and chief administrators of any organization. This is true, not only in cases of death, but even more often in cases where a business is sold or key personnel retire. In family-owned businesses, there is often a desire to pass on the firm to a family member, but frequently family members are not interested or are unqualified to succeed, requiring talented "outsiders" to be brought in and groomed for the job, or for the business to be sold in the equivalent of a "dynastic change."

Organizations that find succession desirable or necessary must not only find a successor, but also develop a process that allows a smooth transition and prepares the new owner or new leader to take over. Patricia Ireland has been president of the National Organization for Women since 1987 and will step down in August 2001. She explains NOW's succession plan this way:

"Unlike the leaders of most other nonprofits, the four national officers of the National Organization for Women run the organization on a day-to-day basis and are elected as a team by the membership. Thus, I have the power to choose a successor to the extent that I can organize NOW's chapter members and persuade them to vote for the team I believe will best serve the organization and its goals.

Ireland said she feels strongly "that a key part of any leader's job is to find and mentor her successor, and that it will reflect ill on my leadership if NOW's new team of officers are not successful." She told us that "partly out of my own pride and mostly because of my commitment to NOW and to the issues we advance, I have taken an active role for the last five or six years in developing the skills of not only someone to succeed me as president, but also others with complementary abilities to team up with her."

To assure continuity, Ireland's term will overlap for thirty days with that of the newly elected president, giving Ireland a chance to "brief her on every aspect of the job I can." After the thirty-day transition, Ireland says that she and the new president will "informally walk that tightrope of giving her the room to take leadership and shape the job to her skills and style and giving her any advice she seeks and the support she deserves."

Succession is always a complicated matter, but it is even more complicated in the case of family businesses, whether they involve the Tudor throne or a steel company. "When you make decisions in business they are almost always objective," according to Barbara Bissett, CEO of Bissett Steel in Cleveland, Ohio. "When you make decisions in the context of family, they are purely subjective. Merging the objective and subjective factors within a family business is very, very difficult. The family says, 'Poor Johnny Ne'er-do-well, he needs a job.' The business says, 'We can't afford to hire incompetent people; they will ruin our reputation in the market place.' So what do you do? There are irresolvable problems in decision making in terms of the objective business and the subjective family."

Bissett describes her own succession as a "full-blown disaster." Her story has some parallels to that of Elizabeth, in that she was a female heiress who had to fight the desires of other family members to obtain and maintain succession. Also, like Elizabeth, Bissett faced problems among the managers that came with the job and had to assemble a new team in order to properly manage the company. Like Elizabeth, she has had to plan for a succession that will go outside the family. Bissett speaks openly and frequently on the topic of succession and she tells her story well. Here it is:

"My father died abruptly in 1988. I was thirty-eight years old. I had been the designated heir apparent, but he had not made any changes in his estate to reflect that decision. A bullet point for advice on this one: Be prepared, don't assume your wishes might be carried out by other parties . . . don't leave it to chance. . . . Don't think for a minute because you see something a certain way that it will be legally conducted that way unless you make specific plans for it. Do not do this to your children. None of them will be better off as a result of it.

"My father had five kids. But I told him he really had six children and the perpetual infant was the business and the business never grew up and would never be able to take care of itself. And it was never going to be able to behave responsibly, so he had better appoint a foster parent to make sure somebody looked after it and make sure it conducted itself properly.

"The bottom line for me was when my dad died I was given the responsibility to run the company. I had a 12 percent ownership stake in it, and there were two generations of stockholders I had to contend with. A number of them came to me a couple years after my father's death and said, 'Listen, we think we want our money and we think you should liquidate the assets of the business and wind it down so we can have our cash.'

"It took me a long time and a lot of money to buy control. For me that was the only way I could actually run the business. I needed control . . . but since my father died abruptly he hadn't made any arrangements to secure my ownership. I had to do that myself. The day before my brothers showed up with their attorney, I had bought out some of my aunts . . . that was the only way I could walk into that meeting with any confidence, knowing that I had achieved ownership of the controlling stock."

In running her steel company, Bissett argues that successful operation of the business must be the top priority of the CEO. "If you don't provide sustenance to the dependent business, the perpetual infant, it will die and nobody will get any benefit from it. So the consequence of the decision making that goes against the objective needs of the business is usually punishing to the family. Maybe not immediately, but down the road. My view is that I look at everything through the lens of what is good for the business. If I can answer that question, 'Is it good for the business?' it usually ends up being good for the family. But frequently it's not an immediate satisfaction to the family. My view is that business decisions are made purely on the objective criteria and if family needs merge with that, great. If they don't, that's because the business is not run to serve the family needs. It's there to serve the customers."

When Bissett first started working at the steel company, (she's been with the company for seventeen years and CEO for twelve) she faced problems with existing managers' abilities to accept and adapt to the changes she put in place. A self-described "intra-preneur," she notes that changing a business can be much more difficult than building one from scratch because "you're fighting people resistant to change."

Over time, most of the resistant managers left the company. "They just quit," Bissett said. "I was devastated. In hindsight, however, it was a blessing."

As the old team left, Bissett said, " I slowly built up a good team with people who could share my vision for change and innovation, and continuing to promote customer service as the most important thing that we do."

Regarding her own succession plans, Bissett had this to say: "My kids are sixteen and fourteen, son and daughter. . . . On a personal level, when you pick a successor, you have to pick one over the other child on the objective criteria of which one is most qualified for the job." Noting that such a decision almost always creates disharmony, Bissett told us she is "going to be selfish and say I'd rather have my kids at the dinner table than to have to decide that one of them has the preference over the other. Their inheritance is whatever cash is left. Green (money) plays no favorites. I don't see that it's a likely chance that my kids will grow up wanting to run a steel distribution company."

In choosing Scotland's James VI (he became England's King James I) as her successor, Elizabeth wanted to extend her legacy of unifying England. The country needed new energy, but did not need a revolutionary departure from the achievements of Elizabeth. That's not always the case. Take, for example, the transition at General Electric when CEO Reginald Jones retired and supported the appointment of current CEO Jack Welch (now about to retire himself) as his successor. Jones was named CEO in 1954 and served as the company's top officer until 1981. Upon his own appointment, Jones began almost immediately to plan for his succession. Like Elizabeth, Jones didn't announce his choice until he had to, but he had begun studying the nature of succession and watching potential candidates and considering his criteria as early as 1957. Jones, a sophisticated, socially adept Englishman, had guided the company during some of its peak years—years in which the company prospered as a result of Jones's consummate public relations skills and his ability to work well with government regulators. Those skills were recognized when he was named by *Fortune* magazine as the most admired CEO in the world in the late 1970s. Diplomacy and lobbying were the rule of the day, and Jones was considered a consummate diplomat who lobbied hard and effectively to minimize government regulations that might have adversely—and, GE argued, unnecessarily—impacted GE's ability to compete. Jones's efforts took place not only in the United States but also in most other countries in which GE did business—in effect, the world. Welch, on the other hand, was something of a "street fighter." The two have often been described as near-polar opposites in terms of approach, demeanor and background. Jones rose through the ranks of a traditional, even hidebound, GE. His background was in finance. He had little operational experience and no technical training. Welch, on the other hand, was trained as an engineer. He came from a working-class New York neighborhood (his father was a ticket-taker on the Long Island Railroad) and was educated as an engineer at state universities in Massachusetts and Illinois. Both men were tough, brilliant, and innovative, but Jones wore Savile Row suits, whereas Welch, when required to wear a coat and tie at all, opted for a blazer and slacks.

As Jones's term progressed, he realized that the competitive world was changing and that GE needed a new type of leadership for an age in which the ability to schmooze with presidents, senators, and foreign leaders was less likely to help GE maintain its profits than were skills that helped the company lower costs, improve quality, and innovate. Welch had come to Jones's attention early in his career when he was managing GE's plastics division. Welch produced results and he was unswerving in his efforts to reduce costs, flatten administrative hierarchy, and toss out antiquated and burdensome paperwork. Jones saw in Welch the type of revolutionary leader he knew GE would need. The wisdom of Jones's choice has been proven by the "new GE's" success, worldwide—and by Welch's selection, in the late 1990s, as the world's most admired CEO— the same accolade Jones himself had earned two decades earlier.

At first the transition was tough for many GE employees. Welch flattened the company's hierarchy, sold off less productive divisions, and dramatically downsized most of those he kept. His actions earned him the nickname "Neutron Jack"—a reference to the neutron bomb that kills people but leaves buildings intact. By cutting fat, however, Welch built a new GE that today produces more types of goods and particularly more services than did the old GE. Arguably, GE has a stronger position in the new economy than it had in the old one for which Jones's style was so well suited. In both worlds, GE was the largest and consistently most profitable corporation in the world.

Part of Jones's legend and legacy stems not only from his choice of successor, but the techniques he used to sift the candidates. Among these was his "airplane interview question" for potential CEOs. With slight variations, the story goes that Jones would schedule interviews with the leading succession candidates and at a key moment he'd asked the candidate to imagine that the two of them are in a plane crash and both of them are killed. "Who," asked Jones, "should be chairman of GE?" Apparently, many people didn't focus on the first part of the question; they imagined they would somehow survive the flight and so put themselves forward as the best candidate for the job. Jones would smile and restate the premise that both he and they had been killed and would be out of the succession picture. Jones wasn't asking the question as a trick to see if his candidate was listening. Rather he was looking for a compelling way to discover the candidate's thoughts on the qualities that the next CEO should have. The answers he got also told him who else in the company might be an acceptable alternative to himself and the candidate at hand.

There's a variation on Jones's technique that can be used in any succession situation: the two-vote method. To understand how it works, let's apply it to Elizabeth's succession dilemma. Imagine it's the year 1575 and Elizabeth has contracted the plague. She and those around her are sure she will die and therefore must act quickly, as in the smallpox episode, to name a successor. She has decided, as she had during her previous illness, that the best candidates to rule England are in her Privy Council. She also knows that if she selects any of them, several, if not all, of the others will likely resign; the concerns over her premature naming of Dudley years before have convinced her of that. To assure that the maximum number of key advisers will stay on board, she calls the top half-dozen men together. Her "shortlist" in this hypothetical situation might have looked like this:

- Burghley, secretary of the Exchequer and former secretary of state
- Dudley, Earl of Leicester, longtime friend, Master of Horse
- Walsingham, spymaster and current secretary of state
- Charles Howard, Lord Howard of Effingham; and
- Thomas Radcliffe, Earl of Sussex.

The queen assembles the men and asks them each to vote by blind ballot for the two people they favor to become Lord Protector. The vote goes like this:

Walsingham and Dudley have worked hand in hand and are united in their militant Protestantism and dislike of Burghley, who often advised the queen to take caution in following their advice. Each of these men casts one vote for himself and one for the other.

Burghley is ready to take on lighter duties, rather than heavier ones. He knows Radcliffe to be a fine candidate, but Radcliffe has been too long away from London (first in Ireland, then on the northern borders). Also, as a Roman Catholic, Radcliffe has no chance of getting enough votes to win, and Burghley will not cast his vote for a lost cause. He also won't vote for either Walsingham or Dudley. He fears their radicalism and has had personal run-ins with Dudley. In the end, he casts a vote for Howard, whom he knows is true to the queen and a man of political moderation. He also casts a reluctant vote for himself.

Howard casts one vote for himself and one for Burghley.

We now come to Radcliffe. He is the only Catholic in the group, but his loyalty to the queen is not in doubt. He has served her in Ireland and was instrumental in suppressing the Northern Rebellion of 1569–1570. He knows that he will get no vote other than his own. He also realizes that he likely has the tie-breaking votes and wants to make sure they count. Believing that loyal Catholics will fare poorly under either Walsingham or Dudley—and having had ongoing conflicts with Dudley—he casts one vote for Burghley and one for Howard.

Elizabeth has the ballots opened and finds the following count:

Burghley 3 votes
Howard 3 votes
Dudley 2 votes
Walsingham 2 votes
Radcliffe 0 votes

The results are indecisive (they usually are), so Elizabeth repeats the process, this time allowing each man one vote, but only for the winners from the first round: Burghley and Howard. Burghley, not anxious to have the top job himself, votes for Howard; Howard votes for himself; Radcliffe feels either man would be excellent, but casts his vote for Burghley, whom he feels has earned the office. Dudley and Walsingham, eliminated by Radcliffe's vote in Round 1, now hold the power in Round 2. Dudley has often worked to counter Burghley's influence so he feels he must vote for Howard. Walsingham, on the other hand, once worked for Burghley and Burghley had not resisted the spymaster's appointment as secretary of state. Sir Francis votes for Burghley. Final vote: Howard 3, Burghley 2. The queen decides Howard

should be Lord Protector. No one resigns: Radcliffe is satisfied that there will be no reign of anti-Catholic terror; Dudley will no longer have to deal with Burghley; Burghley has
kept both Dudley and Walsingham from the Protectorship;
Walsingham will make the best of the situation—which at
least has maintained a Protestant in power. And Elizabeth
has been able to keep her entire cabinet together and assured that, if she dies, her successor will be able to draw on
the same talents that have served her well.

Of course, voting was not a common practice in sixteenth-
century England and the process we just described never oc-
curred at any time (nor did Elizabeth ever contract the
plague!). But it may well have been that Elizabeth, with her
keen sense of balance and her ability to read men as well as
she read books, used a similar process to determine what decision was most likely to send good advisers packing if the
wrong successor were chosen. The key to this kind of succession process—whether it's Reg Jones's airplane interviews or
the type of two-vote process we anachronistically placed in
the Privy Council—is to win everyone's *second* vote. Since,
in most cases, the candidates cast one vote for themselves, it
is the second vote that produces the candidate most acceptable to all others.

Rather than take a formal vote, as we imagined in our example, Elizabeth would simply have done what Reg Jones
did: call each man in for a separate interview and ask who,
in the case of both their deaths, he'd like to see ruling England. Over a period of nearly forty-five years, she had had
lots of time to gather this kind of information on an ongoing basis. She and Burghley regularly went over the qualifi-
cations of suitors. He developed a list of strengths and

weaknesses, a sieve of questions through which every candidate had to pass. Such a sieve was used to argue through the succession question when Elizabeth was feared to be dying of smallpox. On that occasion it produced the names of Hastings and Catherine Grey. Elizabeth, of course, had the final call and exercised the CEO's prerogative of naming her choice at the time — Dudley. Processes like the two-vote method are seldom binding — and should not be — but they can provide critical information in choosing a successor. Reg Jones and other great CEOs have applied it with consummate skill and great success.

Finally, we come to the matter of Elizabeth's ultimate legacy. In our view it is this: She was a great leader because she encouraged the greatness around her. Indeed, the queen is so widely known today because those around her felt her memory was worth preserving. As her worth enhanced that of those around her, so theirs, in turn, has enhanced hers. To understand the power of Elizabeth's legacy to mold the future, consider that during her reign England had an average population of only about 4 million people. Of those, about three dozen are still commonly studied today by amateur and professional scholars. These thirty include well-known figures such as the playwrights Shakespeare, Marlowe, and Jonson; the composers Thomas Tallis and William Byrd; the explorers Drake and Raleigh; the philosopher Francis Bacon; the poets Edmund Spenser and Phillip Sidney; and, the queen's great rivals Mary, Queen of Scots and Philip II. Their names and those of the other lesser, but influential luminaries of her age, are seldom raised without some mention of Elizabeth. If, 400 years from now, a proportional number of names from our time are as commonly known as those of the Elizabethan Age, there will be nearly 2,000 of them! More than 3,600 plays from our recent history would still be performed on the stages of the world in 2400! The major works of more than 300 late-twentieth-century poets would be studied and cited.

Since the queen's death in 1603, an average of a book a year has been written about Elizabeth and thousands of books have been written about those whose work she fostered and the Golden Age she created as a result. Far more than her political, economic, and military achievements, Gloriana is remembered for the intellectual and artistic legacy she nurtured and which, in turn, has preserved her memory. This support of talent in others was the fertile ground in which her memory was planted and that has kept it ever green not only among historians, biographers, and dramatists, but also among modern executives who have learned from her example.

In the comments we gathered from twenty-first-century executives, we found Elizabeth was appreciated for a wide range of reasons. For example, Betsy Reveal, head of the United Nations Foundation, noted that "Elizabeth and Catherine the Great always struck me as extraordinary examples of gender defying the norms of the day—and of today."

IBM's Micki Napp cited Elizabeth's organizational strengths. "Notice that when Queen Elizabeth ascended the thrown, she set very definite priorities," Napp told us. "Ruling her country was all that mattered to her. She set aside her personal life because she had so much to learn and so much to do. Her position required all of her mental and physical energy. Later in her reign, she was able to re-set her priorities and redefine balance. She could once again enjoy cultural activities. She did not marry, but that was for political reasons, not lack of time. She eventually ruled in a calm, relaxed, and easy style which allowed her to enjoy life."

Entrepreneur Sandy Gooch cited "several admirable traits" exhibited by Elizabeth. "She had the courage to choose a different religion from her sister Mary. She had a thorough education. Her monarchical duty was her primary concern. She had a colorful personality. And she chose able and wise advisers. . . . Initially she restored confidence in English money by minting coins, so she thought beyond her prior conditioning and saw how to do something differ-ent with a powerful commodity—money. Foreign trade was encouraged so that England was not insular and was incul-cated with new ideas and products. She was an icon for En-gland and she encouraged her people to investigate the New World. I think a business that is successful incorpo-rates many of these qualities, as does the leader."

Terri Lee Rogers, vice president of sales & marketing for furniture maker O. W. Lee Co. Inc., described Elizabeth as "an admirable leader," but found her life "tragic, in that she had to forsake her identity as a woman to successfully gain the respect and admiration of her subordinates." Lee praised Elizabeth for having had "the conviction to stand by her morals and do what was best for her country, what-ever difficulties it caused her personally."

And, finally, St. Louis–based Flori Roberts, founder of Flori Roberts Cosmetics and SmartCover, told us Eliza-beth was an excellent teacher of the need to be prepared for change. "Think of the changes during her reign from the arts to 'invading' the world. . . She was able to respond unbelievably to the changes she saw in the world at that time. . . . And though she was the boss, she had to be responsive to what was around her—and bring the people in who could help her do it. That makes a great leader."

Perhaps the highest accolade ever paid to Elizabeth was written during the final years of her reign by the playwrights William Shakespeare and John Fletcher in their collaborative work, *The Famous History of the Life of King Henry the Eighth*. In the closing scene of the play, the Archbishop of Canterbury addresses the child Elizabeth and makes a prophecy about the young princess and her legacy:

> This royal infant—heaven still move about her!—
> Though in her cradle, yet now promises
> Upon this land a thousand thousand blessings,
> Which time shall bring to ripeness. She shall be—
> But few now living can behold that goodness—
> A pattern to all princes living with her,
> And all that shall succeed . . .
> . . . Truth shall nurse her;
> Holy and heavenly thoughts still counsel her;
> She shall be lov'd and fear'd. Her own shall bless her;
> Her foes shake like a field of beaten corn,
> And hang their heads with sorrow. Good grows with her;
> In her days every man shall eat in safety
> Under his own vine what he plants, and sing
> The merry songs of peace to all his neighbors.
> . . . She shall be, to the happiness of England,

An aged princess; many days shall see her,
And yet no day without a deed to crown it.
Would I had known no more! But she must die—
She must, the saints must have her—yet a virgin;
A most unspotted lily shall she pass
To th' ground, and all the world shall mourn her.

Although England did, indeed, mourn its great queen's death, the world today celebrates her life and her accomplishments as a brilliant, far-sighted leader, who led a beleaguered realm to greatness and created an age that is synonymous with excellence.

APPENDIX I

Quotes from the Queen

Accuracy

Who seeketh two strings to one bow, they may shoot strong, but never straight.

Advice

I know that in my court, as in the courts of all princes, there are divisions and secret hatreds. I am always careful to discriminate between those who advise me from affection for my services and welfare of my subjects, and those who advise me for other reasons.

This judgment I have of you, that you will not be corrupted with any manner of gift, that you will be faithful to the State, and that without respect of my private will you will give me that counsel that you think best. — November 19, 1558, to William Cecil (later Lord Burghley) upon appointing him secretary of state and swearing him into her Privy Council.

It is dangerous for a prince to irritate too much, through evil advice, the generality of great subjects.

To Nicholas Bacon:
   I have followed your advice, these two years past, in all affairs of my kingdom, and I have seen nothing but trouble, expense, and

danger. From this hour, for the same length of time, I am going to follow my own opinion, and see if I find I do any better.

Give not the rein in God's name to wild horses, lest they should shake you from your saddle.

Anger

The king of France is bursting with rage, and I do not want to make him burst any more.

Clerks

I see that the greatest clerks are not always the wisest men.

Coaching

I have on my part inculcated good lessons on my people, which, I am assured, they will observe.

Competitive Intelligence

Princes have big ears with which to hear far and near.

If you suppose that princes' causes be veiled so covertly that no intelligence may betray them, deceive not yourself; we old foxes can find shifts to save ourself by others' malice, and come by knowledge of greatest secret, specially if it touch our freehold.

Contingency Planning

My peaceful government and security have not so lulled me to sleep that I have not made provision for any accident.

Criticism

To Burghley who wished to resign (May 8, 1583) because he was discouraged by criticism and conscious that he was disliked by some of his powerful colleagues in the Privy Council:
  I have lately seen . . . that if an ass kick you, you feel it too soon.

Ends and Means

If the right must be violated, it must be for the sake of rule.

Education

Indeed I studied nothing else but divinity till I came to the crown; and then I gave myself to the study of that which was meet for government.

Extradition

The king of Spain may have [the traitor's] head if he wants it; but his body shall be left in England!

Finance

When French pirates drove four gold-laden Spanish ships into her ports during the Netherlands crisis, Elizabeth seized the money and put it into her own exchequer. Though England and Spain were at peace, the money was to be used to pay Spanish troops in the Lowlands. Bess knew, however, that the money was still the property of Genoese bankers who were lending it to Spain. When Spain protested, she explained her action to Philip's ambassador, the Duke of Alva:

It being known for a fact that the treasure belonged to the merchants, I thought it well after its due preservation from the perils of the sea, by an act not unreasonable, or contrary to the honourable usages of princes in their dominions, to arrange with its owners, with their goodwill and not otherwise, to borrow it.

Foolhardiness

. . . You will remember that he is very worthy of tripping who enters a net.

Forgiveness

To a lady of Queen Mary's household who, in Mary's reign, had been particularly cruel to Bess, but who later asked most abjectly for Elizabeth's pardon:

Fear not, we are of the nature of the lion, and cannot descend to the destruction of mice and such small beasts.

Fortitude

I know I have the body of a weak and feeble woman but I have the heart and stomach of a King, and a King of England too

Greed

No prince's revenues be so great that they are able to satisfy the insatiable cupidity of men.

Health

Abstinence is the better part of physic.

. . . There can be no folly greater than by fearing that which is not, nor by overgrieving for that which needs not, to overthrow at one instant the health of the mind and body, which once being lost, the rest of our life is labour and sorrow, a work to God unacceptable, and to our friends discomfortable."

Honor

I will never break the word of a prince spoken in a public place, for my honour's sake.

I would rather go to any extreme than suffer anything that is unworthy of my reputation, or of that of my crown.

Can you imagine that the softness of my sex deprives me of the courage to resent a public affront?

Ignorance

Brass shines as fair to the ignorant as gold to the goldsmiths.

Ingratitude

It would be unjust to impute the faults of others to me; but it happens often to kings to do good and receive no recompense.

Can a prince that of necessity must discontent a number to delight and please a few (because the greatest part are often not best inclined) continue a long time without great offence, much mischief, or common grudge?

Justice

I am not so base-minded that fear of any living creative or prince should make me afraid to do what were just; or done, to deny the same.

Language

God's death, my Lords! This day I have been forced to scour up my old Latin that hath lain long rusting.

There is no marvel in a woman learning to speak, but there would be in teaching her to hold her tongue.

Lawyers

You lawyers are so nice and precise in sifting and scanning every word and letter that many times you stand more upon form than matter, upon syllables than the sense of the law.

[Without goodwill] laws become cobwebs, whence great bees get out by breaking, and small flies stick fast for weakness.

Leadership

My state requires me to command that I know my people will willingly do from their own love to me.

Loyalty

To Nicholas Clifford, when he returned from France wearing a decoration presented him by the king:
  My dogs wear *my* collars.

Marriage

For my own part, I firmly believe that my happiness will be only too great for an old woman to whom paternosters will suffice in place of nuptials.

I am attracted to perpetual spinsterhood not by prejudice, but rather by natural inclination. I call the wedding ring, the "yoke" ring.

Mary, Queen of Scots

There seems to be something sublime in the words and bearing of the Queen of Scots that constrains even her enemies to speak well of her.

Meditations

From Lady Elizabeth Tyrwhitt's Morning and Evening Prayers, with Divers Hymns and Meditations, *prepared for Elizabeth by her governess:*
  "Think upon the needy once a day."
  "Further the just suit of the poor."
  "Help to pacify displeasure."
  "Kill anger with patience."
  "Make much of modesty."
  "Be always one."
  "Look chiefly to yourself."

Orders

To Heneage, who had not followed his orders in the Netherlands:

Do that you are bidden, and leave your considerations for your own affairs. For in some things you had clear commandment, which you did not, and in others none, and did.

Oversight

To some of her counsellors who urged her to send more soldiers to the Netherlands:

I will see an account of those already sent over before I yield my assent to the sending over of any more.

Personal Appearance

To Francis Bacon, when the queen was insisting on the importance of the mien and appearance of an official:

Bacon, how can the magistrate maintain his authority, if the man be despised?

Personnel

To the Earl of Lennox, when he asked for money to pay his Scottish troops:

I would rather spend my money in hiring my own folks.

Plain Dealing

Act plainly without reserve, and you will sooner be able to obtain favour of me.

Power

The word "must" is not to be used to princes.

As to liberties, God forbid that your liberty should make my bondage, or that your lawful liberties should anyways have been infringed.

Never tempt too far a prince's patience.

To be a king and wear a crown is a thing more glorious to them that see it than it is pleasant to them that bear it.

Precaution

Precaution and Subtlety [are] unbecoming to great princes.

Quid Pro Quo

To the Spanish Ambassador:
    If the pope or your king sends any help into Ireland, I will let out at Flanders and get the French to go in with me.

Reconciliation

. . . Pilate and Caiaphas were good friends [and] the Innocent died. God keep the innocent from enduring the evil that ill-founded agreements merit. Friendship is better kept between like natures; from reconciled enemies *conservat Deus dominum tuum* [may God preserve your master].

Religion

The king of France and I both know very well what religion the other holds, and I believe firmly that though they differ in certain words, they are not contrary in substance: so that as I hold him to be a Christian prince, who will not break his faith nor his word, so he will find me a Christian princess who will hold to everything I have promised and vowed.

These religious differences are not so great as supposed, and may be adjusted. It is my opinion, that two Christian sovereigns, acting in unison, can settle everything on a better principle, without heeding either priests or ministers.

To the French Ambassador:
   If there were two princes in Christendom who had good will and courage, it would be very easy to reconcile the religious difficulties; there is only one Jesus Christ and one faith, and all the rest is a dispute over trifles.

To Mendoza, the Spanish Ambassador:
   I have never castigated the Catholics except when they would not acknowledge me as their queen; in spiritual matters I believe as they do.

I have heard that some of them of late have said that I was of no religion—neither hot nor cold, but such a one as one day would give God the vomit. I pray you look unto such men.

Rumors

We cannot cover every one's mouth, but must content ourselves with doing our duty and trust in God, for the truth will at last be made manifest.

Silence

Video et taceo. [I see and am silent.]—Elizabeth's favorite motto, honored more in the breach, perhaps, than the observance.

I don't keep a dog and bark myself.

Sincerity

It becometh . . . all of our rank to deal sincerely, lest, if we use it not, when we do [use] it, it will be hardly believed.

Self-Deception

They are most deceived that trusteth most in themselves. —1549 to Somerset.

Succession

Think you that I could love my winding sheet, when as examples show, princes cannot even love their children who are to succeed them?

Tenacity

Tenacious virtue overcomes all. —Written in Latin on the wall of her cell in the Tower of London. She signed the statement: Elizabeth the Captive.

Unwanted Gifts

To a gentleman who had sent some pearls to her which she would not accept:
   My mind is as great to refuse as yours to give.

Youth

Eyes of youth have sharp sight, but not so deep as those of elder age . . .

About Elizabeth

There was never so wise a woman born, for all respects, as Queen Elizabeth, for she spake and understood all languages; knew all estates and dispositions of princes. And particularly was so expert in the knowledge of her own realm and estate as no counsellor she had could tell her what she knew not before. —Lord Burghley

To say the truth I cannot tell your majesty what this woman means to do with herself, and those who know her best know no more than I do. —Spanish Ambassador Feria to Philip II

Lord! The queen is a woman! —One of her subjects upon first seeing her

Appendix II

Chronology

1533   Elizabeth Tudor, the daughter of King Henry VIII and Anne Boleyn, born at Greenwich [September 7].

1536   Anne Boleyn beheaded for treason.

1537   Edward Tudor, son of Henry VIII and his third wife, Jane Seymour, born. Seymour dies shortly afterward of complications stemming from childbirth.

1540   Henry VIII marries and divorces Anne of Cleves, then marries Katherine Howard.

1542   Henry orders execution of Katherine Howard. Birth and accession of Mary, Queen of Scots.

1543   Henry VIII marries Katherine Parr.

1547   Death of Henry VIII. Edward Tudor ascends to the throne as the boy-king Edward VI. Lord Somerset serves as Lord Protector of England during Edward's minority.
       Katherine Parr marries Thomas Seymour.

1553   Edward VI dies on July 6, willing the kingdom to his cousin Lady Jane Grey. Jane reigns for nine days before being deposed by Mary Tudor (Queen Mary I).

1554   Sir Thomas Wyatt, opposed to Mary I's proposed marriage to Prince Philip (later King Philip II) of Spain, leads unsuccessful rebellion against Mary. Wyatt and others, including Jane Grey, are executed. Suspected of supporting Wyatt's rebellion, Elizabeth is imprisoned for two months in the Tower of London in March, but later is released and placed under house royal estate at Woodstock. Mary I marries Philip.

1555   Mary restores England to Catholicism. In the coming three years, the burning of more than 300 Protestant dissidents, including the Smithfield Martyrs, will earn her the nickname "Bloody Mary."

1558   Mary, Queen of Scots, marries Francis, heir to the French throne.

Mary I dies, childless. Elizabeth becomes queen [November 17].

William Cecil named Elizabeth's secretary of state [November 20].

1559   Philip II proposes marriage to Elizabeth. She declines his offer.

Elizabeth's coronation ceremony [January 15].

First Parliament is called to session [January 23]. The session passes the Act of Supremacy, which separates England from the Roman Catholic Church. It also passes the Act of Uniformity, which establishes a Protestant church for England.

Elizabeth rejects marriage suit of Charles, Archduke of Austria, a Catholic.

Francis II and Mary, Queen of Scots, become king and queen of France.

1560   Amy Robsart, wife of Robert Dudley, dies.

England and France sign the Treaty of Edinburgh.

Francis II of France dies.

1561   The widowed Mary, Queen of Scots, returns to Scotland and asserts her claim to the English throne.

1562   Elizabeth survives smallpox.

1563   Elizabeth calls Second Parliament for purpose of levying taxes. Parliament demands that she either marry or name a successor. She does neither.

Parliament passes Act of the Artificers, regulating wages and conditions of employment.

1564   William Shakespeare born [April 23].

Robert Dudley elevated to peerage, named Earl of Leicester [September 28].

1565 Mary, Queen of Scots, marries Lord Darnley (Henry Stuart). Elizabeth had previously proposed Robert Dudley as a husband for Mary.

1566 Elizabeth battles with Third Parliament over succession issues.

James VI of Scotland, Elizabeth's eventual successor, is born. He is the son of Mary, Queen of Scots, and Henry Stuart, Lord Darnley.

1567 Lord Darnley, husband of Mary, Queen of Scots, is murdered. Mary soon after marries the Earl of Bothwell, who is suspected of Darnley's death. The scandal surrounding Darnley's death leads to Mary's abdication and imprisonment in Scotland.

1568 Mary, Queen of Scots, escapes prison, flees to England, and is imprisoned by Elizabeth.

1569 Rebellion of the Northern Earls [November].

1570 Pope Pius V excommunicates Elizabeth.

Elizabeth entertains proposals of marriage from the persistent Charles of Austria, and from Henri, Duke of Anjou (who will later become Henri III of France).

1571 Elizabeth elevates William Cecil to peerage as Lord Burghley.

Burghley's spies uncover the Ridolfi plot.

Elizabeth's Fourth Parliament, in reaction to the queen's excommunication, makes calling the queen a heretic an act of treason. The queen, however, prevents the Parliament from requiring Catholics to attend Protestant services or pay a fine for not doing so.

1572 Fifth Parliament opens and urges execution of Mary, Queen of Scots, and Thomas Howard, leader of the Ridolfi plot. Puritan members seek, without success, to alter structure of Church of England.

St. Bartholomew's Massacre of Protestants in France [August 24].

Francis Drake captures Spanish treasure ships in the West Indies [August 29].

1573   Drake returns from West Indies with captured Spanish treasure.

Nuptial discussions begin between Elizabeth and Francis, Duke of Alençon.

Sir Francis Walsingham named secretary of state [December].

1574   Roman Catholic seminary priests arrive in England.

Elizabeth makes extensive summer progress, tours Bristol and the western counties.

1576   Sixth Parliament opens and again petitions Elizabeth to marry.

1577–80 Francis Drake circumnavigates the globe.

1578   James VI succeeds to Scottish throne at age twelve.

Robert Dudley, Earl of Leicester and the queen's favorite, secretly marries Lettice Knollys Devereaux, Countess of Essex.

1581   Seventh Parliament opens in mid-January. Makes converting to or being Catholic an act of treason.

Duke of Alençon comes to London to finalize marriage arrangements with Elizabeth [November].

1582   Elizabeth returns ring to Alençon, abruptly decides against marriage [February].

1584   Elizabeth grants Sir Walter Raleigh the right to put English colonies on American soil in March; in April, Raleigh dispatches an exploratory mission to America.

William of Orange, the Dutch Protestant leader, is assassinated [July 10].

Eighth Parliament, called in late November, passes the Acts of Association, aimed at preventing Mary Stuart from claiming the English throne. The acts banish all Catholic priests from England and prescribe death as penalty for conspiring to overthrow or kill Elizabeth.

1585   The Netherlands revolts from Spain and England intervenes on the side of the Dutch [May].

Drake embarks for raid on Spanish America [September].

Robert Dudley sails with army of 6,000 to fight in the Netherlands [December].

1586   Anthony Babington and six others executed for their role in plot to replace Elizabeth with Mary, Queen of Scots [September 20].

Trial of Mary Stuart. She is found guilty of treason for involvement in the Babington Plot [October 14].

Ninth Parliament opens and petitions Elizabeth to order Mary's execution [October 15].

1587   Execution of Mary, Queen of Scots [February 8].

Drake attacks Spanish ships in harbor of Cadiz [April 21].

Dudley replaced as commander of English forces in Netherlands.

1588   Spanish Armada leaves Lisbon [May 20].

English fleet engages Armada in a series of battles in the English Channel from July 28 to August 8. Following Battle of Gravelines, the Spanish fleet is driven north by storms. Sailing around England and Ireland, the remains of the fleet are destroyed by storms off the Irish coast on September 11.

Elizabeth addresses troops at Tilbury [August 8].

Robert Dudley, Earl of Leicester, dies September 4.

Marprelate Tracts begin circulating in London [October]. The tracts criticize Anglican bishops who opposed Puritan reform efforts.

1589   Tenth Parliament opens; Puritan members again failed to alter structure of the Anglican Church.

Drake launches unsuccessful Portugal Expedition against Spain [April].

1590   Walsingham dies [April].

Robert Cecil, son of William Cecil, is named secretary of state.

1591   The Earl of Essex leads English troops to France to aid French King Henri IV.

1592 London's mayor asks the Archbishop of Canterbury to stop performances of plays and close playhouses because of their corrupting influences [February 25].
First performance of a play by William Shakespeare.

1593 Eleventh Parliament is called, passes measures punishing Puritans and other Protestants who refused to conform to Anglican Church.
Playwright/spy Christopher Marlowe murdered in tavern brawl.
Plague hits England in June and July.

1594 Beginning of a three-year period of rainy summer weather; food prices rise throughout England owing to poor harvests.

1595 Drake and Hawkins raid the West Indies [August 28].

1596 Francis Drake dies at sea [January 29].

1597 Twelfth Parliament opens and petitions Elizabeth for redress of monopolies. It passes a new Act for Relief of the poor.

1598 William Cecil, Lord Burghley, dies [August 4].
Philip II dies [September 13].

1599 Globe Playhouse built in London.
Essex appointed Lord Lieutenant of Ireland [March 12]. On September 8 he concludes a truce.
Essex returns from Ireland without the queen's permission.

1600 Elizabeth pardons Essex, but places him under house arrest and deprives him of most of his offices.

1601 Essex leads rebellion in London [January 8]. On February 25 he is executed.
Robert Cecil opens secret correspondence on succession with James VI of Scotland, Elizabeth's probable heir.
Thirteenth and final Parliamentary session of Elizabeth's reign meets and again petitions the queen to reform monopolies.
Elizabeth delivers the "Golden Speech" [November 30].

1603 Elizabeth dies. James VI of Scotland takes English throne as King James I. Tudor dynasty ends; Stuart dynasty begins [March 24].

Notes

Unless otherwise noted, all comments from contemporary business executives quoted in *Leadership Secrets of Elizabeth I* were made in interviews with the authors or in written response to the authors' questionnaires between February 15 and April 25, 2000.

Introduction

xiii   SHORTLY AFTER 7 O'CLOCK: from Jane Resh Thomas, *Behind the Mask*, p. 2.

xxxi   TODAY THE RELIGIOUS HATREDS: from Jasper Ridley, *Elizabeth I: The Shrewdness of Virtue*, p. ix.

Chapter 1: Leadership

5   THERE WERE THOSE WHO GRUMBLED: from Hibbert, *The Virgin Queen: Elizabeth I, Genius of the Golden Age*, pp. 139–140.

7-15   THE SIX STYLES OF LEADERSHIP: See Goleman, "Leadership that Gets Results," *Harvard Business Review*, March-April, 2000. pp.78–90.

10   ACKNOWLEDGING THE DEPRIVATION . . .: See Luke, *Gloriana: The Years of Elizabeth*, p. xii.

12-14   THE TURKISH COMPANY: The story of the Turkish Company and Harborne's appointment is drawn from an essay on the topic by George Born Manhart, in Rowland and Manhart's *Studies in English Commerce and Exploration in the Reign of Elizabeth*, Philadelphia: University of Pennsylvania Press, 1924.

16-17   SCHLESINGER ON LEADERSHIP: from Introductory Essay "On Leadership," in *Mary, Queen of Scots* by Sally

Stepanek. The quotations may be found, respectively on pages 7 and 11.

Chapter 2: Finance

28   "FINANCE IS THE ESSENCE": from Neale, p. 294.

28-30   CURRENCY CONVERSIONS: Determining the relative purchasing power of an Elizabethan sovereign (or pound) compared to a Year 2000 pound sterling or U.S. dollar is problematical. In our research we found estimates ranging from one

Elizabethan sovereign equaling £500 modern pounds sterling currency (about US$800) to £1,500 (US$2,400). The wide variance occurs in part because of the rampant price fluctuations that characterized Tudor England both before and during Elizabeth's reign.

30   CECIL ON THE QUEEN'S PARSIMONY: Hibbert, p. 108.

30   WHEN OPPORTUNITIES TO MAKE MONEY: Hibbert, p. 108.

Chapter 3: The Art of "Spin"

50   WHEN ELIZABETH WENT TO STAFFORD: See Somerset, p. 373.

Chapter 4: Building and Managing Teams

63   IT WAS A REASSURING SPEECH: Perry, *Elizabeth I: The Word of a Prince*, p. 130.

67   ELIZABETH DESIRED: from Neale, p. 55.

67-69   CAMPBELL's CABINET: For a more detailed account of Kim Campbell's process for selecting her cabinet, see her *Time and Chance*, pp. 313–324.

75-78   TEAMS AND CONFLICT: See Kathleen M. Eisenhardt, Jean L. Kahwajy and L.J. Bourgeois III, "How Management Teams Can Have a Good Fight," *Harvard Business Review*, July-August 1997, pp. 77–85.

78   TEAMS AT THE TOP: See Katzenbach, "The Myth of the Top Management Team," *Harvard Business Review*, November-December 1997, pp. 82–91.

Chapter 5: Vision, Mission, Commitment

94   NORDSTROM EMPLOYEE HANDBOOK: Reprinted in Spector, Robert and Patrick McCarthy, *The Nordstrom Way: Inside America's # 1 Customer Service Company*, pp. 15–16.

96-97   WAL-MART CULTURE STORIES: The Sundown Rule and other Wal-Mart culture stories may be found on the company's website, *walmart.com*.

97   WHERE THERE IS NO VISION: The Biblical quote is from *Proverbs* 29:18.

105-108   A FEW EFFECTIVE MISSION STATEMENTS: The cited mission and values statements may be found on each company's website, listed in the Bibliography.

Chapter 6: Decision-Making

113   PERSIAN DECISION-MAKING: Herodotus describes the drunk/sober method of decision-making in Book 1, Section 133 of *The History*; in Grene's translation see pp. 95–96.

Chapter 7: Vast Intellect

130   ASCHAM QUOTE: Cited in King, *Elizabeth, The Tudor Princess*.

Chapter 8: Style

146-148   ELIZABETH's CONCERN FOR PROPER DRESS: from Somerset, *Elizabeth I*, p. 340.

149   . . . WHEN LADY MARY HOWARD: from Hibbert, p. 254.

150   DUDLEY's DIET: from Harrison, *The Letters of Queen Elizabeth*, pp.125–126.

151   FART STORY: from Hibbert, p. 117.

152   "HOWEVER THEY DISGUISED": Neale, *Elizabeth I*, p. 67.

160   STYLE IN TODAY'S WORKPLACE: See Ellen Joan Pollock's article, "Deportment Gap in the Workplace," *The Wall Street Journal*, February 7, 2000.

Chapter 9: Gender Politics

165   DEBORAH: The story of Deborah is told in chapters 4 and 5 of the Old Testament book *Judges*.

166   "BLOWN OUT OF SEASON": Quoted in Neale, p. 64.

166   NOT LIKELY TO BE DISTURBED . . .: See Neale, p. 64

169   YOUNG MEN—AND OLD MEN—IN LOVE: See Neale, pp.65–66.

174-175   MYERS-BRIGGS: The Myers-Briggs Type Indicator is a proprietary psychological profiling tool that identifies personality types on the basis of four factors. The MBTI is commonly used by corporate Human Resources departments and management consultants. Myers-Briggs Type Indicator and MBTI are registered trademarks of Consulting Psychologists Press Inc.

Chapter 10: Competitive Intelligence

183   FIVE FORCES THEORY: For this and other aspects of competitive intelligence, see Porter, *Competitive Strategy: Techniques for Analyzing Industries and Competitors*, pp. 39–79.

194-195   BIZRATE.COM: Descriptions of the company and its services are taken from its website.

198-201   WALSINGHAM's SPIES: An excellent account of Walsingham's secret service and its codebreakers appears in Simon Singh's *The Code Book*, pp. 1–44.

Chapter 11: Her Greatest Triumph

220-222   FORMULA 409 AND P&G: For the complete story on this marketing battle see Solman and Friedman, *Life and Death on the Corporate Battlefield: How Companies Win, Lose, Survive*, pp. 26–30.

Chapter 12: Succession and Legacy

236-239   SUCCESSION AT GE: The Reg Jones-Jack Welch succession story and the descriptions of the two men and their styles has been drawn from Slater, *The New GE*, pp. 17–18 and pp., 47–49; O'Boyle, pp. 46–66; also see, Vancil, "How Companies Pick New CEOs," *Fortune*, January 4, 1988, p. 74.

Selected Bibliography

Books about Elizabeth I

Chamberlin, Frederick, *The Sayings of Queen Elizabeth*, London: John Lane, The Bodley Head, 1923.

Harrison, G.B. (editor), *The Letters of Queen Elizabeth*, London: Cassell and Company, Ltd., 1935.

Hibbert, Christopher, *The Virgin Queen: Elizabeth I, Genius of the Golden Age*, Cambridge, Mass.: Perseus, 1999.

King, Marian, *Elizabeth, The Tudor Princess*, New York: Frederick A. Stokes Company, 1940.

Luke, Mary M., *Gloriana: The Years of Elizabeth I*, New York: Coward, McCann, Geoghegan, 1973.

Neale, J.E., *Queen Elizabeth I*, Chicago: Academy Chicago Publishers (reprint), 1999.

Perry, Maria, *Elizabeth I: The World of a Prince (A Life from Contemporary Documents)*, London: The Folio Society, 1990.

Ridley, Jasper, *Elizabeth I: The Shrewdness of Virtue*, New York: Viking, 1988.

Somerset, Anne, *Elizabeth I*, New York: Alfred A. Knopf, 1991.

Thomas, Jane Resh, *Behind the Mask: The Life of Queen Elizabeth I* (young readers), New York: Clarion Books, 1998.

Wilson, Charles, *Queen Elizabeth and the Revolt of the Netherlands*, Berkeley: University of California Press, 1970

The Battle of the Spanish Armada

Graham, Winston, *The Spanish Armadas*, New York: Dorset Press, 1987.

Martin, Colin and Geoffrey, *The Spanish Armada*, New York: W. W. Norton & Company, 1988.

Mattingly, Garrett, *The Armada*, Boston: Houghton-Mifflin Company, 1959.

Milne-Tyne, Robert, *Armada! The Planning of the Battle and After*, London: Robert Hale, 1988.

Usherwood, Stephan, *The Great Enterprise: The History of the Spanish Armada*, London: The Folio Society, 1988 (reprint), original 1978)

The Elizabethan Age

Ashley, Leonard R.N., *Elizabethan Popular Culture*, Bowling Green, Ohio: Bowling

Green State University Popular Press, 1988.

Jones, Norman, *The Birth of the Elizabethan Age: England in the 1560s*, Oxford, UK: Blackwell, 1993.

Loomie, Albert J., *The Spanish Elizabethans: The English Exiles at the Court of Phillip II*, New York: Fordham University Press, 1963 (reprint, Westport, CT: Greenwood Press, 1983)

Rowland, Albert Lindsay, and George Born Manhart, *Studies in English Commerce and Exploration in the Reign of Elizabeth*, Philadelphia: University of Pennsylvania Press, 1924.

Wagner, John A., *Historical Dictionary of the Elizabethan World*, Phoenix, AZ: Oryx Press, 1999.

General

Barty-King, Hugh, *The Worst Poverty: A History of Debt and Debtors*, Phoenix Mill, Gloustershire, UK: Sutton, 1991.

Brinton, Crane, *Ideas and Men: The Story of Western Thought*, New York: Prentice-Hall, 1950

Fischer, David Hackett, *The Great Wave: Price Revolutions and the Rhythm of History*, New York: Oxford University Press, 1996.

Herodotus, *The History* (David Grene, translator), Chicago: University of Chicago Press, 1987.

Machiavelli, Niccolo, *The Prince: A Bilingual Edition*, (Mark Musa, editor and translator, New York: St. Martin's Press, 1964.

Singh, Simon, *The Code Book*, New York: Doubleday, 1999 (Chapter 1: "The Cipher of Mary, Queen of Scots")

Supporting Characters

Kamen, Henry, *Phillip of Spain*, New Haven: Yale University Press, 1997.

Nicholl, Charles, *The Reckoning: The Murder of Christopher Marlowe*, Chicago: University of Chicago Press, 1992.

Stepanek, Sally (with introductory essay on leadership by Arthur S. Schlesinger, Jr.), *Mary, Queen of Scots*, Philadelphia: Chelsea House Publishers, 1987.

Sugden, John, *Sir Francis Drake*, New York: Simon & Schuster, 1990.

Business & Leadership

Bethel, Sheila Murray, *Making a Difference: 12 Questions that Make You a Leader*, New York: Berkley Publishing Group, 1990.

Campbell, Kim, *Time and Chance: The Political Memoirs of Canada's First Woman Prime Minister*, Toronto: Seal Books (McClelland-Bantam, Inc.), 1996.

Decker, Charles L., *Winning with P&G 99: 99 Principles and Practices of Proctor & Gamble's Success*, New York: Pocket Books, 1998.

Goleman, Daniel, *Working with Emotional Intelligence*, New York: Bantam Books, 1998. *Emotional Intelligence*, New York: Bantam, 1995.

O'Boyle, Thomas F., *At Any Cost: Jack Welch, General Electric and the Pursuit of Profit*, New York: Alfred A. Knopf, 1998.

Porter, Michael E., *Competitive Strategy: Techniques for Analyzing Industries and Competitors*, New York: The Free Press, 1980.

Slater, Robert, *Jack Welch and the GE Way*, New York: McGraw-Hill, 1999. *The New GE: How Jack Welch Revived an American Institution*, Homewood, IL: Business One Irwin, 1993.

Solman, Paul and Thomas Friedman, *Life and Death on the Corporate Battlefield: How Companies Win, Lose and Survive*, New York: Signet (reprint), 1984.

Spector, Robert and Patrick McCarthy, *The Nordstrom Way: Inside America's #1 Customer Service Company*, New York: John Wiley & Sons, 1995.

Vernon, Lillian, *An Eye for Winners: How I Built One of America's Greatest Direct-Mail Business*, New York: HarperCollins, 1997.

Business Articles

Goleman, Daniel, "Leadership That Gets Results," *Harvard Business Review*, March-April, 2000. pp.78–90.

Kathleen M. Eisenhardt, Jean L. Kahwajy and L.J. Bourgeois III, "How Management Teams Can Have a Good Fight," *Harvard Business Review*, July-August 1997, pp. 77–85.

Katzenbach, Jonathan R., "The Myth of the Top Management Team", *Harvard Business Review*, November-December 1997, pp. 82–91

Pollock, Ellen Joan, " ", *The Wall Street Journal*, February 7, 2000, p. 1

Vancil, Richard F., "How Companies Pick New CEOs," *Fortune*, January 4, 1988, p. 74.

Selected Web Sites

Business and Organizations

amazon.com
bellatlantic.com (Bell Atlantic)
bizrate.com
bnsf.com (Burlington Northern Santa Fe Railway)
costco.com
fordfound.org (Ford Foundation)
ge.com (General Electric)
nordstrom.com
starbucks.com
walmart.com

Elizabethan

LUMINARIUM
www.luminarium.org/renlit/elizface.htm
This prize-winning site features excellent photographs of images of Elizabeth, period music, biography and essays. Regularly updated with new material, Luminarium describes itself as " the labor of love of Anniina Jokinen. The site is not related to any institution, is sponsored by no one, nor does it generate any profit—except to those who benefit from the knowledge and pleasure it provides.

ELIZABETH—THE MOVIE

www.elizabeth-themovie.com

Lush web site devoted to the 1998 movie Elizabeth starring Kate Blanchett. The site is filled with as much error as the movie itself, but features a fascinating on-line games that take you into the Elizabethan period in an engaging and exciting way. Counter this one by going to:

ELIZABETH I

www.elizabethi.org

This Welsh site, created and maintained by Heather Thomas provides interesting and credible material on Elizabeth. It's non-commercial, not-for-profit and, in addition to its own fine offerings, provides links to many other Elizabethan sites. As of this writing, the site was moving. The address above was to be its new location as of May 2000.

Index